# 'WHAT ARE YOU THINKING OF, DAD?'

# 'WHAT ARE YOU THINKING OF, DAD?'

NICK WISBEY

Matador
5 Weir Road
Kibworth Beauchamp
Leicester LE8 0LQ, UK
Tel: (+44) 116 279 2299
Fax: (+44) 116 279 2277
Email: books@troubador.co.uk
Web: www.troubador.co.uk/matador

ISBN 978 1848764 811

British Library Cataloguing in Publication Data.
A catalogue record for this book is available from the British Library.

Typeset in 11pt Garamond by Troubador Publishing Ltd, Leicester, UK

**Matador** is an imprint of Troubador Publishing Ltd

Printed in Great Britain by the MPG Books Group, Bodmin and King's Lynn

*To Joanna*

# ONE

Uncle Ralph missed the undertaker by a matter of inches. Reversing had never been his strong point and the stress of arriving late and finding nowhere to park compounded the situation. Considering the undertaker resembled an octogenarian, might have had a wooden leg and needed a stick to shuffle about with, he moved remarkably quickly to dodge the fast reversing Cortina Mark 4. As the protagonists squared up Auntie Joan got out of the passenger seat and made good her escape. She needed a Benson & Hedges to steady the nerves.

"No harm done," said Ralph inspecting his nearside rear door for signs of scuff marks.

"Don't you worry about your car," replied the undertaker. "You're lucky you didn't have two funerals on your hands."

"I think you're over reacting," said Ralph.

"Well that's the closest I've come to being run over at a funeral."

"Is that so?"

"Yes, by a mile."

"Well I apologise then. No hard feelings."

"No hard feelings. Just sort your reversing out."

"That's a deal. I'm Ralph."

"Mr Talisman."

They smiled and shook hands.

"Not a bad day for a funeral," said Ralph.

"No, could be worse. Were you related?"

"Yes, Stan Wisbey was my brother-in-law. He'd been ill a long time."

"That's right. Mrs Wisbey said he had a stroke back in sixty three."

"Good Lord, I don't remember it being that long ago."

They were joined by Nick who'd witnessed the near calamity.

"That was a good bit of parking Uncle. Have you actually passed your test?"

"Hello Nick. Now who was it helped me with my driving all those years ago?"

"I've no idea."

"You should have concentrated on my reversing on those Sunday mornings round Leytonstone."

"You wouldn't let me. You were so impatient. Talk about sleepless nights."

"Come on Nick, I wasn't that bad."

"Well, what do you say Mr Talisman. Have you seen reversing like that before?"

"No, comment," replied Mr Talisman.

"You're being polite. I hope he didn't make contact with you."

"Almost, but not quite."

"No bones broken then, that is a relief. And how are you Ralph?"

"I'm okay, no bones broken."

The three of them smiled. You couldn't beat a smidgen of humour at a funeral to take your mind off the sombre proceedings.

"I meant did you have a good journey up?"

"Yes, fine. We did it in just over two hours. I don't know why we're late."

"It takes good practice."

"What do you mean?"

"Well you like to cut it fine."

"Do I?"

"Without fail Ralph, but it's good to see you."

"Good to see you too Nick. How's your mum been?"

"Okay. There's been such a lot to do she hasn't had time to sit down and think about things."

"That's normal. It's after the funeral when it hits you. Then you can have too much time."

"You're right. But she's pleased that so many have made it today."

"Good. I bet there's some that haven't met up for years. Like at weddings. A rare opportunity to get together."

"I suppose so."

"How many funerals are you doing today?" enquired Ralph of Mr Talisman.

"Just the two. It's a quiet day for us."

"What's the most you've done in a day?"

"I think we made double figures back in the seventies."

"That's a lot of funerals."

"You're right, very tiring."

"That must have been when the public service workers were on strike? Well afterwards. Old Callaghan's government."

"I think you're right."

"When the dead were piling up like dirty laundry."

"I don't know about that but there were certainly delays in funeral arrangements."

"A stressful time then" said Nick. "Having to wait to say your goodbyes. That's not what you want."

"I think a week is long enough," said Ralph. "Then try and get on with your life again."

"Well its six days since dad died so that's been pretty quick."

"We always do our best," said Mr. Talisman."

The three of them crossed the road and walked towards the bungalow. It wasn't a bad day for a funeral. Well dry at least. Just that depressing November murkiness that enveloped the fine city that Norwich paraded itself as.

"The grass needs cutting," said Ralph inspecting the front la~

"No, that'll keep until the spring," replied Nick. "It's too
~ ."

hat you think."

's  ppy with."

's hibernating anyway."

isman gave mum the nod

ice started in twenty min~

3

it should have left five minutes ago. But then had a cortege ever arrived late?

"I hope we're not late," said Uncle Alan.

"They know what they're doing," said Uncle John.

"I suppose so. When did we last get together?"

"God knows, years ago."

They shook their heads. It certainly seemed an age. Alan was Stan's brother and John his brother-in-law. And although they lived within a few of miles of each other in the East End their paths hadn't crossed for years.

"Probably at Joanna's wedding," continued John.

"When would that have been?"

"About twenty years ago."

"She's a lovely girl. I bet Stan was proud of her."

"Four well turned out boys as well. They're all here today."

"Good for them."

They made their way outside to watch the cortege set off. Hopefully it wouldn't coincide with a bus pulling up at the request stop. A downside of living on a main road. Passengers would disembark while mum minded her business mowing, digging and pruning. Being a naturally shy person she would scuttle indoors rather than indulging in small talk. Today though, thank God, the coast seemed clear.

"Can you remember when Stan had his stroke?" asked Alan.

"Now you're asking. The early sixties?"

"I think you're right. It could have been that severe winter of sixty ⁓ee."

"Can you believe it though – all those years?"

⁓know. What a life for the pair of them."

⁓t's why he survived so long," said John. "Joan's love and

what about the quality? Was it worth surviving all that

⁓uld answer that one."

⁓s only forty nine when he had the stroke."

⁓ow, do you?"

4

"No. Do you think his boxing had anything to do with it?" said Alan.

"What caused his stroke? I've never thought of that. I wouldn't have thought so. He didn't have that many fights."

"But he did get knocked out."

John looked gob smacked. "Did he? Stan! Knocked out! I thought he was unbeaten."

"No, he definitely took the count on one occasion."

"Well, well, well. So top heavyweight prospect Captain Stan Wisbey wasn't invincible after all. I don't remember him letting on about that."

"He still had a pretty impressive record though," said Alan. "Won twelve and lost one."

"Yes, but not the same as being unbeaten."

"They still wanted him to turn professional."

"True. But I don't think Joan was keen on the idea. They'd only just got married."

"Stan wasn't either. He saw boxing as something he did in the army. He always intended going back to the office after the war. Although they would have promoted him to Major if he'd stayed in."

"A Major," said John. "They must have thought a lot of him."

"They did. Poor old Stan. Come on we'd better get going. Don't want to be late for a funeral."

# SEPTEMBER 1962

The family's eighth annual summer holiday had almost lived up to expectations. This year the Wisbeys, with Nana Bailey, had spent a fortnight in B & B accommodation in Weymouth. If it was to be their last holiday together, because Nick had reached the grand age of fifteen and might not wish to participate with the family again, then it had been a satisfying swansong.

Previously they'd visited such memorable resorts as Hemsby, Camber Sands and Dymchurch. They'd even journeyed north to Saltburn and Whitby on the Yorkshire coast. Unheard of for

Londoners because families from the capital rarely ventured past Great Yarmouth. The north wasn't considered cool. But then other families didn't have an Aunt Iris in Middlesbrough. That was definitely cool. Up there they drank Newcastle Brown in working men's clubs, left their front doors open twenty four hours a day and said things like *burss and burter.*

With one reservation the consensus was that Weymouth had been the best holiday so far. Why? Well for starters the weather had been good. And with the sun shining every holiday destination can look a million dollars. Weymouth didn't buck the trend. It simply exuded laughter and a let's have a good time feel.

Secondly, there'd been no tantrums. Everybody had played their part to ensure a relaxing fortnight. In fact they'd got on really well. They'd sat on the beach, walked along the promenade, played crazy golf, visited Portland Bill and seen Morecombe & Wise ably supported by Matt Monroe. And they had the box camera black and white photographs to prove it.

On one particular afternoon they'd split up and done their own thing. Mum and Joanna had seen the film the Music Man. Dad had opted for the possibly more exciting El Cid. Nick had chosen Weymouth Town's tricky Southern league fixture against Bath. While Nana Bailey had infuriated Mrs Cuthbert, the landlady, by spending the afternoon in the lounge listening to the play on the home programme. But that's another story.

It was dad who had the tallest of tall tales when they later rendezvoused. As El Cid (Charlton Heston) and his troops entered Valencia he'd spotted one of the production crew on camera. That's right, a stubby middle-aged bloke wearing a flat hat. Indeed an Andy Capp of the middle ages. No, he wasn't mistaken. He'd witnessed a classic "It'll Be Alright on the Night" blooper. He suggested the whole family viewed the film to back up his observation. But there were no takers. An error like that in a blockbuster didn't ring true. Dad must have been mistaken. Dad smiled knowingly. He knew what he'd witnessed.

The one drawback on the holiday had been the B & B itself. Due entirely to the attitude of Mrs Cuthbert the landlady, a loose cannon of gigantic proportions. At the time of booking she'd clearly stated there wouldn't be a problem with the family returning to their room during the day. She ran a very relaxed and hospitable establishment. Residents could come and go as they pleased. In other words, treat the place like home. Oh yes, well you could have fooled me landlady. The *fuss* she made on the few occasions the Londoners returned to their digs during daylight hours was totally out of order.

"You should have gone for self-catering if you wanted to use your rooms during the day," she shouted on more than one occasion.

"There's no need to shout," said mum.

"I'm not shouting," shouted Mrs Cuthbert.

"You said there wouldn't be a problem if we popped in during the day," said dad.

"I don't think I did."

"You did."

"I don't think so."

The family were united. If ever there was a time when dad could have put his boxing skills to good use then this should have been it. Give her a right uppercut she'd remember for the rest of her life.

She'd also made a big thing about not allowing pets on her premises – which suited fine because the family weren't pet orientated. But then she owned a stupid cream coloured Pekinese called Brumus. (Named after a character in El Cid no doubt.) That dog was the pits. Totally out of control it had the complete run of the B & B. That included jumping up on the breakfast table and nicking the odd sausage or rasher. But God forbid if you took revenge by swatting it with a piece of toast. Pandemonium ensued with the threat of a call to the RSPCA if the action was repeated.

In her defence was the confusion of Joanna and Nana Bailey sharing a bed. Mrs Cuthbert could never work that out. When she brought up the tea in morning she'd be confronted by only one of the occupants of the double bed. It wasn't a deliberate policy to confuse Mrs Cuthbert – it just so happened that every morning either Joanna or nana would be fast asleep under the covers. So she'd go away scratching her head. "A thirteen year old school girl? I could have sworn yesterday a sixty six year old grandmother took the tea."

Other excitement included a couple of potential life threatening incidents. On the Tuesday dad and Joanna had taken a canoe out to sea. Dad had joked about canoeing to France. Joanna had taken him seriously. She was at that impressionable age. A few months earlier she thought she'd walked from Leyton to Scotland with Christine Allen. Well, within ten minutes of being afloat the canoe started taking on water big time. Joanna panicked and screamed, "I'm never going to see my friend Christine Allen again." Dad kept a stiff upper lip, told her to be quiet, did a U turn and paddled back in double quick time. They made it just before the canoe disappeared beneath the waves

Then, on the Friday, Nick, possibly, saved somebody from drowning. It wasn't clear whether the seven year old boy needed to be saved but Nick wasn't taking any chances. There were no adults at hand and the kid appeared to be out of his depth splashing about frantically. In his own indomitable style Nick grabbed the boy's feet and dragged him ashore. Once saved the boy was dumped ceremoniously on the beach and left to sob his heart out. Nick, meanwhile, melted into the background, shunning the publicity guaranteed by a heart rending story in the Weymouth Gazette.

Like all their holidays the sunny resort had been reached by rail. The family didn't yet own a car – though there had been talk about that possibility. Dad had recently been promoted at the shipping office. Now earning the decent wage of £20.00 per week things were looking up. Add the £7.00 mum earned as a cashier at Henry Taylor's, plus a small contribution from Nick and Joanna, from earnings received from chopping up quality orange boxes and selling it on as bundles of firewood in their capacity as members of the Nottingham Road gang, then anything might be possible.

But if truth be told another reason why a car might be on the agenda were the neighbours. The Watts and the Jaycocks had recently bought their first motor vehicles – and in the same week. Even more of a coincidence they'd both opted for the middle of the range Singer Gazelle. So the Wisbeys thought it time they climbed on the bandwagon. But they'd go for the more up market Singer Vogue. That would certainly cause a stir.

The train journeys were invariably a lot of fun. Okay luggage had gone astray – but infrequently. On this particular holiday the ex army trunk that'd been forwarded five days earlier had been discovered in the guards van. Joanna had actually sat on it when reading her Girl Guide comic. When dad mentioned this to the station master he was taken to task. The family should be thankful for small mercies because the trunk could easily have turned up after they'd returned home. Then what would they have done? Quite.

On the return journey Nick took the earlier train. His beloved Leyton Orient were at home to neighbours West Ham. Excitingly they achieved their first victory in the top flight. To this day Nick bores people with the ultimate trivia question. Which team won promotion to the first division alongside Shankley's Liverpool? Of course, everybody's second favourite team, Leyton Orient. Forty five years on and Liverpool are still there. But did the O's and their supporters enjoy their one season with the big boys? You bet they did. You ask Nick.

The family arrived home to discover that mum's brothers, Ralph, Tom and John, had been as good as their word and painted the front of the house. The three bedroom terrace in Nottingham Road positively gleamed in the September sun. Although dad couldn't recall vetting the pillar box red front door.

"I thought we were having a brown front door again?" he said.

"Brown?" replied mum. "I don't think so. That wouldn't have gone with the cream window frames."

"Wouldn't it?"

But whatever, the Watts and the Jaycocks would now be under pressure to spruce up their houses. They might own new cars but in both cases their front paintwork left a lot to be desired. And they'd better get round to it quickly because within six months there could be a top of the range Singer Vogue parked in between their Gazelles. That would really put the cat amongst the pigeons.

"I can't wait until we buy the car," said Joanna. "Christine Allen will be so jealous. What colour are we getting?"

"Oh I haven't thought about a colour yet," said dad. "There's plenty of time for that. We've still got some saving to do."

9

"But we might have it in time for next year's holiday?"

"We might. I'm not promising though."

"Well I'm going to mention it to Christine anyway. I'll tell her it's going to be red to match our front door."

"Red?" said dad. "I'm not sure about that. Just wait and see."

"I can't," said Joanna. "I'm too excited."

# TWO

The cortege moved at a respectful snails pace down Bowthorpe road with Mr Talisman extremely wary of a Mark 4 Cortina that appeared to be cruising in his slipstream. If he braked suddenly then that would be it – a traumatic outcome to an already stressful situation. He wondered what Ralph had against him.

Travelling in the car were mum, Nick, Joanna, her husband David, and their four boys (Tim, Duncan, Will and Robert). Robert just nine years old, an age mum considered too young for funeral duties. But Joanna disagreed and argued he wanted to attend, that he needed no coercing but simply wished to say goodbye to grandpa. That was the end of the matter. Making mountains out of molehills wasn't something the family indulged in. Clearly born out on the vexed question of a burial or cremation. While mum preferred the modern day latter, her daughter would have gone for the more harrowing and muddier former. But there would be no disagreement. The decision was mum's – end of discussion. Whether they'd have been so close if dad hadn't had his stroke we don't know, but certainly the experience of living with an invalid husband and father for so many years did bond the family.

"Ralph's driving close," said Tim.

"Yes," said Joanna. "We don't want any accidents."

"He almost ran over Mr Talisman when he arrived," said Nick.

"He did what?"

"Yes, he was attempting to reverse. He blamed me. He said I didn't teach him properly back in the seventies."

"You taught Ralph to drive?" said David.

"Well not just me, but I did my bit."

"It's a shame I never learnt," said mum. "Did you know I had forty lessons."

"I do remember," said Nick. "How many driving schools?"

"Three or four, I can't remember now."

"I suppose it didn't help when I sold my car. You didn't get the extra practice."

"I don't think it would have made any difference how much practice I got. I just couldn't concentrate."

"Still, you had no mishaps," said Joanna.

"I wouldn't say that. I remember going round the Green Man roundabout the wrong way."

"Did you?"

"The instructor said that was a first. But I didn't believe that. It's easy to get confused at a roundabout. The fuss he made. I mean I didn't hit anything."

"That's a coincidence," said Nick. "Uncle Ralph did that twice with me at the Green Man roundabout."

"Twice?" said David.

"Yes, and on the same morning. He wouldn't have it the first time he was in the wrong and set off again to make doubly sure. Talk about scary. This time the police stopped us. And guess what? Ralph blamed me and they let him off with a warning and advised me not to take up a career with BSM."

There were smiles as the family imagined Ralph driving round the Green Man roundabout in an anti-clockwise direction. They knew that grandpa would have seen the funny side. But Ralph was certainly driving close. Too close for comfort.

"Auntie Joan doesn't look too happy," said mum.

"I'm not surprised," said Joanna. "She'll need another Benson & Hedges when we arrive."

"Look," said Duncan. "He's giving us the thumbs up."

"I wouldn't have thought you did that on the way to a funeral," said mum.

"He'll be hooting next," said Nick.

"I suppose he doesn't want to lose us," said David.

"There's no chance of that. I reckon he could arrive before us."

There were more smiles and chuckles – but all in good taste.

# DECEMBER 1962

The Singer Vogue had been put on hold for a while. Since the holiday dad hadn't been enjoying the best of health. For starters he'd been experiencing a numbness down his right side. This could occur at any time and on one occasion caused him to drop the tray and break the bone china teapot as he came downstairs. There'd also been severe headaches and a general feeling of being unwell. The doctor had diagnosed "worrying" and dad had sort of accepted it without really believing it.

But then, over breakfast, he complained about a headache and shouted out something about a hot water bottle to mum and Joanna. It was complete gobbledygook and most upsetting. Then he started crying. Then Joanna started crying. Mum tried to comfort the pair of them.

After a while dad returned to bed and Joanna prepared for school.

"Are you okay?" asked mum.

"Yes, I'll be alright," said Joanna. "But I do think dad should see the doctor again."

"Yes, you're right. I'll make sure he goes along this week. But I'd be happier if we found a new one."

"Christine Allen's got a good one."

"Where does she go?"

"Somewhere near Markhouse road. I'll find out."

"Okay then. Have a good day at school."

After she'd gone mum went to check on dad. She was relieved to find him snoring loudly. She sat with him pondering his health problem. All sorts of explanations entered her head – from the serious to the not so. But she knew you simply couldn't attribute his condition to "worrying" as the doctor had suggested. That didn't make sense. They needed a second opinion. She returned downstairs to start on the Monday wash and the house work.


## A WEEK LATER


"Come along Nick," said mum. "Put the tape recorder away. Dad should be back soon."

Nick sighed then reluctantly packed up his pride and joy. Boy did he love his Stella, reel to reel, tape recorder purchased from Underwoods at Leyton Midland for £38.00. It had opened up a brand new world. Tracks, such as 'Breaking up is hard to do', 'Don't ever change', 'Love me do' and the Z cars theme song were his personal pick of the pops. Rarely without his Stella he'd have slept with it if feasible. At meal times he'd offer to provide the musical entertainment. Alas the offer wasn't always taken up – tonight being one of those occasions. But to think the recorder had cost dad two weeks wages. Nick felt sorely indebted to his parents for their kindness.

"So what did the doctor say?" said mum when dad returned.

"He still puts it down to worrying," said dad.

"Worrying? That doctor's a waste of time. It's a shame old Hutchinson isn't around."

"Yes, but he isn't."

"We should look for another one."

"I know, but it's such a lot of bother."

"It'll be worth it in the long run."

"Have you noticed how he tears strips off the bottom of his prescription pad?" said Nick.

"That must be nerves," said mum. "He's not confident about his diagnosis."

"So what did he say you should do?" asked Joanna.

"Take some time off work," said dad.

"And that's it?" said Mum.

"I'm afraid so. He gave me the impression he didn't believe I'd ever suffered from angina."

"That's ridiculous."

"Well when reading through my notes I could tell he thought the heart problems were imaginary. He's got me down as a worrier."

"I'll give him imaginary. You must get a second opinion Stan."

"You're probably right, but I'm not taking any time off work at the moment. I'll see how it goes."

What a pity Doctor Hutchinson had suffered a fatal heart attack whilst driving a few months earlier. He'd actually crashed into a tree in Nottingham road just fifty yards from their house. With him at the helm dad's health would have been sorted. Well at least he'd have referred him to hospital.

The family sat down for dinner. Being a Monday that meant another scrumptious Shepherds pie. Amazing what one could do with Sunday leftovers. And for afters a delicious homemade apple pie with custard. In those days there was invariably a pie or a tart to finish the meal. Well flavoured yoghurts weren't around to tempt the shopper to cut corners.

"Nick, I've told you before," said mum. "It's not afters it's dessert."

"Sorry."

"Afters sounds awful."

"Everybody at school calls it afters."

"I don't care what they call it at school."

"At our school they call it sweet," said Joanna.

"Well that's better than afters," said mum.

"At the office they call it pudding," said dad.

"That's better than afters as well."

"No, it's not," said Nick.

"It is if your mum says it is," said dad.

Nick conceded defeat and got on with his dessert. He had a lot on his mind at the moment – primarily the form of his beloved Leyton Orient. Their first spell in the top division had turned out to be a disaster. With less than half the season gone relegation already loomed. A fact more worrying than the G.C.E exams looming. But then Nick wasn't a studious scholar. He found it hard to apply himself at the secondary modern. Unlike Joanna who appeared to be doing well at the grammar school. At the age of thirteen she'd already decided to go into nursing after her A levels.

"Can I borrow the tape recorder?" asked Joanna.

"Well as long as you look after it," said Nick. "And no recording over my pick of the pops."

"No, I've got my own tape. Christine Allen gave me one. We're going to do a Christmas story."

"That's a nice idea," said mum.

"That sounds great fun," said Nick sarcastically. "I can't wait to hear it."

"Well you'll have to until Christmas," said Joanna.

"Oh dear, it'll be difficult but I suppose I'll have to then."

"Don't be so sarcastic," said mum.

"That's right," said dad. "Listen to what your mum says. Now who are the O's going to lose to this Saturday?"

That got a laugh from everybody. Not that dad was a soccer fan. He much preferred cricket. In the fifties he'd regularly taken Nick, with his pals Peter and Michael, to the Lords and Oval test match. What a fantastic day out. A six thirty start, with a packed lunch of course, commenced with a twenty minutes walk to the underground station. Followed by a one hour's tube journey and than an orderly ninety minute queue. Finally you competed in a mad dash to get a decent patch of boundary grass – where you had the best chance of obtaining the fielders autographs. If you asked politely that is.

On top of that it was invariably hot and sunny and England held the upper hand. Dad and Nick had even appeared on the tele. There they were applauding when Godfrey Evans got his century in double quick time. Unfortunately mum and Joanna missed it. The family didn't yet own one of those modern day inventions and were only aware of the tumultuous event when Mrs Forest, from two doors down, came banging on the door.

"Stan and Nick are on the television celebrating Godfrey's hundred," she shouted. "Nick's catching flies." But by then it was too late.

The next time they'd be invited in to watch their neighbours twelve inch black and white would be for the annual boat race. When the best team, Oxford, invariably lost.

"Dad, why do we support Oxford?" asked Joanna time and again.

"Because that's our team."

"But we live closer to Cambridge."

"That doesn't matter."

"All my friends support Cambridge."

"I don't care."

"But Oxford lose every year."

"They're going to win next time."

"If they don't can I support Cambridge?"

"We'll see."

After dinner the family went their separate ways. Joanna took the tape recorder to her bedroom to start on the Christmas story with Christine Allen. Nick went to Boys Brigade. Mum got her Singer sewing machine out. While dad did the washing up before settling down with his favourite read, the boxing magazine, The Ring.

At Boys Brigade it was P.T. night. The highlight of the evening being hand ball. Not yet an Olympic sport but it wouldn't be long. Similar to football, but played with the hands, you scored a goal by fisting the ball between the chairs at lower than waist height. When Nick sided with his pals, rocket Ray Shaw and wizard Keith Newbon, they proved a formidable outfit.

"Are you going to summer camp next year?" asked Mr Lewis.

"Where is it we're going?" replied Nick.

"Sheringham in Norfolk."

"Will we be camping on the cliff top?"

"I don't know. Does that make a difference?"

Of course it made a difference. At last years camp in Cornwall Nick had sleepwalked for the first time. It wasn't until a stones throw from the cliff top that he did an about turn and saved himself. The experience had unnerved him somewhat. The officers at camp had probably been more unnerved by a returning, and still sleepwalking, Nick removing his pyjamas in their tent.

"Oh I see," said Mr Lewis. "Your sleepwalking adventure. I'll find out for you."

"And no stripping off next time," said Ray.

"You know it doesn't make sense," said Keith.

"I'm never going to live that down, am I?"

"Probably not," said Mr Lewis.

Meanwhile Joanna and Christine Allen were having great fun with the tape recorder. But it wasn't a children's story they were producing. Instead they were recording their version of the popular TV game show, Take Your Pick. The top prize being a ticket for the Christmas dance at the boy's grammar school. When they tired of that they amused themselves singing popular songs of the day such as 'Michael row the boat ashore'. One of the songs that had kept them going when they thought they'd walked to Scotland.

"Christine," shouted mum. "Your dad's here."

"She's just coming," shouted Joanna. "We're doing one last song."

"Well hurry up."

"Okay. It's the Beatles."

"The Beatles?"

"The song we're doing. 'Love me do' by the Beatles."

"I haven't heard of them. Are they like the Shadows?"

"Mum, they're nothing like the Shadows."

Christine Allen started tittering. "I can't believe your mum said that."

Joanna was embarrassed but preferred not to make a big song and dance about her mothers faux pas.

"She probably didn't hear me. I know mum likes the Beatles."

But Christine Allen wasn't convinced.

Mum had finished her sewing for the evening. She'd been doing the new curtains for Nick's bedroom. Pale yellow ones to match the green lino and brown paintwork. Next on the agenda would be a bed, then a chest of drawers and replacement sash cords. Since mum had started the part time cashiers job at Henry Taylor's the family were able to afford more of the luxuries available in the early sixties. As she packed the sewing machine away Joanna came in to say goodnight.

"Can I have a bigger chest of drawers as well?" she asked.

"You really haven't got the room," said mum.

"Well can we change bedrooms then?"

And that was the crux of the matter. While Nick slept in the spacious seventeen by twelve feet double bedroom Joanna had to make do with the miniscule eight by five box room. Growing up she'd never had enough room to swing her favourite teddy. An ongoing debate as to whether the two should swap had recently intensified. Granted Nick was the eldest but girls needed more space. That's what Joanna said anyway. Mum and dad were staying out of it at the moment.

Dad, meanwhile, had been in the back room reading about the new boxing sensation Cassius Clay. Evidently a future world champion. Well that's what he'd predicted for himself – the cocky young upstart. Prior to every fight he'd name the round in which he'd win in the form of a rhyme. So far he'd been proved right. Beginners luck no doubt. To think he only turned professional in 1960 after winning the Olympic title. Dad smiled. He knew he'd get his comeuppance before too long. Probably against the new British sensation Billy Walker. Now there was one hell of a fighter. The blonde bombshell as he liked to be known. Although Uncle John, the other boxing enthusiast in the family, disagreed.

"He may look pretty but I bet he can't take a punch," he argued.

"Course he can," said dad.

"We'll have a bet if they do meet up."

"That suits me, how about two and six?"

"Yes, that's fine. Make it five bob if you like."

But dad wasn't that confident.

Suddenly Dad could feel one of his headaches coming on. He put down the magazine and shut his eyes. He was concerned about his health. Something wasn't quite right, but he didn't think it stress related as the doctor suggested. He couldn't think of anything worrying him. He had no work problems. He enjoyed his job at Vavasseurs where he'd recently been promoted to Export Manager. He could cope with the added responsibility.

He'd also completed an evening class course that had given him extra qualifications as an honoured member of the Institute of Export. Three years of hard graft but now the diploma took pride of place hanging in the hall. No, the doctor hadn't a clue.

When dad opened his eyes he'd lost the side vision out of the right one. That really worried him. What did it mean? He had a feeling it could be serious. Now he desperately needed a second opinion.

# THREE

The cortege arrived safely with five minutes to spare. Everybody sighed with relief. Not because they were on time but because Ralph hadn't driven into them. The protagonists squared up for a second time while Joan sidled off for another Benson & Hedges.

"Thanks for not driving too close," said Mr Talisman.

"I think you're being sarcastic," said Ralph.

As family and friends mingled the sun came out. The November murkiness had gone. Now you couldn't have wished for a nicer day for a funeral. An added bonus being the fact there were no rogue mourners present. According to Alan everybody knew somebody that had embarrassingly turned up at the wrong funeral. Usually the same absentminded person that made the mistake at weddings. Although, granted, that would be more of a laugh. Paying your last respects to a stranger while friends and family at the chapel opposite tried frantically to figure out the reason for your non appearance would be unforgivable.

"I don't know anybody," said Joanna.

"You don't?" said Alan.

"No. People turning up at the wrong funeral! Are you sure?"

"It happens all the time."

Joanna walked away unsure what to believe but decided now wasn't the right time to bring up the subject with family and friends.

"Hello Kit," said mum. "I'm glad you could make it."

"Hello Joan. How are you?"

"I'm okay. You know it's for the best but it still comes as a shock."

"Of course it does. But if it hadn't been for you Stan would have died years ago."

"Perhaps that would have been for the best. Well after the second stroke definitely."

"It must have been difficult for both of you."

Mum nodded. No, it hadn't been easy. But that was married life. For better for worse, for richer for poorer. She loved dad and so for over half of their married life she'd cared for him. His condition necessitated it. There were no regrets. Although in hindsight she wished she'd made that decision to put him into a nursing home earlier. Those last few years had been terrible. There'd been so much tension due to his deteriorating mental state. As he became more confused so their relationship suffered. They continually fought, vying for the upper hand, having the last word. In some respects mum lost sight of the fact that dad had suffered for all those years. That at the age of forty nine he'd had a stroke which had rendered him speechless and unable to work. While likewise dad overlooked the fact that mum had tried her best to make his life as comfortable as possible.

But even though their life together had became intolerable the idea of putting dad into a home hadn't been an option. Definitely one step too far. Now she realized the last twelve months of his life in the home had been a blessing in disguise. Okay, without her one to one care he declined physically but on the other hand he seemed more contented. No, perhaps contented was the wrong word. A more resigned person. Resigned to the fact that without mum's care he wouldn't be around much longer. That it'd been her love and devotion that had kept him going throughout the years. And he could cope with that.

From a distance mum could again put into perspective his lot. The years sat in the rust coloured moquette armchair behind the lounge door contemplating. But contemplating what? The days when he could speak? Living a normal family life? The dances at the drill hall Leytonstone where they'd met. His army exploits? The fact he'd rather be dead because his quality of life being such it wasn't worth living. But whatever, because of his loss of speech and his inability to write down his thoughts how much dad could remember from the good old pre stroke days would forever remain a mystery.

"Hello Mary," said Joan.

"Hello Joan. No, it wasn't fair. You think of all those villains that enjoy good health. Especially that bloke from Plaistow who got away with West Ham's cup final tickets. Did you read about that? Where's the justice in it?"

"No, there isn't any."

"You can say that again. He's laughing at us right now. Its one law for us and one for them."

"Yes, Mary, Anyway it's good to see you."

"And you Joan."

Kit and Mary were Stan's unmarried sisters. They'd lived in the family home in Hainault since their teenage days. In the beginning there'd been eight of them. Mum and dad, the two girls and four brothers. They'd kept chickens,which they fed on potato peelings. Owned a lovely obedient mongrel called Muffit, which they also fed on potato peelings and befriended countless cats that moved on once they realized potato peelings were the staple diet.

Granddad worked on the railway. If late he'd improvise by taking a shortcut over the back fence and walk along the track. Fortunately in those days it wasn't electrified. Nana made a delicious Yorkshire pudding. A lovely dignified lady who kept everything ticking over nicely. The real star of the show.

After the brothers married there'd never been any other men in Kit and Mary's life. According to tittle-tattle Kit hadn't experienced the joy and strife of courting while Mary had just the once. But they weren't really anti men – just that growing up with four lazy brothers had sown the seed of doubt in their mind. "Is this what it's all about?" they'd mutter regularly. "The men do sod all while we keep the wheels turning."

On top of that after grandma died they'd spent a great deal of time looking after granddad who didn't enjoy the best of health. For years he'd suffered severe respiratory problems. Even on a good day he could be a cantankerous so and so. So men were relegated further and further down the popularity stakes.

The memories of Nick and Joanna of their granddad was of somebody who spent their entire life in bed. Whenever they visited they'd be ushered into the downstairs back bedroom to say hello and later to say goodbye. On each occasion receiving a rather unpleasant wet moustached kiss.

A much nicer memory would be the warmth afforded them by their aunties. This manifested even before they arrived. As the underground train pulled into Hainault they'd spot Kit and Mary waving from their back door. But not an ordinary wave. This one heralded the fact that everything seemed okay with the world. Peace and goodwill reigned. So what the heck if you were compelled to drink the strongest tea imaginable. It was brewed with love and accompanied by a delicious homemade jam sponge.

On top of that they owned a genuine Dansette record player. A real treat that for Nick and Joanna. They had great fun sifting through the huge pile of singles and long players. Everything from Elvis and the Everley Brothers to the Drifters and Dennis Lotis. You could say their appreciation of pop music had begun in earnest. Although, to be honest, Dennis Lotis wasn't their cup of tea.

But there was another side to life in Hainault. Some might say a racier side. Kit was granddad's bookie runner.

"A what?" Joanna enquired.

"She puts bets on for granddad," said mum.

Joanna looked at mum in amazement. "Our Aunt Kitty bets on the horses."

"Are you sure?"

Mum smiled. "Yes, I'm sure. She has an account."

"What like the Co-op?"

"I suppose so."

"She gets a divi from betting on the horses?"

"Well, not exactly."

"Would she put a bet on for me?" asked Joanna.

"No, she wouldn't. You're too young."

"That's not fair. I bet you let Nick?"

"No, I don't."

"He said you let him help dad with the football pools."

"That not the same."

"Why isn't it?"

After their brother had his stroke in 1963 Kit and Mary were as supportive as sisters could be. Kit had especially found it difficult coming to terms with her brothers stroke at the age of forty nine. Indeed she'd found it impossible to visit him in hospital. Being her big brother he'd always been there for her. She couldn't accept the fact he couldn't talk and would be unable to again.

Every fortnight they'd take the underground train to Leytonstone and then walk to Nottingham road. If they were lucky they'd get a lift back to the station courtesy of Nick. Stan certainly enjoyed seeing his sisters. They invariably had a tale to tell and half a dozen Guinness with a bar of Cadbury's fruit and nut. They were excellent therapy. They made Stan laugh. And the whole street could hear Stan when something tickled him. Though, granted, sometimes he laughed at the most inappropriate things. For example a disaster causing great loss of life. But that's a stroke sufferer for you. The inappropriate laughter syndrome.

# JANUARY 1963

After dad discovered he'd lost the side vision from his right eye he did get a second opinion. He popped into Moorfields eye hospital on the way to work. They confirmed the worse. He probably had a neurological problem and needed to be admitted to hospital for tests. Dad felt more relief than worry. At least a diagnosis had been forthcoming.

A month later and the appointment still hadn't come through. A worrying time for the family. Dad's health had deteriorated to the point where packing up work looked a probability. The numbness feeling down his right side and headaches were making concentration at the office extremely difficult. On top of that he found the loss of his side vision disconcerting. The hospital were contacted on numerous occasions. They always confirmed that his was a priority case. So life went on.

"It says in the paper," said Nick. "That we've had twenty

consecutive days with the temperature remaining below freezing."

"Yes, it's cold but not as bad as forty seven," said mum.

"That must have been bitter then?"

"Dreadful, the coldest winter for more than two hundred years. I was carrying you so I remember it well"

"I should be used to the cold then."

"You should be."

"So the Hollow ponds would have been frozen?" said Joanna.

"I expect so," said mum.

"It's really good fun playing on the ice."

"Well just be careful," said dad.

"It's okay," said Nick. "The ice must be at least two foot thick."

"Two foot! I don't think it is."

"Well I saw a car on it yesterday."

"You saw a car on the ice?"

"Yes, this family had parked on the ice and were skating round it," said Joanna.

"That sounds dangerous," said dad.

"I wish I could ice skate," said Joanna.

"You can roller skate," said mum.

"That's not the same. I want to ice skate like Christine Allen. She says it's easier then roller skating once you get started. That's old fashioned anyway."

"Is it now?" said dad.

"Of course it is."

"Where does Christine go ice skating?" asked mum.

"I'm not sure."

"I know they've got a rink at Richmond but that's the other side of London."

"No, she can walk there from home."

Mum and dad looked at each other and shook their heads. An ice rink within walking distance? That certainly didn't ring true.

"She can," said Joanna.

But boy was it cold. The snow had arrived unexpectedly on Boxing day. When Nick made his way to bible class with neighbour and good friend Mike, whose father owned the maroon Singer Gazelle, it was through a snow drift. Granted not a big one but the snow definitely pushed up against the school railings.

Peter, another neighbour and good friend, whose father didn't possess a car, chucked snowballs at them. He wasn't going to bible class. For some reason he'd joined the scouts. That didn't make sense to Nick. For a start you didn't play handball in the scouts.

But whatever, more than a month later the freeze continued to hold firm.

"There is one good thing about this cold weather," said dad.

"And what's that?" said Nick.

"The O's can't lose any more matches."

Everybody laughed. As yet there hadn't been any football this year. The deep freeze had curtailed all outside sporting events. So the O's were able to languish at the foot of the table with a dismal thirteen points without falling further behind.

"Things will be different when they start up again," said Nick. "They've already played all the top teams."

But he didn't sound convincing.

"I'm just wondering," said dad. "Whether I'll get admitted to hospital before the big freeze ends."

"It can't be long now," said mum. They keep saying you're at the top of the list."

"I know. How long is it since I went to Moorfields?"

"At least a month."

"That's what I thought."

"We'll have to ring up again."

At that moment they heard the letter box rattle. The post had arrived. Now would it include a letter from the hospital? Nick went to see – not so much for that letter but for tickets for the Beatles concert at Southend he'd requested ages ago.

He returned forlorn and handed a letter to dad. "This could be what you're waiting for. Unfortunately there's nothing for me."

"I think you could be right," said dad. "Now let's see what they have to say."

There was anticipation as he opened the letter.

He smiled, "Monday the eighteenth of February."

"At last," said mum.

"Yes, at last," said dad.

They kissed and hugged. What relief. They were moving forward.

"I think I'll give up with the Beatle tickets," said Nick.

"That's right," said mum. "You make sure you get your priorities right."

"Sorry dad," said Nick.

"That's okay," said dad. "Now are the Beatles similar to the Shadows?"

# FOUR

The crematorium was situated in the golden triangle area of Norwich. Estate Agent jargon for a much sought after district with inflated prices. Strange when the majority of properties were the basic two up and two down. You walked from the street into the lounge bemoaning the absence of the hall.

The crematorium itself resembled an unattractive sixties style South Bank building. But it looked clean and the waiting room and toilets smelt of freshly applied Pledge furniture polish and Pine disinfectant respectively. So not an unpleasant place to wile away some time while the party before you paid their respects.

The adjoining cemetery was a massive affair with paths crisscrossing in every direction. Here you could easily lose yourself down the avenue of life and death, of hope and despair, of accomplishment and failure. The graves and verges looked well tended but in a wild and rambling way. When the autumn mist descended you could imagine Holmes and the good doctor laying in wait for Moriaty. Or, alternatively, a party of ramblers seeking directions to the ring road.

"I'm afraid they're running late," explained Mr Talisman to mum.

"Oh dear, why's that?"

"Well the previous party were held up because of an accident and once that happens it's impossible to catch up. I am sorry."

"Don't worry it's not your fault. I'd better tell everyone."

"That's like golf," said Cousin Peter on being informed of the delay. "The party before you are late teeing off and they hold up everyone for the rest of the round."

"I don't think it's quite the same," said Cousin Jacqueline.

"Well no, but it is annoying."

The cousins had travelled up together to pay their respects on behalf of their deceased father's. That's dad's older brothers Fred and Ron. They tried to recall the last time they'd seen Uncle Stan.

"I reckon it could have been Joanna's wedding," said Peter.

"Yes, didn't it snow?" said Jacqueline.

"Snow? Not that I remember."

"You must do?"

"I don't."

"I'll check with Joanna."

"Okay, but I'm sure you're getting your weddings mixed up."

Because of the delay there was more time for the cortege party to mingle with relatives and friends that had arrived independently. Some that had considered meeting up at mum's bungalow but on second thoughts had headed straight for the crematorium in case mum's directions weren't up to scratch and there ensued a stressful last minute dash. There were those that knew exactly what to say and those that shied away from all pleasantries. But that didn't matter, mum was pleased to see everyone.

"Hello Nick," said Iris. "I was talking to your mum about the time you called in after seeing Leyton Orient play Middlesbrough."

"That's right, when the team was doing well in the seventies. I only had half an hour to spare before the train left. A good job you lived near the ground. There were only eight of us who made the journey."

"Eight!"

"Well it's a long way to come midweek. You know, getting the time off work and then a six hour train journey. We made a lot of noise though. You could hear us above the home supporters."

"I think we won."

"You certainly didn't. You scraped a lucky draw. Daylight robbery. Or more like floodlight."

"Uncle Ted gave you some barley wine."

"Yes, I didn't enjoy it."

"You said you liked it."

"I know, I wasn't being totally honest. I liked the Newcastle Brown though, another of uncle's recommendations. You can buy that from the supermarket these days. But I've never seen barley wine. It probably didn't catch on."

"Well I won't tell Ted your secret."

Iris was mum's sister and had travelled down the night before with her daughter Lyn and elder sister Joyce. Mum was pleased they'd stayed overnight. She'd being able to share some happy family memories. They were a close unit and over countless cups of tea they reminisced about Joan's tyrannical form teacher Miss Saunders. (If anybody deserved to be cast into a vat of boiling oil for eternity she did.) Joyce's in service employment with the Figgis family. (That high profile household with IRA connections.) And Iris's transition from life in the East End to life in the Yorkshire Ridings after meeting Ted.

They remembered Marjorie, the sister that had tragically died of T.B. at the age of twenty one. They talked about their four brothers. Because while Stan had been one of six Joan could go two better. They wondered how their mother had coped with such a large family – especially after dad had died in his early fifties at the outbreak of the second world war. But she had because like Stan's mother she was the star of the show. She just got on with life. No fuss and no tantrums.

Nick and Joanna had fond memories of their grandmother. They remembered a quiet dignified person extremely grateful for any small treat. As for a big treat, such as going round her daughters after church and watching Last of the Summer Wine served up with scrumptious homemade meringues with strawberries and cream. Well, that just took the biscuit.

Uncle Ted was not at the funeral. He rarely ventured far from home nowadays – not even for the cup final. Thirty years ago that would have been a must. He'd annually travel down on the Saturday morning in Bill's Humber Snipe. (Bill, his workmate, being one of the few people in Middlesbrough who owned such a prestigious vehicle.) They'd call in at Leyton for lunch and then continue on to Wembley.

After the match they'd drive home non stop. To think in those days they had few motorways and even fewer Little Chef's.

"How is Ted?" asked mum.

"He's okay," said Iris. "I left him a casserole."

"That's good. He won't starve then."

"No, I was trying to remember the last time he actually ventured out of Middlesbrough."

"Didn't he come down to Lowestoft after we moved to Norwich? We met up a couple of times."

"I think you're right."

"He didn't really enjoy it."

"You can say that again. It put him off holidays for good. Well it put him off going anywhere for good. Touch and go whether he'd go to Sue's wedding. His own daughter! Can you believe it?"

"But he did. I've seen the photos. He looked quite happy at the bar with a pint and a cigarette."

"That must have been early on. By nine o'clock he couldn't wait to get home. In a dreadful mood. We both decided then it wasn't worth making the effort. That he'd be better off staying at home with all his comforts."

They were joined by another Ted – Stan's old army friend. And the only person able to persuade Stan to visit the local after his stroke. A fact that had always narked Nick. Well he'd wanted that privilege. It was his dad and fathers and sons did that occasionally. Not that the Five Ways had anything going for it. Except that you could walk there in five minutes and buy a pint of dad's favourite tipple, Guinness, without being crushed in the rush.

"Hello Joan," said Ted. "Not a bad day for a funeral."

"No. How's Gwen?"

"The leg's improving. She sends her condolences."

"Thanks for coming Ted."

"That's okay. I wouldn't have missed it. Stan was a good man. They thought a lot of him in the army. Somebody you could trust and respect. That's why they wanted him to stay on after the war. Promote him up to Major."

"I know Ted," said Joan. "He did enjoy those years. He made

31

some good friends. And he always appreciated your visits after his stroke. You had the knack of making him laugh."

"Well I wasn't always sure how much he remembered from the old days but we did have a laugh. Poor old Stan, you just don't know what's round the corner."

# 18th FEBRUARY 1963

You could describe it as the irony of ironies that dad suffered his stroke on the very day he prepared for admittance to hospital for neurological tests. Weeks of waiting, the big day finally arrives, and dad has a stroke. What rotten luck. But they were the facts. At precisely ten past eight on the morning of the eighteenth of February he collapsed in the bathroom whilst shaving. Life would never be the same for the Wisbey family.

The rest of the family were downstairs having breakfast. Nick and Joanna were shortly off to school while mum had the Monday wash and a Shepherds pie to complete before a one o'clock start at Henry Taylor's. They all heard the bump as dad collapsed and rushed upstairs.

"Stan," said mum. "Can you hear me?"

Dad didn't answer. He appeared to be in a state of semi-consciousness slumped on the floor by the side of the bath. The bathroom seat had toppled on top of him and his razor lay in pieces in the washbasin. His glasses were perched in an undignified manner on the end of his nose. His breathing seemed loud and laboured. He looked a sorry sight. But his eyes were open. That must be a good sign – surely. Although they seemed glazed – as though he couldn't take in his surroundings. He looked at his watch with puzzlement. Then his expression changed. Now he had a resigned look on his face. As though he knew his luck had just run out.

"Dad," said Joanna. "Can you stand up?"

Dad stared ahead. He dribbled. He looked again at his watch. He pointed to it as if there was some great significance with the time.

"I'll go and phone for the doctor," said Nick.

"Okay," said mum. "But we'll probably have to wait until after surgery."

"It's only twenty past eight," said Joanna. "He wouldn't have started yet."

"Yes, but you know what Jarvis is like."

"Well I'll do my best," said Nick.

He shot off to the telephone box at the top of Griggs Road convinced he'd be able to persuade the doctor to attend to dad before morning surgery.

Mum picked up the bathroom seat and removed dad's glasses. She carefully placed them in her apron pocket. She cradled him in her arms. He looked so helpless. The thought crossed her mind he'd suffered a stroke. But no, not at that age, surely. Dad eyes were shut now. His breathing more regular but weaker. Was that a positive or negative sign?

"Stan, can you hear me?" she repeated. "Stan, please answer me."

But he didn't. He'd either fallen asleep or slipped into unconsciousness.

"It's a good job he didn't collapse against the door," she said. "We'd never have opened it."

"Or if he'd locked the door," said Joanna.

Together they attempted to make dad more comfortable on the floor. But it was a hopeless struggle. Dad weighed more than fourteen stone. Every time they tried to pull him up into a sitting position he resisted. After a while they gave up.

"I'm surprised how heavy he is," said Joanna.

"Yes, you're right. I think dad could have had a stroke."

"A stroke? That's serious, isn't it?"

"They can be."

"I thought only old people had strokes. Dad's not old. Are you sure?"

"No, I'm not. We'll see what the doctor says."

"Hello, could I speak to Doctor Jarvis please?" said Nick.

He was determined to stay as calm as possible. Just relay the facts and persuade the doctor to call in before surgery commenced.

33

But unfortunately Doctor Jarvis hadn't yet arrived so a pre surgery visit looked out of the question.

"Well, when do you think he'll be able to make it?" said Nick.

The receptionist didn't know. It depended on how busy morning surgery was.

"You've got no idea" said Nick.

She reiterated that she didn't but assured him that Dr. Jarvis would be around as soon as possible.

"We might as well have rung for an ambulance," said Nick and slammed down the phone.

But ringing for an ambulance wasn't normal procedure in the sixties. In the first instance you called the doctor. Society would have deemed ringing nine, nine, nine, as way over the top. Unless you were convinced you had a near fatality on your hands. And Nick wasn't.


"You won't believe this," said Nick on his return home."

"He can't make it before surgery," said mum. "I told you that's what he'd say."

"Actually he hasn't arrived yet."

"Hasn't arrived? He cuts it fine."

"That's what I thought."

"We'll have to ring for an ambulance. Or have you already done that?"

Nick looked guilty. "No, sorry I should have. I did think about it but thought that might be over reacting."

"I know what you mean," said mum. "You didn't want to make a fuss. But I think we should now."

"Okay, I'll go back. How is dad? It looks like he's sleeping. Has he said anything?"

"No, but his breathing seems better."

"That's a good sign then, isn't it?"

"I hope so."


This time Nick arrived at the phone box to find it engaged. A situation he hadn't considered. Fortunately he recognized the occupier.

"Hello Mrs Farrow," said Nick, nervously opening the door. "We've got an emergency at home."

"An emergency?" replied an agitated Mrs Farrow.

"Yes, dad's not well. He's collapsed. And the doctor hasn't got time to visit before surgery. So we need an ambulance."

"Hasn't got time?" said Mrs Farrow. "I would have thought there's plenty of time."

"That's what I thought."

"You'd better ring nine, nine, nine then. These doctors don't like to put themselves out, do they?"

"We used to have a good one," said Nick. "But he had a heart attack."

"You mean Hutchinson. Yes, he certainly knew his job. A real shame that. So you're with Jarvis now?"

"Unfortunately we are."

"Actually he hasn't been too bad with us. Give him his due. He's got some irritating habits mind you."

"You mean like tearing strips off the bottom of his prescription pad," said Nick.

"That's right. Why does he do that? I find it really off putting."

"I don't think he realizes."

"No, you're probably right. Anyway, I hope your dad's alright."

"I hope so."

As Nick dialled nine, nine, nine he had his fingers crossed that an ambulance would be despatched immediately. That dad could be admitted to hospital without delay.

# FIVE

The service started ten minutes late. Those expected to turn up had and on time. The Rev. Turner welcomed everybody and got off on the right foot by getting dad's name right. According to Alan, who else, everybody knew somebody that had attended a funeral where the priest made a right hash of the deceased's name. In one embarrassing instance even substituting Mark for Mary.

"I don't know anyone," said Joanna.

"You don't," said Alan.

"No. Getting the name wrong! Are you sure uncle?"

"Positive."

The proceedings commenced with the old favourite, The Lords my Shepherd. A hymn guaranteed to lift the rafters.

"Oh no," said Nick. "I've left my glasses at Mum's."

"I didn't know you wore them," said Nicole.

"I've just started. Give it a few years and you'll be wearing them."

"I don't think so."

"It's inevitable with age."

"We'll see about that."

Nick and Nicole had recently split up after six years of marriage. Things were still a little fraught. There were issues to sort out. For instance, which aggrieved party took ownership of the twenty year old metallic green Morris Marina with a piffling fifty thousand on the clock? Who could be persuaded to take on the cumbersome and unwieldy filing cabinet?

But disregarding those conundrums Nick appreciated his ex for making the effort to attend. For lending her support at his time of need. But then she'd always had a soft spot for dad. She invariably felt more comfortable in the company of children and because of his stroke dad fitted that criteria perfectly. Somebody who needed the care of an adult. As for mum, well they got on okay but she detected a certain detachment in her company. No, it wasn't her imagination as Nick suggested.

"If mum does appear cold," said Nick earlier that day. "It's probably to do with you saying you couldn't guarantee to look after me if I had a stroke. That you might stick me in a home."

Nicole looked horrified. "I said that?"

"Yes, it might have been bravado but that's probably what mum remembers."

"That does sound a bit selfish, doesn't it?"

"A little bit. But not to worry it's irrelevant now."

"On second thoughts I would have managed. I'd have pushed you in your wheelchair if necessary."

"That is reassuring, I'll let mum know."

"So long as it was downhill."

With their services presently not required Mr Talisman relaxed with his colleague, and grandson, on a bench in the Garden of Remembrance. The November sun continued to shine.

"It's really nice now," said Mr Talisman.

"You're right," said Tommy. "A pity about the delay though."

"Yes, a good job we're not busy. That would have put a spanner in the works."

"You can say that again."

"I remember back in the seventies when we made double figures."

"So you've said hundred of times."

"Well it's true. That would have tested you."

"I like hard work," said Tommy.

"I haven't noticed."

"At least I don't make a habit of arguing with the families. What was that all about?"

"Well did you see his driving? He almost ran me over reversing outside the house. Then he's up my rear all the way to the crematorium."

Mr Talisman and grandson Tommy didn't get on. They put up with other. Well they had to carrying a coffin in and out of a chapel. Could you imagine undertakers squabbling over which end to carry? The problem was Tommy had taken up the profession reluctantly. He'd been coerced into it to keep the family business going. He'd much rather sell second hand cars like his best mate Darren. What a life he led. A different late registration car parked outside the house every night.

"Do you know what car Darren's driving now?" said Tommy.

"I've no idea and I really don't care," replied a bored Mr Talisman.

"Only a Porsche. What do I drive?"

"I've forgotten."

"An 1100. A bloody Austin 1100."

"Okay, but it's not his car, is it? He just takes it home."

"You don't get it, do you? The girls see him in a Porsche, they see me in a 1100."

# AUGUST 1963

After being admitted to Whipps Cross hospital, where he'd been due on the eighteenth, dad transferred to the National Hospital for Nervous Diseases in Holborn W.C1. The hospital that afforded you the best possible treatment if you'd suffered a stroke. There he stayed for six weeks.

From the outset Dr Heathfield declared dad was unlikely to talk again. His stroke had been very serious and regaining ones speech didn't normally occur. But on the positive side, over the next three years there should be some physical improvement. Although besides dad's gammy left hand there wasn't much physical evidence of a stroke. He retained the good looks and posture of Captain Stan Wisbey – ex 2nd World War Anti-aircraft Division latterly stationed in the Orkneys and Canvey Island. Indeed if you passed in the street you'd be hard pressed to pick up on an affliction.

Within the three years time scale dad might also regain the ability to write down his thoughts. What he wanted, what irked him, what memories he had. Obviously that would make life easier if he remained speechless for the rest of his life. But for the present dad could only say Eeeeeee. Eeeeeee and wave his arms about when trying to make himself understood.

Hospital visits for the family entailed a walk to the Bakers Arms and then the No. 38 bus to Theobalds Rd. Approximately an hour from door to door. Mum, Nick and Joanna did the trip most days. Supporting each other and hoping against hope that the next time they visited dad might be talking. Wouldn't that be great? And there was one false dawn with Auntie Joyce reporting back that Stan had spoken a few words. For a couple of hours the excitement mounted, the rumour mill worked overtime. But sadly it wasn't to be. When they next visited dad's vocabulary remained restricted to Eeeeeee. Eeeeeee.

While dad remained hospitalised the winter did its utmost to make life even more miserable. The temperature remained below freezing and the Boxing Day snow refused to melt. The coldest winter in living memory some people said. Naturally mum disagreed. Nothing compared with forty-seven.

If they had time before the bus home they'd pop in the café on the corner of Theobalds and Red Lion Street. Where, on mum's recommendation, the children tasted their first rumbabas. Wow, what a sumptuous gooey sickly texture. You certainly wouldn't want two.

While there they listened to the Beatles singing 'Please, Please, Me' on the radio. Their very first number one. The Liverpool sound had taken off big time. Vocal groups were all the rage and the Shadows and Tornados were sulking. Although the family's particular favourite at the time happened to be the non Liverpudlian brother and sister act, the Springfields, with their 'Island of Dreams'. What a beautiful uplifting tune at such a sad time.

"Dad, have you heard of the Beatles?" asked Nick.

"Eeeeeee."

"They're a group from Liverpool."

"Eeeeeee."

"They're my favourite."

"Eeeeeee."

Nick smiled. He knew from dad's reaction that on this occasion he understood. Obviously his regularly recorded pick of the pops at the dinner table had registered. Suddenly dad grabbed his hand and shook it with his gammy one. He regularly did that – to prove his grip was improving.

"Eeeeeee. Eeeeeee."

"Yes, it's getting stronger," said Nick.

"Eeeeeee. Eeeeeee."

"You'll be breaking my hand soon."

They both smiled and Nick went away humming the Beatles 'From Me To You'. For some obscure reason he wondered whether Dr Jarvis had heard of the Beatles. Whether he approved or otherwise of the mop tops? He shook his head. That doctor had a lot to answer for. Although having said that he did make it round to Nottingham Road on the eventful morning of the eighteenth -albeit fifteen minutes after the ambulance. Rather sheepishly he agreed with their diagnosis of a stroke. But of course he wasn't about to admit he wished he'd been more on the ball previously. That he should have referred dad to the hospital for a second opinion. He just shrugged his shoulders and, "Oh well we all make mistakes," came to mind. Actually that wasn't what the family were thinking.

So life changed on the eighteenth. And mum gave up smoking. Never again would she indulge. Well, what more incentive could there be. The future looked uncertain. She needed the extra cash. No, it wasn't a health thing. In the early sixties smoking was acceptable – even cool. Over half the adult population indulged. Mum had smoked her players as she ironed and vacuumed. Nick and Joanna could never work out how she managed to retain the fag in her mouth for such a time without choking. And as with any accomplished smoker she knew just how much ash would collect before it dropped on her best nylon blouse.

For security reasons she'd sellotape the packet of ten Players to the living room mantelpiece. Well, cigarettes had gone astray and drastic measures were needed. Nick, the chief suspect, always denied the crime but mum knew better. He had guilt written all over his face.

Dad had never indulged. His army cigarette allowance went straight to mum. Sometimes she'd been completely overwhelmed by the amount of fags he'd bring home on leave. The whole regiments supply he joked. Undoubtedly the war years were good fag years for mum.

Everybody pulled together after the eighteenth. Family, friends and neighbours all did their bit. Offered help where needed. None more so than Nana Bailey who moved in with the family when dad came home from hospital. She wanted to be with her daughter at this time of crisis and readily accepted her invitation. She helped run the household while mum tried to sort out a routine with dad. She eased the pressure. She spent time with the children. Because what did they think of it all? Their dad unable to communicate. The head of the household relegated to minor duties.

"Hello dad, how do you feel today?" said Joanna,
"Eeeeeee. Eeccccee."
"You've finished your porridge."
"Eeeeeee. Eeeeeee."
"I'm going to have my breakfast now."
"Eeeeeee. Eeeeeee."
"No, I prefer cornflakes."
"Eeeeeee. Eeccceee."
"Then I'm off to school."
"Eeeeeee. Eeeeeee"
"See you this evening."

"It must be so frustrating for dad," said Joanna over her bowl of cornflakes.
"I know," said mum. "You just don't know how much he can understand. It'd be so much easier if he could write down what he wanted to say."
"It doesn't seem fair."
"No, but at least he can get about."
"That's true."
"I don't know what would be worse," said mum. "Like he is, or

able to speak but confined to a wheelchair. They're funny things strokes. It depends on which side of the brain is affected."

"Which side was dad's?" said Joanna. "I've forgotten again."

"The left hand side."

"I'll try and remember."

But life did get into a sort of routine. A month after dad came home mum went back to her part-time job and nana moved out. One hundred percent dad's decision. Mum would have preferred her support for a few more weeks but dad had had enough. She irritated him. He needed more space.

"But she's only trying to help," said mum.

"Eeeeeee. Eeeeeee."

"I know Stan. I know it's difficult."

"Eeeeeee. Eeeeeee."

"Okay, I'll have a word with her."

There were things that dad could do. For instance: Get the shopping. (Well mainly the fruit and vegetables from Godlontons and the bread from Mays. They knew dad from his pre stroke days so he handed over his list and they obliged.) Put the oven on – so long as mum wrote down the time. And make a cup of tea. That he did from memory. So to a minor degree his brain could still function.

Every morning he'd have breakfast in bed, porridge followed by eggs and bacon, shave and then come down and sit in the armchair behind the dinning room door. He'd read the paper, the labour party supporting Daily Herald and the boxing magazine the Ring. He gave the impression he understand most of what was happening in the world.

At ten he'd have a coffee and a ginger nut, followed at eleven thirty by a Guinness. At twelve thirty he'd have lunch, which was normally a tin of ravioli. Mum then went to work and dad either ate again at six thirty, when dinner would be served, or, and if his brain was up to it, make himself a cup of tea with another ginger nut sometime in the afternoon.

After dinner, which always included a dessert, there'd be a coffee with another ginger nut at eight thirty. At ten thirty dad retired for the night. Mum needed that routine as much as dad – probably more so.

Weekly he reluctantly took the bus to a day centre in Walthamstow. The social worker said it would be good for dad – but dad couldn't see that. He would much rather have stayed at home. They weren't going to teach him to speak again so why bother? At the centre he did menial tasks like putting sweets into a jar. But at least he made it there and back on the single-decker without mishap.

Then, bizarrely, there was the Algipan saga. Dad had always suffered from lumbago. Since the stroke the condition had deteriorated. Well that's what mum deduced from dad's gesticulating and moaning.

"Is it your back Stan?"

"Eeeeeee. Eeeeeee."

"The lumbago?"

"Eeeeeee. Eeeeeee."

"We'll see what the doctor says."

After an examination Dr Jarvis prescribed two tubes of Algipan. (The popular backache ointment of the day). It didn't improve the condition but every morning mum did dad's back regardless. Undeniably a comfort thing dad needed the cream and mum wasn't about to say "It's a waste of time Stan." As for the doctor, well after the stroke diagnosis debacle he dared not refuse the request. He never examined dad's back again but just kept on with the prescriptions. Dad's back got greasier and greasier and Algipan's shares rocketed.

In the August Vavasseur's stopped paying dad's wages. The decision had been expected. They'd been generous to keep it going for six months. In that time his work colleagues regularly visited. They told some great stories about dad. How they missed him, his integrity and sense of humour. They hoped he'd be able to return. And you could tell they meant it. But now they'd stopped his wages. That was final. Dad wouldn't be working again. Thankfully the decision coincided with the mortgage being paid off. A coincidence or an act of God mum pondered?

Also that month Nick started his first job. Earning five pounds a week as a shipping clerk. Coincidentally just around the corner from Vavasseurs. If it hadn't been for the fact that Mr Purchase, the office manager, knew dad from his army days Nick probably wouldn't have got the position. At that time his interviewing skills left a lot to be desired. He debated on how much housekeeping money he should give mum. Would ten shillings be okay?

Needless to say there wasn't a family holiday in sixty three. The continuous run since fifty four had been broken – probably for good. There had been talk of getting dad into a respite centre. But mum decided against it. She thought it unfair that dad should have to cope with that upheaval after what he'd been through. Perhaps that would be an option next year.

And suffice to say Leyton Orient were relegated.

# SIX

When the hymn finished the majority sat down. There were a few unsure of protocol, who chose to remain standing until the realization they stuck out like a sore thumb. But unlike the concert hall nobody actually shouted, "Sit down," at the top of their voice.

"It doesn't say sit down on the service sheet," said John.

"They take it for granted that everybody knows," said Dot.

"We're not all churchgoers."

"That's true."

John and Dot were friends of Joanna and David. They had been since the latter moved to Norwich in nineteen seventy eight. The girls had teamed up at the local branch of Amnesty International. Nowadays supporting that worthy cause and having a laudable attempt at aerobics went hand in hand with bringing up the children. That's Joanna's four and Dot's three.

"I think I'll stay seated from now on," said John.

With everybody seated the Rev. Turner said a few words about dad. Their paths hadn't crossed but with the information gleaned from mum he had a good picture of his life before and after the stroke. Growing up as one of six in downtown Leyton and then rural Hainault. The war years stationed in such diverse places as the Orkneys and Canvey Island. Back in civvy street, this time the posh part of Leyton, opposite the grammar school, married with a mortgage. The three bedroom terrace purchased for seven hundred and fifty pounds. (A significant amount for a house in those days) The advent of fatherhood and the joy that brought. A successful career in the export trade. But then the stroke – the complete change around. No longer the breadwinner but reduced to carrying out simple errands. And that was in the early days prior to his condition greatly deteriorating.

It seemed amazing he'd survived twenty eight years. Obviously Joan's love had something to do with that. He observed her dignity and surprising lack of bitterness (Well, except when discussing their doctor's role in the tragedy). But instead pride because Stan had been such a good husband and father prior to the stroke. And afterwards, well he couldn't be blamed for the increasing irrational behaviour as the years passed. The brain was malfunctioning. An unfortunate fact of stroke life.

He noted they were a close family. That the children had been most supportive throughout the years. That without their love and, at the appropriate time laughter, life would have been more of a struggle. More recently she'd been grateful for the support of her son-in-law and grandchildren. Her four lovely boys, as she called them. She'd been fortunate indeed to see them grow up – to be part of their life. Yes, she did have lots to be thankful for. But poor Stan. The Rev. nodded and sympathized.

# 1964

A year after dad's stroke he'd once again been admitted to hospital. This time for investigation of a stomach ulcer. Probably caused through the frustration of being unable to speak. Well that's what Dr Jarvis reckoned and although he had a poor track record it did make sense. Daily one witnessed dad's frustration. His gesticulations, his shouting and his aggressiveness as he tried to make himself understood. Life would have been easier if he could have written down his thoughts. But unfortunately twelve months on that ability hadn't yet returned.

"I'm not late," said mum as dad pointed to his watch when she arrived at his bedside.

"Eeeeeee. Eeeeeee."

"Yes, I'm okay Stan. How are you?"

"Eeeeeee. Eeeeeee."

Dad looked agitated. He had something on his mind.

"Eeeeeee. Eeeeeee."

"I'm sorry Stan but I don't understand."

"Eeeeeee. Eeeeeee."

"Your brothers?"

"Eeeeeee. Eeeeeee."

"Kit and Mary?"

"Eeeeeee. Eeeeeee."

"My brothers?"

Dad nodded, now they were getting somewhere.

"John?"

"Eeeeeee. Eeeeeee."

"Ralph?"

Dad nodded again.

"What about Ralph?"

"Eeeeeee. Eeeeeee."

"How is he?"

"Eeeeeee. Eeeeeee."

"His job?"

"Eeeeeee. Eeeeeee."

"Oh, I know what you're going on about. You want me to hide the Southern Comfort when he visits?"

Dad nodded for a third time.

"That's a bit mean Stan."

"Eeeeeee. Eeeeeee."

"You don't think so."

"Eeeeeee. Eeeeeee."

"Okay, I'll put it in the wardrobe. But he's not likely to pop round while you're in hospital."

"Eeeeeee. Eeeeeee."

"No, I won't forget. But your brother Ron is just as bad."

"Eeeeeee Eeeeeee."

"That's because he's your brother. You're biased."

Unlike the previous winter this one had been mild. So that hadn't been the reason dad gave up on the day centre. He'd just had enough. He'd much rather be stuck at home. They couldn't do anything about his speech so why attend? Needless to say the social worker didn't see it like that. She tried to convince mum that he should persevere. That mentally it would benefit him. But mum had badgered enough. It was too damn stressful having a weekly confrontation about the subject. Thankfully with dad hospitalized the emotive topic didn't arise.

"He's doing very well," said the nurse.

"Oh that's good," said mum.

"He went round with the drinks trolley last night."

"Really?"

Mum found that hard to believe. That Stan had wheeled the patients nightcap trolley round the ward. Okay, so that was the hospitals quirky tradition, the ablest patients encouraged to volunteer as drinks waiter. But how could Stan have coped with handing out such a variety of beverages? Tea, coffee, cocoa, Horlicks, and Bournvita to name just five.

"Are you sure?" said mum.

"Yes, and he'll probably be doing it again tonight. Won't you Mr Wisbey?"

"Eeeeeee. Eeeeeee."

"Good for you. Well I've finished for the day now. I'll see you tomorrow. Goodnight."

They watched as she walked away. Mum reckoned she originated from the Middle East. Well she had a slightly tanned skin and her name was Nasrin. So no way could you mistake her for an Irish national, where ninety per cent of the nursing staff originated from.

"She's a nice girl," said mum.

"Eeeeeee. Eeeeeee."

Dad obviously agreed. He smiled and gave her the thumbs up.

"I wonder what nationality she is."

Dad shrugged his shoulders.

"It could be Egyptian."

Dad laughed sarcastically. As far as he was concerned Nasrin wasn't Egyptian.

"Well she's not Irish," said mum.

Dad nodded. That didn't need much working out.

After a week in hospital dad came home. He'd undergone a couple of barium meals and that was that. No surgery but a course of medication to improve his condition. He immediately made for his favourite armchair and slumped down. He breathed a sigh of relief. You couldn't beat being at home – especially when you were a stroke sufferer. One needed the security of family life. Although, granted, there were times when he didn't appreciate what Joan did to make his life as comfortable as possible. He found it so frustrating being unable to talk. He wanted to share things with Joan, with Nick and Joanna. He was missing out on such a lot. He'd be better off dead. He put two fingers against his forehead as though to shoot himself. No, he shouldn't think like that. There were people worse off than himself. Although at that precise moment he couldn't think of anybody.

"How do you feel dad?" asked Nick.

"Eeeeeee. Eeeeeee."

"Would you like a cup of tea?"

"Eeeeeee. Eeeeeee."

"You know the O's?"

"Eeeeeee. Eeeeeee."

"Well they had their biggest ever attendance the other week. The cup match against West Ham. Over thirty four thousand turned up."

"Eeeeeee Eeeeeee."

"Yes, they lost."

"Eeeeeee Eeeeeee."

"No, they won't get relegated again. They're holding their own this season."

Nick had been at work for six months now. He enjoyed it. His wages had recently been increased to five pounds and ten shillings. After giving mum ten shillings he had enough remaining to enjoy the good things in life. Such as venturing down Leyton Baths on a Monday to see a top group like the Yardbirds or the Kinks. Supporting his beloved Leyton Orient. And three nights a week, plus a Sunday morning, participating in Boys Brigade activities.

At Christmas he'd actually received a one hundred pound bonus. A complete surprise. With half the money he'd been tempted to buy five hundred Beatles shares. Their music publishers, Northern Songs, were offering loads at the very reasonable price of two shillings each. But the advice from his work colleagues and, more importantly, the well respected Investors Chronicle didn't pull any punches, "Buying Beatles shares? Don't be silly. What does a pop group know about investing money on the stock market? Put it in a dependable unit trust sonny." So reluctantly he did. Unicorn Trust to be exact.

Joanna hadn't changed her plans for the future. She still wanted to be a nurse. But that remained a couple of years away. In the meantime she did a paper round plus Saturday jobs at Woolworth's and the transport café down the Southend Arterial. She attended the Guides and played teenage games with friends Christine Allen and Pauline Sadler. (Their favourite being whom is the best looking sixth former at the Boys High School?) And she kept up the swimming. Something that dad as a member of Leyton Swimming Club had encouraged from an early age. Both her and Nick had learnt by the age of five. They'd also learnt that waiting outside the William IV pub with a bag of chips and a pickled onion while dad had a quick half before returning home was par for the course.

Unfortunately mum couldn't swim and no amount of encouragement from the family could persuade to have a go. She'd had a nasty experience while at school. The infamous Miss Sanders, who else, had pulled her in too quickly with the rope. A drowning attempt? Only the old trout would have known the truth. Sadly the end result was that mum swallowed gallons of water and never again took the plunge.

Dad's hospitalisation had been a welcome break for mum. It had given her time to recharge her batteries. Like being on holiday. She could please herself without worrying about dad's frame of mind. Listening to him going, "Eeeeeee. Eeeeeee." God, that could make her feel so uptight. Yes, she knew he couldn't help it but it irked her. How could she be expected to understand what he meant every time? She did her best.

But she was pleased to have him back home where he belonged. Her Stan, for better for worse. How apt that sounded today. They had many great memories. Their courtship days, those dances at the Drill Hall and trips to the West End to see a show. The marvellous Christmas parties they hosted. Watching the children grow up healthy and sound. How things had changed.

Although from appearances you wouldn't have guessed dad's lot. He still retained his good looks and posture. Indeed at six foot one and fourteen stone he caught the eye as he walked to the Bakers Arms for the weekly errands. How appearances could deceive.

At least with her part-time job mum had a life outside home – some independence. She really enjoyed the cashiers work at outfitters Henry Taylor's. In the local area they were the people to see for your school uniform. State or private they were unrivalled. Well that's what mum repeatedly drummed into family and friends alike.

"It's only a school uniform," said Joanna.

"That's where you're wrong," said mum.

"Christine Allen says there's a shop in Ilford that sells much nicer uniforms."

"That's our other branch."

"I didn't know there was another Henry Taylor's."

"No, of course you didn't."

Mum enjoyed the camaraderie at work – even the backbiting. Henry Taylor's employed two other cashiers, Mrs Walker and Miss Warner. They didn't always see eye to eye. In fact they were known as the troublesome trio. But all in good faith because where customers were concerned they were a united front. Rivalries were overlooked and a pleasant smile greeted each shopper. Each night though the family looked forward to the latest gossip on the outfitters front. Who had upset whom? Which of the trio had delivered the first sarcastic comment?

Unfortunately mum didn't have time to hide the Southern Comfort when Uncle Ralph turned up unannounced on the Friday evening. Very spooky that, as if he knew dad's intentions and wanted to get one over him. And you should have seen the look on dad's face when he realized the identity of his visitor.

"Hello Stan," said Ralph. "How are you? I wouldn't mind a Southern Comfort if there's one going."

"Eeeeeee. Eeeeeee."

"Yes, just a small one."

No, that wasn't what dad had in mind. But Ralph didn't pick up on the negative vibes emanating, being totally consumed with discussing the forthcoming general election.

"Okay," said mum. "I'll get you a small one."

"Thanks Joan. I think Labour will get in this time."

"Eeeeeee. Eeeeeee."

"Yes, it's going to be close. Are you voting Stan?"

Dad nodded. He'd always voted – and invariably Labour. But at this particular moment was more concerned with seeing how small the Southern Comfort measure would be. From past experience mum tended to overdo it.

"Did I tell you that Harold Wilson offered me a job? "Ralph said.

"Eeeeeee. Eeeeeee."

Dad's eyes were fixed on the filling glass.

"Yes, as his press secretary, but it would have meant moving up to his constituency. I didn't fancy that. Joan wouldn't have either."

"I'm not surprised," said mum. "Huyton in Lancashire wasn't it?"

"That's right."

"Is that enough Ralph?"

"Eeeeeee. Eeeeeee."

"No, that's plenty Stan," said Ralph. "Don't want to overdo it."

Dad seethed. Plenty wasn't the word. He'd never seen such a large, small measure. Why did mum have to be so generous with the spirits?

"Well cheers," said Ralph. "Here's to a Labour victory."

"Let's hope so," said mum.

"Eeeeeee. Eeeeeee."

"Did you want a drink Stan?" said mum.

Dad shook his head. He wasn't in the mood.

"Do you know," said Ralph. "Its thirteen years since we had a Labour government. Can you believe that?"

"Eeeeeee. Eeeeeee."

At that moment they were joined by a solemn looking Nick and

Joanna. The school disco in Walthamstow had been a let down. Plenty of Glen Miller and Tony Bennett but no Beatles or Stones. A really pathetic affair.

"Hello you two," said Ralph.

"Hello Uncle Ralph," said Joanna.

"Hello Uncle Ralph," said Nick.

"You're back early," said mum.

"They didn't play any Beatles," said Joanna.

"Did that matter?"

"Of course it did. Glen Miller, who wants to listen to him?"

"Did you know he died in a plane crash?" said Ralph.

"That's what they said," said Nick. "But they never found his body."

"No, you're right," said Ralph. "Now do you fancy seeing Harold Wilson at the Assembly Rooms, Walthamstow?"

Nick gulped. He'd been caught off guard. Okay, he did have an interest in Politics. He'd probably vote Labour when old enough – but did he want to listen to their leader?

"Eeeeeee. Eeeeeee."

"You want to go Stan?" said Ralph.

"Eeeeeee. Eeeeeee."

"No," said mum. "I think he wants Nick to go."

"Eeeeeee. Eeeeeee."

"Do you Stan?" said Ralph. "So what do you say Nick."

Well what could Nick say?

"Yes, okay."

"Good for you. It'll be a night to remember."

Nick nodded but was already having second thoughts. Unless Uncle Ralph could get an introduction to meet Harold Wilson. Now that would go down well with his mates.

"He's got a weak handshake," said Ralph. "I think that says a lot about a person."

"In which way?" said Nick.

"It means they're lacking in confidence."

"Is that so? Well I'll make sure I give his hand a real squeeze then.

If I get the opportunity that is. What do you think Uncle? Is there any chance of an introduction?"

"It's possible."

"That'll be great."

"I said possible."

# SEVEN

Mr Talisman sat down with a heavy heart. He hated having words with his grandson but surely at the age of nineteen he should be more mature.

"But I'm only nineteen," said Tommy. "Did you know everything at my age?"

"I left school when I was fourteen."

"What, to go up the chimney?"

"See, you're being childish again."

They were joined by an out of breath elderly silver haired lady. They waited while she took enormous gulps of air trying desperately to compose herself.

"Is this the funeral for Brenda Patterson," she eventually blurted out.

"No," said Mr Talisman. "Stanley Wisbey."

She visibly aged. She held her head in her hands and began to sob.

"I'm lost" she shouted. "They've directed me to the wrong place."

"You probably want St. Faiths," said Tommy. "It happens all the time. You'll have to get a taxi – if you're lucky that is. You don't see too many of those round here."

Distraught she cupped her hands over her ears. Mr Talisman patted her shoulder.

"Now, now that won't do any good. Come on, we can sort this out. Have you any directions Mrs…?"

"Watkins," she said.

She wiped her eyes and opened her shiny black leather handbag. She handed Mr Talisman a manila envelope. On the back were some directions. He studied them carefully. After a minute he grinned broadly.

"It's tomorrow. Look, one thirty on the sixteenth. You've got the wrong day."

Mrs Watkins snatched back the envelope. She too studied it closely. She smiled broadly.

"You're right. Oh thank God for that. What a relief. I can go home and relax now."

"Okay, we might see you tomorrow then," said Mr Talisman. "We're back here for two funerals."

Back at the service Joanna had started the reading. John 14 verses 1-6.

"Jesus said to his disciples: Do not let your hearts be troubled. Believe in God, believe also in me."

"What does that mean?" whispered Robert to his dad.

"Ssh, I'll tell you later,"

"Does mum know what it means?"

"Yes."

"That's good then."

The reading concluded. "Jesus said to him, I am the way, and the truth, and the life. No, one comes to the Father except through me. Amen."

"Amen," said Robert. "I suppose God knows what it means."

# 1965

Dad looked forward to his trip to the fish shop. He had his list and the correct money (according to mum that is) in one pocket and an extra two shillings in another – just in case. Harry's Fish Bar wasn't a regular destination for dad. Indeed this would be his first visit since the stroke. Needless to say mum had the jitters. Okay dad could regularly find his way to the greengrocers and bakers but the fish shop could pose a problem.

She would have preferred one of the children to accompany him. But Stan wouldn't hear of it. He knew exactly where to go. In the good old days a stroll to the Bakers Arms on Saturday to fetch the traditional delicacy went without saying. And today his damaged brain wouldn't let him down. Although he didn't recall the establishment being called Harry's Fish Bar.

"Right, now are you okay Stan?" said mum. "You know where you're going?"

"Eeeeeee. Eeeeeee."

"Alright, you don't have to shout. Just take care."

Stan held his hand up in apology. Then he touched her cheek gently. Of course she worried about him. Dear Joan, what would he do without her?

She held his hand tightly. "That's okay Stan. You have a nice walk."

"Eeeeeee. Eeeeeee."

As soon as he'd gone she checked the time. Twelve thirty, that meant he'd be back about one fifteen. No logical reason to worry until then – but she did.

"I wish you'd gone with him Joanna," said mum.

"But he didn't want me to. You could see that."

"Perhaps you could follow him."

"Mum! I'm not going too."

"The only thing is," said Nick. "I don't think the place is called Harry's Fish Bar."

Mum looked aghast. "Isn't it?"

"No, Harry's Fish Bar is the one round the corner. You know, next to Bidmeads."

"Is it?"

"Well done Nick," said Joanna. "I wasn't going to mention that. Something else for mum to worry about."

"No, it's not," said Nick. "Dad knows where he's going."

"I hope you're right," said mum. "But why did we go all the way to the Bakers Arms when there's a fish shop round the corner?"

"Because you said Harry didn't wash his hands before frying," said Joanna. "You wouldn't let us go there."

Mum stared at Joanna in disbelief.

"You did mum. You said you hoped he fell in the fryer."

"I said what?"

"That's right," said Nick. "And you said he was rude when you told him he used too much batter."

"I've got no recollection of that."

"It's a long time ago now."

"Well I do hope dad's okay."

"He'll be fine mum. Down to the Bakers Arms, turn right and then left down Boundary road."

"Well if he's not back in forty five minutes he's lost."

"No, they might be busy," said Joanna. "You know how popular that place is – whatever it's called? You've got to give it at least an hour."

"I don't think it had a proper name," said Nick. "Just the Fish shop. Now would you like a cup of tea? That usually helps in these situations."

"Okay," said mum.

She smiled. What would she do without their support? Often she thought it'd be nice to have a heart to heart. To talk about dad's stroke and how they felt. But being a naturally shy person she found that difficult. And they were only eighteen and sixteen respectively. Too young to be burdened with her frustrations and insecurities. So instead she bottled up her feelings.

It'd been two years now. The time had flown by. There hadn't been much change in dad's condition. Physically things were okay – well except for his gammy hand that hadn't really improved. But he remained speechless and the odds were that wouldn't change.

She tried to imagine what it must be like unable to converse. To lose that ability you take for granted. Your brain is telling you what to say but it's all Eeeeeee. Eeeeeee. Well that wasn't quite true. He could say tea and coffee and yes and no in a sort of exaggerated childlike way. Obviously a part of the brain had enabled dad to achieve a vocabulary of four.

As for writing down his thoughts, well except for signing his name on a good day he still couldn't. So those in a similar position able to communicate by this method were fortunate indeed. Obviously Dad's stroke must have registered ninety nine out of a hundred on the severity scale.

Dad reached the Bakers Arm and turned right. In a few minutes

Boundary road should come up on the left. The number of times he'd done the trip in the past. Come rain or shine, fish and chips on a Saturday. He assumed the word had got around about his stroke? Obviously his presence had been missed. He'd been on first name terms with the husband and wife owners. In the old days they invariably made a fuss of the children. So much so that Nick had got fed up going. Too much silly talk, he said. He felt apprehensive as he turned into Boundary road.

"Hello there," said the fifty something year old fish fryer. "It's Stan, isn't it?"

"Eeeeece. Eeeeeee."

"Yes, we heard you had a stroke. I'm so sorry about that."

"Eeeeeee. Eeeeeee."

"I know it's no consolation, but you look well Stan. In fact you don't look any different."

Stan had heard that plenty of times since the stroke. No, it wasn't any consolation but he understood people mentioning it. He smiled and handed over the list.

"Do you remember my name?"

Dad shook his head.

"Ron, and my wife Winnie. She died nine months ago. She had cancer Stan. Bloody breast cancer. It came right out of the blue. It was so quick."

"Eeeeeee. Eeeeeee."

"Yes, a terrible shock. But that's life. Look at you Stan."

Dad felt really compassionate. He offered Ron his hand.

"Oh thanks Stan, I appreciate that. It is good to see you."

"Eeeeeee. Eeeeeee."

Stan recognized Ron now. He looked a lot older – probably losing his wife and all that. The jury was still out on whether he'd rather have cancer than a stroke. Today he felt quite positive but there were times when despair consumed him. When cancer seemed the better option.

"You haven't changed your order then," said Ron. "Two cod and two skate. How are the kids?"

"Eeeeeee. Eeeeeee."

"Nice children. Nicholas and Joanna isn't it?"

"Eeeeeee. Eeeeeee."

"They'll have to come in and say hello. And how's Joan? Is she still at Henry Taylor's keeping the other cashiers in check?"

"Eeeeeee. Eeeeeee."

"It must be very difficult for both of you."

"Eeeeeee. Eeeeeee."

They reminisced while the fish and chips cooked. Dad looked relaxed and Ron seemed to understand what he was intimating. They were on the same wavelength.

"Well here you are Stan. It's been really good to see you. You've made my day. Say hello to the family."

"Eeeeeee. Eeeeeee."

"I hope to see you again Stan. You must bring the kids in."

Dad walked back with a smile on his face. Mission accomplished. He'd been given a lift. He felt like a normal human being – a rarity these days. Perhaps the Saturday trip to the fish shop would return to the calendar. On the other hand he might not feel up to it again. One thing would be certain though, Nick's negative reply to the suggestion that he popped in to see Ron. And he couldn't count on Joanna's support either.

"I enjoyed that," said mum as she consumed the last chip. "We should do that more often."

"Eeeeeee. Eeeeeee."

"What?"

"Eeeeeee. Eeeeeee."

"His wife dying of cancer?"

"Eeeeeee. Eeeeeee."

"Have they got any children?"

"Eeeeeee. Eeeeeee."

"I don't know what you mean Stan."

"Do you mean the name of the fish shop?" said mum.

"Eeeeeee. Eeeeeee."

"It's not Harry's Fish Bar?"

"Eeeeeee. Eeeeeee."

"No, Harry's Fish Bar is the one round the corner. Next to Bidmeads."

"Eeeeeee. Eeeeeee."

"Why don't we go there?"

"Eeeeeee. Eeeeeee."

"Mum wouldn't let us," said Joanna.

"Eeeeeee. Eeeeeee."

"Because Harry used too much batter."

"Eeeeeee. Eeeeeee."

"And he didn't wash his hands before frying," said Nick.

Dad looked puzzled.

"It's true, isn't it mum?" said Joanna.

Mum looked rather sheepish.

"Eeeeeee. Eeeeccee."

"I don't remember saying anything of the sort."

"Eeeeeee. Eeeeeee."

"It's a long time ago Stan."

Dad smiled then pointed at mum. He put his arms together in front of him as if preparing to dive.

"What do you mean Stan?"

Dad repeated the actions.

"That's a difficult one dad," said Nick.

"Eeeeeee. Eeeeeee."

"Oh I see. You mean Harry falling into the fryer."

"Eeeeeee. Eeeeeee."

"That's how he died?"

"Eeeeeee. Eeeeeee."

"How could you fall into a fryer?" said mum. "I've never heard anything so ridiculous."

"Eeeeeee. Eeeeeee."

"That's right," said Joanna. "Perhaps somebody pushed him because of the amount of batter on their cod."

Dad started laughing and having one of the most infectious laughs imaginable soon had everybody else joining in.

After dinner dad sat in his armchair and read the Sun. The old Daily

Herald had changed its name to the former about six months ago. Dad wasn't happy. Okay it still supported the Labour party but it had gone down market. And now there was talk about it going tabloid to compete with the Mirror. Dad shook his head. He loved his broadsheet. After a while he put down the paper and had a snooze.

While dad snoozed mum and Joanna went to Bearmans in Leytonstone. The biggest departmental store in that part of London. They were looking for a chest of drawers for the box room. Unfortunately Nick still hadn't conceded the point that his sister needed more space than him – because girls just did. So mum, reluctant to get involved and in an attempt to pacify her daughter, had agreed to her request for new furniture. Although the room being only eight by five meant there'd be limited choice. But Joanna apparently knew just what she wanted. Christine Allen had bought the ideal size chest of drawers from Bearmans a couple of weeks ago.

"But are you sure Christine's room is the same size as yours?" asked mum.

"It's probably smaller."

"I thought you had the smallest bedroom in the world."

"I have."

Nick meanwhile studied the letter from the unit trust where he'd invested half of his bonus. He was absolutely flabbergasted. The interest paid amounted to less than the two and a half per cent the post office gave. He compared that miserly figure with the impressive amount Northern Songs would have guaranteed seeing that their two shilling shares were now worth one pound four shillings.

"What!" he shouted. "That's a twelve fold increase. That's six hundred pounds – I think. Now why did I listen to the Investors Chronicle? What do they know? I should have gone with my feeling. What an idiot I was."

He woke dad and explained the situation. Dad was sympathetic.

"Never again," said Nick.

"Eeeeeee. Eeeeeee."

"No, I've learnt my lesson."

"Eeeeeee. Eeeeeee."

"I can't believe the poor return."

"Eeeeeee. Eeeeeee."

"Yes, less than the post office dad. Who gives less than the post office?"

"Eeeeeee. Eeeeeee."

"What, stop going on about it?"

"Eeeeeee. Eeeeeee."

"Sorry dad. I won't mention another word. I'll leave you to it."

"Eeeeece. Eeeeeee."

"Fish and chips next Saturday?"

"Eeeeece. Eeeeeee."

"Yes, too soon to say. Perhaps I'll come with you if you do decide."

"Eeeeeee. Eeeeeee."

"He'll probably ruffle my hair like in the old days. Do you remember dad?"

Dad smiled. He certainly did remember those days but who knows if he'd return to the Boundary road fish shop again.

# EIGHT

The sermon followed and although the Rev Turner wasn't renowned for his, let's grab your attention preaching, he was sincere. He accepted the vast majority present weren't churchgoers. Indeed some wouldn't remember their last visit. So there'd be no point harking on about the message of the Lord. Instead he made an analogy, some might say a curious one, between dad's wartime boxing career and his religious calling. Both had resulted in sacrifices. Dad, although tipped for a title, had given up the sport after the war to return to Joan and civvy street. While the reverend had followed his belief and enrolled at the theology college instead of pursuing a more lucrative career as a city stockbroker. Evidently his friends considered him bonkers.

"I agree with them," whispered Uncle John. "Completely bonkers."

"John, behave yourself," said Auntie Eileen.

"Okay, but that's not right what he said about Stan's boxing career."

"What's not?"

"That he remained unbeaten. His brother Alan said he'd been knocked out."

"Are you sure?"

"Positive."

"Well perhaps he never told Joan. He thought she might worry."

"She probably would have. I'll check with Alan again after the service."

"Does it matter now?"

"Yes, I'd like to know. I always thought Stan had thirteen fights and won the lot."

"Well only losing once is still a good record."

"Yes, but not the same as being unbeaten."

"Please don't make a big thing about it."

"As if I would Eileen."

# 1966

The year hadn't started well for dad. He seemed more depressed. Less willing to do the shopping errands and making the occasional cup of tea. He certainly hadn't returned to the fish shop. He lost his temper more regularly. He mostly sat in his armchair and watched the tele. Even reading his once favourite boxing magazine didn't have the same appeal. He looked a sorry sight staring into space and contemplating his lot on that Saturday morning in March.

"Here's your coffee Stan," said mum.

Dad, agitated, snatched the coffee and put it down. He flayed his arms about. Obviously something was on his mind.

"Eeeeeee. Eeeeeee."

"What day is it?"

"Eeeeeee. Eeeeeee."

"The children?"

"Eeeeeee. Eeeeeee."

"Kit and Mary?"

"Eeeeeee. Eeeeeee."

"Your brothers?"

"Eeeeeee. Eeeeeee."

"My brothers?"

"Eeeeeee. Eeeeeee."

"I'm sorry Stan."

He sighed, shook his head and aggressively gestured for her to leave. He'd had enough trying to make himself understood. Why bother?

Mum returned sheepishly to the kitchen. She felt guilty. Why? Because she had a pretty good idea what dad was on about. That evening's army reunion at the Drill Hall where Nick had agreed to act as his escort. A few days ago he'd been all for it. He'd given the thumbs up. But now more than likely he'd decided he wouldn't be attending. That he wasn't in the right frame of mind to reminisce about the war years. And mum didn't want to hear those negative words. She could see dad needed a change of routine. That he'd regret not going. She'd have to choose her moment carefully and bring up the subject.

"Nick," said mum. "Do you want to mention the reunion to dad?"

"Me. Isn't it better coming from you?"

"No, he'll lose his temper with me."

"Okay then, but I don't think he'll be going."

That would have suited Nick. Then he could have joined his friends, Peter and Mike, up the Tottenham Royal. The regular Saturday night haunt with resident band, The Dave Clark Five. Travelling there by bus (two actually) was a pain but you suffered in silence if you wanted the chance of meeting that special sixteen old. Joanna and her friend Christine often tagged along but tonight they were doing their own thing. A disco at St Andrews church hall where they'd been reliably informed that half a dozen of the most eligible sixth formers would be attending.

"If you believe that you'll believe anything," said Nick.

"Well how do you know they won't be there?" said Joanna.

He shrugged his shoulders. Of course he didn't know. He was simply playing devils advocate and more concerned with gauging the right moment to question dad about his attendance at the reunion.

"Hello dad," said Nick. "How do you feel today?"

"Eeeeeee. Eeeeeee."

"I'm sorry about that."

"Eeeeeee. Eeeeeee."

"I don't know dad."

"Eeeeeee. Eeeeeee."

"I suppose you don't feel like the army reunion tonight?"

Dad looked surprised. Obviously he'd forgotten all about it. But then, surprisingly, he nodded and gave a flabbergasted Nick the thumbs up.

"Eeeeeee. Eeeeeee."

"You want to go. Oh that's great dad. We'll see how many of your old friends are there."

"Eeeeeee. Eeeeeee."

"What Ted? Yes, he should be there."

"Eeeeeee. Eeeeeee."

"You had some good times in the army."

Dad's demeanour had changed completely. He smiled broadly.

"Eeeeeee. Eeeeeee."

"What, on the guns at Canvey?"

"Eeeeeeee. Eeeeeee."

"How many planes did you shoot down?"

Dad shook his head.

"None, what in all that time?"

"Eeeeeee. Eeeceee."

"You got close though. You just needed a few more years."

They both smiled.

"Eeeeeee. Eeeeeee."

"I know what you mean dad. When the four of you collected your pooh and dumped it on the officers desk."

"Eeeeeee. Eeeeeee."

"It sounded disgusting."

"Eeeeeee. Eeeceee."

"Yes, he must have been a bastard but you had to clean up the mess."

"Eeeeeee. Eeeeeee."

"He learnt his lesson. Well it was worthwhile then. Perhaps he'll be there tonight."

"Eeeeeee. Eeeeeee."

"He's dead?"

"Eeeeeee. Eeeeeee."

"Oh you hope he's dead."


Right up until the time dad and Nick left for the reunion mum had convinced herself there'd be a sudden change of plan. That dad would announce he wasn't going. But he didn't. He looked really smart in his tweed jacket, grey trousers and trilby.

"You're not wearing your medals Stan?" said mum.

"Eeeeeee. Eeeeeee."

"You don't wear them for reunions," said Nick.

"When do you wear them?" said mum.

"Dad said you only wear them on remembrance Sunday."

"Eeeeeee. Eeeeeee."

"I didn't know that. Well what about a coat Stan? It's not that warm tonight."

"Eeeeeee. Eeeeeee."

"No, that's okay," said Nick. "We've got a lift."

"A lift?"

"Yes, Mr Watts offered."

"Are you sure?"

"Yes, he's going to Abbots Park."

"That's not the same way as the Drill Hall."

"Mum, he offered."

"Well what about coming home?"

"Oh mum! Dad do you want a coat?"

"Eeeeeee. Eeeeeee."

"See, now don't worry. We'll be okay."

There was a knock on the door.

"That'll be Mr Watts," said Nick. "Come on dad. See you later mum."

Dad went across and gave mum a peck on the cheek.

"Yes, you have a good time Stan. Now Nick, try and remember who turns up."

"I'll do my best."

"Write down their names. You know what you're like. Have you got a pen?"

"Yes, mum."

"Concentrate."

Never had a truer word been spoken. The previous September mum and Joanna had holidayed in Minehead while dad went into respite. Due to an oversight mum realized she hadn't taken sufficient funds and wrote home requesting a sub. Nick received the letter but unfortunately didn't digest the important part. So mum, embarrassed, ended up visiting the police station and borrowing ten pounds. Obviously feelings were running high when mum returned home and confronted Nick. He adamantly denied mum had requested anything of the sort and would prove it because the letter had been kept. But dear oh dear, one up to mum, because there in black and white were the words, *Please forward ten pounds.*

The Drill Hall was packed when they arrived. Both looked apprehensive. Dad because of the worry of how his buddies would react to his disability and Nick because he hadn't acted as his fathers escort before. They headed straight for the bar.

"Do you want a pint of Guinness dad?"

"Eeeeeee. Eeeeeee."

"I think I'll have a pint of Brown."

"Eeeeeee. Eeeeeee."

"No, I don't like Guinness. I prefer something sweeter."

"Eeeeeee. Eeeeeee."

"You used to drink Brown?"

"Eeeeeee. Eeeeeee."

"So perhaps I'll change when I'm older then."

At the age of nineteen Nick hadn't yet perfected the art of ordering a pint in a crowded bar. It took an age to catch the barman's attention. The more he gestured the more the barman appeared to deliberately ignore him and the more self-conscious Nick felt. It was an inauspicious start to the evening. They were saved by old army friend Ted.

"Hello Stan. How are you?"

"Eeeeeee. Eeeeeee."

"Great to see you."

"Eeeeeee. Eeeeeee."

"Yes, we heard Stan. Really sorry to hear that"

"Eeeeeee. Eeeeeee."

"Yes, your son Nick. Good of you to bring Stan. What are you both drinking?"

"Hello Ted. Well I'm trying to get a pint of Guinness and a pint of brown but not having much luck."

"I'll get the drinks. That barman's an expert at ignoring people. Watch this."

He cupped his mouth and shouted at the top of his voice. "Hello. Yes, you barman. Up this end mate, we haven't got all bloody night. It was easier getting a drink at Alamein with Monty. That's better."

Everybody within earshot laughed. But the nearest Ted had got to the action had been Canvey Island. That's right, on the ack–ack guns with Stan and the rest of the crew. He'd never hit anything either.

"That's the way to do it," said Nick.

"You learn with age," said Ted. "Anyway cheers. Here's to a good evening."

"Eeeeeee. Eeeeeee."

They clinked glasses and sipped.


The evening flew by. Stan spent most of it laughing. It'd been a great tonic. A welcome chance to reminisce about the good times. And they had been good. Primarily because of the comradeship encountered. But then Stan had the ability to get on with people. He commanded respect from privates and officers alike. Tonight had been no exception. They admired him for attending although unable to communicate. That took courage. Thankfully his brain held up remarkably well. Incidents relayed twenty to the dozen were recalled with clarity. Well, except for one. The little matter of him being knocked out in the first round. He wouldn't have forgotten something as catastrophic as that. No, he remained the unbeaten heavyweight. Obviously his pals were trying to goad him by suggesting otherwise. They'd forgotten he'd been asked to turn professional.

The only regret had been the non-appearance of the officer whose desk they'd dumped the pooh on. Thus depriving them of the opportunity to ridicule. But there was a perfectly good reason. According to Colonel Craig, dad's respected commanding officer, he'd recently passed away. There were smiles and cheers all round.

"Every cloud has a silver lining," said Ted.

"God moves in a mysterious way," said George.

"Hallelujah," said Bob.

"I'll drink to that," said Ernie. "Another round chaps?"

Nick smiled but felt somewhat uncomfortable at the euphoria that greeted the announcement of the officers demise. Could he have been that despicable?

"So will we see you next year Stan?" asked Bob.

Dad shrugged his shoulders. Who could say what would be happening next year. He might not be around then. Another stroke could be on the cards.

"I'll have to come and visit," said Ted.

"Eeeeeee. Eeeeeee."

"That would be nice," said Nick. "I'm sure mum would appreciate it."

"Well make sure you've got some beer in," said Ted.

"Eeeeeee. Eeeeeee."

"There's always plenty of Guinness in the house," said Nick. "Dad likes his daily half."

"Good for you Stan. That's my man."

"Eeeeeee. Eeeeeee."

"Until the next time then," said Ted.

They shook hands. And then Ted, overcome by emotion, gave Stan a hug.

"It's been really good to see you Stan. You've made my night."

"Eeeeeee. Eeeeeee."

"We were a good team. I can't believe we didn't down any enemy planes. Talk about unlucky."

Everybody within earshot started laughing.

"So did you have a good time Stan?" asked mum when the pair of them walked in at precisely eleven fifteen.

"Eeeeeee. Eeeeeee."

"That's good."

"Eeeeeee. Eeeeeee."

"You look as though you've enjoyed yourself."

"I've never seen dad laugh so much," said Nick.

"I'm pleased. Now did you make a list?"

Nick sighed then produced a piece of paper from his trouser pocket.

"Yes, mum. I made a list. Now let's see who we've got. There's Ted, George, Ernie and Bob."

"Bob? I don't remember a Bob."

"Well he was one of those that piled the pooh up on the desk."

"Eeeeeee. Eeeeeee."

"Well I don't remember Stan."

"He died recently," said Nick.

"Who died?"

"The officer whose desk they piled the pooh on."

"You mean Colonel Craig?" said mum.

"Eeeeeee. Eeeeeee."

"No, mum," said Nick. "That wasn't Colonel Craig. Dad liked him. He's the one that told us about the other officer dying."

"Eeeeeee. Eeeeeee."

"Yes, it's true to say he was disliked intently. I think hated would be the appropriate word."

"Eeeeeee. Eeeeeee."

"Sorry Stan," said mum. "I'm getting mixed up. Of course you liked Colonel Craig. I remember him well. Very distinguished. How was Ted?"

"Eeeeeee. Eeeeeee."

"Yes, your best friend in the army."

"On good form," said Nick. "He told some funny stories."

"Eeeeeee. Eeeeeee."

"Yes, I don't know how he remembers them all," said mum.

"No, and I don't know how many were true."

"Eeeeeee. Eeeeeee."

"What do you mean Stan?" said mum.

"Eeeeeee. Eeeeeee."

"Ted said he'd like to visit," said Nick.

"Oh that would be nice. Perhaps he'll bring Gwen along. How is she?"

"She still has problems with her legs."

"Oh dear. Now did you enjoy yourself Nick?"

"I did actually. Well once we'd managed to order the drinks courtesy of Ted."

"Wouldn't they serve you? You're old enough."

"I know that. I was getting ignored."

"Oh I see."

"Ted reckoned if dad had stayed in the army he'd have been promoted to major."

"Yes, that was on the cards."

"Wow, my dad a major. What's the next rank up after that?"

"A colonel."

"A colonel! What like Colonel Craig? Now that is something to tell your friends."

Dad smiled and gave the thumbs up.

"So we might be on for next year then?" said mum getting carried away with the euphoria of dad enjoying himself.

"Eeeeeee. Eeeeee"

"No, of course not Stan. We don't know what's around the corner."

"Eeeeeee. Eeeeeee."

"That's right," said Nick. "One year at a time."

"Eeeeeee. Eeeeeee."

"Well I'm going to bed," said Nick.

"Okay then," said mum. "Thanks for taking dad. And by the way, Joanna wanted you to know that at the disco she got chatted up by the head boy from William Morris. So you don't know everything."

# NINE

The service continued with The Lords Prayer. A chance for the occasional visitor to show they'd remembered something from their worshipping days. But they were only partially successful There remained a sizeable minority that persevered with the perverse, "In Earth as it is in Heaven."

"Did you say In Earth?" said Duncan.

"In Earth?" queried William.

"Yes, In Earth instead of On Earth."

"Why would I say that?"

"Can you two be quiet," said Joanna.

Duncan and William were the middle two of Joanna and David's children. Sixteen and fourteen respectfully they were, so far, composed attending their first funeral. Paying their respects to the Grandpa they'd never had the privilege to have a conversation with.

The Collect followed. The majority had a recollection of reciting that at sometime in the distant past.

"Amen. I always enjoy the Collect," said Joyce. "The words are really appropriate."

"Yes, they are," said Lyn.

But if truth be told Lyn wasn't concentrating on the words. She was more concerned with trying, unsuccessfully, to recall the last time she'd seen Auntie Joyce. But what she had heard didn't sound like the Collect. She wondered whether Auntie Joyce could be confused with the Nunc Dimittis.

"So that was the Collect," said Lyn.

"That's right," said Joyce.

# 1967

Content to read the paper in his favourite armchair dad didn't take kindly to mum barging in and putting the tele on. But John and Eileen had called in and Eileen being an avid tennis fan had suggested watching Wimbledon. And unfortunately for dad mum considered that an excellent idea.

"Hello Stan," said John. "Do you follow the tennis?"

"Eeeeeee. Eeeeeee."

"No, neither do I."

"Eeceeee. Eeeeeee."

"That's right. It doesn't compare with boxing."

"Well I'm going to Wimbledon tomorrow," said Eileen.

"You are lucky," said mum.

"I don't know what's lucky about it," said John. "You wouldn't catch me there."

"That suits me fine," said Eileen. "Do you remember when we went Joan?"

"I do. Wasn't it hot? Now who did we see?"

"Rod Laver on centre court."

"That's right. He was good. You used to get tickets from work Stan."

Dad shook his head. Tickets for Wimbledon? No, that didn't ring a bell.

"Well you did Stan."

"Eeeeeee. Eeeeeee."

"You've forgotten. Who are you going with Eileen?"

"My sister, Pam. She goes every year."

"More fool her then," said John.

Dad laughed, stood up and started shadow boxing.

"Yes, that's a much better idea Stan," said John. "Is there any boxing on the tele?"

"Now behave yourselves you two," said mum. "We're watching the tennis."

"Thanks Joan," said Eileen. "We might see Ann Jones if we're lucky."

"Ann who?" said John.

"You know," said mum. "The great British hope."

"Don't take any notice of him," said Eileen. "He knows perfectly well."

"Well if she's British she's got no chance," said John. "When did we last win anything at tennis?"

"Actually she's got a good chance. Billy Jean's past her best."

"Billy who?" said John.

So to dad's obvious displeasure they sat down and watched the tennis. Not that they were missing anything on the other channel. In nineteen sixty seven daytime television, except for special events, amounted to the showing of test cards. There wasn't, supposedly, an audience for daytime viewing. But things were about to change. This year had seen the advent of colour TV. Wimbledon being the first outside event broadcast in that medium. The media excitedly announced that people were getting hooked. Although you wouldn't have guessed that in Nottingham Road

"Has anybody in your road got a colour TV?" asked John.

"Not that I've heard," said mum. "Although Mrs Forrest was talking about buying one. What about Matlock road?"

"No, I don't think so."

"Eeeeeee. Eeeeeee."

"What do you mean Stan?"

"Eeeeeee. Eeeeeee."

"The Forrests? How can they afford a colour television? I don't know. But they were the first to buy a black and white set back in the fifties."

"Eeeeeee. Eeeeeee."

"Yes, we were invited in to watch the boat race."

"You mean watch Oxford lose," said John. "I've never understood why you support them. Cambridge is just up the road. That's your local team Stan."

"Eeeeeee. Eeeeeee."

"I think Stan likes to support the underdog," said mum.

"Well they're certainly that," said John.

"Eeeeeee. Eeeeeee."

"What, next year Oxford will win? I don't think so."

"Eeeeeee. Eeeeeee."

"You want to have a bet?"

"Eeeeeee. Eeeeeee."

"Okay, half a crown?"

"Eeeeeee. Eeeeeee."

"No, Stan," said mum. "Half a crown is plenty."

"You're on Stan," said John. "Half a crown it is."

They shook on the deal and returned to discussing the merits of colour television.

"Anyway," said John. "Give it a few months and colour sets will be down in price."

"It'd be good to see Wimbledon in colour," said Eileen.

"Not as exciting as the boxing. All that blood."

"Eeeeeee. Eeeeeee."

"That's right Stan, better than tennis any day."

Dad couldn't believe that John and Eileen stayed for almost three hours. Talk about overstaying your welcome. Three hours watching bloody tennis. And what was all the fuss about Ann Jones? She looked very Miss Average. Fortunate indeed to progress to the quarter finals. She wouldn't stand a chance against the redoubtable Billie Jean King.

The only positive thing about the afternoon, as far as dad was concerned anyway, had been the fact that, unlike his brother Ralph, John didn't have a penchant for Southern Comfort. He'd been quite content to wile away the time with a cup of tea and some fruit cake.

"Well I hope you enjoy your day out," said mum as John and Eileen departed.

"I'm sure I will," said Eileen. "I must remember to take the camera."

"What do you want to do that for?" said John. "You won't be able to take a decent picture."

"I might. Perhaps I should take the autograph book as well."

"Yes, you do that Eileen," said mum. "You might see Ann Jones arriving."

"An autograph book?" said John. "You must be joking. Now do you see what I have to put up with Stan?"

"Eeeeeee. Eeeeeee."

"It's hard work I tell you."


"Well that was a nice afternoon" said mum after the guests had departed. "They both looked well."

Dad nodded and went to the drinks cabinet. He took out the Southern Comfort, smiled and gave mum the thumbs up.

"Eeeeeee. Eeeeeee."

"What do you mean Stan?"

"Eeeeeee. Eeeeeee."

"What, John didn't have a Southern Comfort like Ralph?"

"Eeeeeee. Eeeeeee."

"Oh you do go on about things. Poor old Ralph. You wait until your brother Ron visits. We'll see how much he drinks."

"Eeeeeee. Eeeeeee."

"I know I'm right. You're biased because he's your brother."

So far this year hadn't been too bad for the family. You could say that dad had been on an even keel. Regularly he took a walk, either around the block or to the Bakers Arms to get the errands. He put the oven on when required and on a few occasions had successfully made a cup of tea. But for the majority of the time he sat in his chair and read the Ring magazine, snoozed or stared into space.

His quality of life would have been improved if he'd been able to write down things. Think how much frustration could have been avoided if he'd jotted down things like, "How is Joanna getting on with her nursing?" Instead there could be endless questions and answers before arriving at the correct outcome. Or, alternatively, dad just gave up and stormed out. As four years had now passed since the stroke they had to accept that faculty had been lost for ever.

Mum continued her part time cashier's job at Henry Taylor's. Working from one o'clock to five thirty. She preferred the afternoon shift because of a busy morning schedule. She continued to give dad breakfast in bed then ensured he was dressed, washed and comfortable. That included applying the Algipan to dad's back – an exercise ongoing for four years now. No, mum wasn't about to question the pros and cons of applying that amount of cream, though in her view it was a complete waste of time, because dad needed the Algipan reassurance and the guilt ridden doctor happily continued to prescribe a couple of tubes a week.

The downside of working afternoons meant dad could be agitated when she arrived home. She might not be late but dad wanted his dinner and all reasoning went out of the window. But all in all she didn't worry too much about dad while at work. There'd been no emergencies to speak of. No, burning down the house while attempting to light the oven.

She was thankful for being able to hold down a job. Not everybody in a similar position could say that. She'd been at Henry Taylor's ten years now and continued to keep the family amused with stories about her colleagues. If you believed mum's version of events then the three gossiping cashiers certainly didn't hold back with their sarcastic comments.

"So which one is Mrs Walker?" said Joanna.

"She's got fair hair. Miss Warner is much darker."

"Right, so next time I'll come in I'll have a close look at the pair of them."

"Well don't go saying anything."

"Mum, I'm not that silly."

Joanna had recently started her three year SRN nursing course at Westminster hospital. She enjoyed it. She'd already come into contact with Petula Clark's florist and Wilfred Brambel's milkman. But certainly couldn't discuss their conditions. She shared a flat in Pimlico with a couple of nursing friends and enjoyed the independence. The senior nurses were a friendly supportive bunch – and that included the infamous matron. As for the doctors – well they were just a tiny bit up themselves. But she'd been warned about that. It certainly didn't stop her socializing with them from time to time.

Nick meanwhile had changed jobs and now worked as a stock control clerk for Rootes the car manufacturers at their Knightsbridge office. The job was boring but there were perks. You could purchase one of their vehicles, for example a Sunbeam Alpine or Humber Hawk, at a huge discount. But, more importantly, the Beatles manager, Brian Epstein, lived around the corner and there were countless comings and goings from the fab four. Not that Nick ever saw John, Paul, George or Ringo, but he spotted their minis with the blacked out windows on numerous occasions. Rumour had it there were production problems with their new album. Its release had been put back three months already. But if it was to be their best album then Nick could afford to wait.

With the visitors out of the way dad turned off the tele and returned to reading the paper. But it wasn't long before mum reappeared.

"Stan, dinners ready."

"Eeeeeee. Eeeeeee."

"You're not hungry?"

"Eeeeeee. Eeeeeee."

How ironic thought mum, usually dad badgered and badgered because of his perceived notion that dinner was late but tonight just the opposite.

"But we always have dinner at six thirty."

"Eeeeeee. Eeeeeee."

"Liver and bacon. It's your favourite."

"Eeeeeee. Eeeeeee."

Dad couldn't recall liver and bacon being his favourite.

"Well just eat some of it then."

Reluctantly dad got up and followed mum into the living room convinced that mum had prepared dinner early. But she hadn't. She needed a routine as much as dad and at six thirty on the dot dinner would be served. She watched as dad picked at the liver before taking a mouthful. The omens didn't look good.

But surprise, surprise dad enjoyed his meal and gave mum the thumbs up.

"Eeeeeee. Eeeeeee."

"That's good Stan. What about some apple pie and custard? That's your favourite as well."

"Eeeeeee. Eeeeeee."

Dad took mum's word for it and waited for the dessert.

"Joanna should be home soon."

"Eeeeeee. Eeeeeee."

"No, she's not working this weekend. Nick's picking her up from the station. On his way back from playing cricket."

"Eeeeeee. Eeeeeee."

"Yes, she seems to be enjoying the nursing. She's made some friends."

"Eeeeeee. Eeeeeee."

"A boyfriend? I don't know about that."

"Eeeeeee. Eeeeeee."

"Nick?"

"Eeeeeee. Eeeeeee."

"Well he doesn't say much about the job but I think its okay. You know your brother Fred was asking him about the discount he gets on the cars."

"Eeeeeee. Eeeeeee."

"You didn't know. Well he's thinking of buying... Is it a Humber Snipe? Anyway that's a Rootes car and Nick could get twenty five per cent off."

"Eeeeeee. Eeeeeee."

"No, it probably won't come to anything – although Nick's keen. He might make something out of it."

"Eeeeeee. Eeeeeee."

"What Fred?"

"Eeeeeee. Eeeeeee."

"His driving?"

"Eeeeeee. Eeeeeee."

"He learnt in the army?"

"Eeeeeee. Eeeeeee."

"He's never passed a test. No, you mentioned that before"

"Eeeeeee. Eeeeeee."

"But it still doesn't sound right Stan"

"Eeeeeee. Eeeeeee."

"I know what you're saying. If you drove during the war you were exempt from ever taking a test."

"Eeeeeee. Eeeeeee."

"So you could have driven as well."

"Eeeeeee. Eeeeeee."

"Alright Stan I'll take your word for it."

But she wouldn't. She'd check with her brothers when she saw them.

After dinner mum went to chat over the back fence with Mrs Watts while dad did the washing up – a task quite within his capabilities. Excused putting the crockery away on the grounds that only mum knew where things went dad went to work diligently. He'd just finished, and neatly hung up the tea towel, when Nick and Joanna arrived home.

"Hello dad," said Joanna. "How are you?"

Dad smiled, shrugged his shoulders and kissed his daughter.

"Eeeeeee. Eeeeeee?"

"I'm enjoying it."

"Eeeeeee. Eeeeeee."

"Yes, I've made some good friends."

"Any boyfriends?" said Nick.

"No, just friends."

"Eeeeeee. Eeeeeee.?"

"We lost," said Nick. "Mr Lewis reckoned we were useless but it was just one of those things."

"Eeeeeee. Eeeeeee."

"We were all out for twelve."

Dad looked dumbfounded. Perhaps he'd misheard.

"Eeeeeee. Eeeeeee."

"Yes, twelve. Not a big score I know."

"Eeeeeee. Eeeeeee."

"You should have seen the pitch dad. One of those coconut matting types where the ball bounces all over the place. Really dangerous. They were fortunate we batted first."

"Eeeeee. Eeeeeee."

"No, they didn't lose a wicket. We conceded ten byes in the first over and that was about it."

Dad smiled. He wondered when a team had last been dismissed for such an abysmal score.

"Eeeeeee. Eeeeeee."

"Did I get any runs? Hmm, let me see now. No, I've got to be honest. Out first ball. The first time ever."

"That's what you said last week," said Joanna. "Where's mum?"

"Eeeeeee. Eeeeeee."

"In the garden?"

"Eeeeeee. Eeeeeee."

"Talking to Mrs Watts?"

"Eeeeeee. Eeeeeee."

"They're probably discussing the Forrest's buying a colour tele."

"So we might be able to see the boat race in colour," said Nick. "It might bring Oxford some luck."

"Eeeeeee. Eeeeeee."

"I support Cambridge now," said Joanna.

Dad looked surprised.

"I'm sorry dad but I'm old enough to support who I want."

"Eeeeeee. Eeeeeee."

"That's right," said Nick. "You can't change back again when Oxford start winning."

"I think I can live with that," said Joanna.

"Eeeeeee. Eeeeeee."

"Yes, I'm sure about that dad."

# TEN

The service continued without a hitch and finished within the allotted twenty five minutes. Family and friends departed by a side door while the next group of mourners congregated around the front. The parties oblivious to each other. Each consumed with their grief.

"What a nice service," said Kitty.

"Yes," said Joanna. "Considering the vicar didn't know dad he made it sound personal."

"I don't know how your mum managed all those years. "

"No."

"That doctor's got a lot to answer for."

"Yes, he wasn't up to much. Well except for tearing strips off the bottom of the prescription pad."

"Why did he do that?"

"I don't know. Nerves or a guilty conscience. It's a shame our old doctor, Hutchinson, died a few months earlier. He wouldn't have let us down. Well at least he would have referred dad to hospital."

"That might have changed everything," said Kitty. "We had some great times growing up. I always looked up to your dad – my big brother."

She started to cry. Joanna put her arm around her and led her though the remembrance garden to where an impressive array of flowers were laid out.

"What a lovely selection," said Kitty as mum joined them.

Mum nodded and smiled, content she'd made the right decision. Originally she'd opted for a gift to the Stroke Association as the best way of remembering dad. Nowadays donating to the charity responsible for the person's death seemed the appropriate course of action. But when it came to informing family and friends of her wishes she couldn't continue down that avenue. For the special day she needed the beauty and fragrance of fresh flowers to help her through. She knew Stan and the Stroke Association would understand. Of course mourners could send flowers and donate to the charity.

"Alright mum?" asked Nick.

"Yes. Now can I rely on you to collect the name tags on the flowers?"

"Name tags?"

"Yes, so that I can say thank you."

"Oh I see. Yes, of course."

"I'll ask the vicar if he wants to come back for the buffet."

"He looks as though he enjoys a nosh up."

In dribs and drabs family and friends inspected the flowers. Spending just the right amount of time bent over the assembled wreaths and sheaths. Checking the names on the cards and making a mental note. Wondering whether the flowers would subsequently be despatched to the local hospital or left to rot.

Then they drifted away to catch up with family gossip, which in some cases went back more than a decade. Everybody composed and showing great fortitude. Lots of handshakes and kisses, a few smiles even laughter. Especially from dad's brother Alan, but that was okay. That's what dad would have wanted. Anyway, nobody had laughed as loudly at a wake as dad at his brother Fred's funeral. So loud there'd been raised eyebrows and mutterings. Mum had been furious and reprimanded him in no uncertain manner. In his defence you could say that his brothers, Ron and Alan, had egged him on and because of his stroke dad often laughed at the most inappropriate time. A strange involuntary action seemed to take place. Anyway the berating did the trick and things calmed down. But the memory of that occasion in nineteen seventy five lingered on.

"Are you ready to go?" asked Mr Talisman

"Yes," said mum. "I think it's about time. Would you like to pop in for a cup of tea and a sandwich?"

"That's a nice idea but I've promised my grandson I'll get him back to Dereham by three."

"Of course, your grandson."

She pointed at the lad lounging on the bench who gave the distinct impression he'd rather be elsewhere. Probably at his mates second hand car business.

"It must be comforting working together in your profession."

"I won't answer that one."

"Oh I see. I suppose there can be problems working with families."

"More than you think actually."

# 1968

Dad had just finished shaving. He checked the mirror then rubbed his hand over his face. Yes, not too bad today. Well, adequate enough. For the past three months he'd been coming to terms with an electric razor, the rotary Philishave. Finding it difficult to shave in a circular mode using the correct amount of pressure. It hadn't been his idea, a wet shave suited fine, but mum reckoned an electric razor would be safer. True he occasionally nicked himself, but that happened to every wet shaver from time to time. It wasn't a problem. When you weighed up the pros and cons there was one undeniable fact. You couldn't get as close a shave with an electric. It had nothing to do with his stroke and ability to shave. But unfortunately mum couldn't see it.

"Let's have a look at your face Stan," said mum.

She slowly ran her hand over it.

"No, it's not that good Stan. You've missed a few places."

"Eeeeeee. Eeeeeee."

"Alright Stan, you don't have to shout."

"Eeeeeee. Eeeeeee."

"I know, you always say that. It's the razor."

"Eeeeeee. Eeeeeee."

"I don't think it is."

"Eeeeeee Eeeeeee."

"No, it's not a good idea to go back to your other one."

"Eeeeeee. Eeeeeee."

"You know why. You used to cut yourself."

"Eeeeeee. Eeeeeee."

"It's true Stan."

With that dad flapped his hands in front of mum and walked out the bathroom in disgust. No, point in arguing. Mum wouldn't listen. She never did.

Mum sat on the side of the bath and sighed. The day hadn't begun well. She felt really low. The last couple of weeks had been terrible. Dad had been such a pain for most of that time – so unreasonable and impatient. Didn't he realize she was doing her best? Okay dinner had been ten minutes late yesterday, but there'd been an accident outside Henry Taylor's. The bus had been delayed. It wasn't intentional.

She wished she could talk to somebody about her frustrations. But that wasn't her way. She chose to bottle things up. Often she blamed Stan for their predicament. Illogical but that's how she felt. Her criticism of his shaving had more to do with her mood than the actual shave. But it didn't help matters – it just made him more bad tempered.

Accordingly she could have done without this weekends visit to Kit and Mary's. This wasn't a good time for Stan's routine to be altered. He'd be in such a foul mood when she reminded him. But unfortunately Nick had booked the house for his twenty first birthday party. As many as thirty five were expected.

She sighed and made her way downstairs. She remembered she'd promised to make Nick some of his favourite Jimmy Young lemon butter bake. Perhaps that would take her mind off more depressing things. Like informing dad of the forthcoming visit to his sisters.

"Hello mum," said Joanna. "What's that you've made?"

"Oh hello Joanna, I didn't hear you come in. Don't you recognize Jimmy Young's lemon butter bake?"

"No, I don't. Can I have a piece?"

"Yes, I'm sure Nick won't mind. There's plenty there."

Mum was pleased to see Joanna. She'd come home for the big

party. Her first time in a month because of her shifts. She missed her daughters company. The shopping expeditions to Bearmans or Walthamstow market. The cinema visits. The cosy chats over a cup of tea – although nothing too heavy. She didn't think Joanna wanted to listen to her moaning about dad. That wouldn't be fair.

"It tastes really nice," said Joanna.

"That's good."

"I'm sure it'll go down well at the party."

"I hope so."

"What time are you off to Hainault?"

"Six o'clock. I'm not looking forward to it. Dad's in a foul mood."

"Oh dear, why's that?"

"I don't know. He's been like it for a couple of weeks. He's not happy using the electric razor for a start."

"So why don't you let him go back to the old one?"

"It's not safe."

"Oh mum, is it worth arguing about?"

"Yes, it is Joanna. I don't want dad to injure himself."

"Alright. I'd better go and say hello."

"Well perhaps you could remind him where we're going tonight. I'm sure he's forgotten."

"Okay."

Dad sat in his favourite chair reading the Ring magazine. When he saw his daughter he stood up and gave her a hug.

"Hello dad. How are you?"

"Eeeeeee. Eeeeeee."

He motioned her to feel his face. To confirm he hadn't had too bad a shave.

"Eeeeeee. Eeeeeee."

"That's not too bad dad."

"Eeeeeee. Eeeeeee."

"What mum?"

"Eeeeeee. Eeeeeee."

"She didn't think much of it?"

"Eeeeee. Eeeeeee."

"I don't know what to say dad."

"Eeeeee. Eeeeeee."

"Yes, it must be. Have you remembered where you're going tonight?"

"Eeeeeee. Eeeeeee."

"You've forgotten? Kit and Mary's."

Dad looked angry. He crossed his hands in front of him to convey the message that he wasn't going anyway.

"Eeeeeee. Eeeeeee."

"Why? It's Nick's twenty first birthday party tonight. There's about forty five invited. It's going to be noisy here dad."

Dad thought about it for a minute then nodded. The lesser of the two evils by a mile had to be Kit and Mary's. Forty five people in the house! That didn't bear thinking about.

"Eeeeeee. Eeeeeee."

"Yes, that does sound a lot."

"Eeeeeee. Eeeeeee."

"I assume mum knows. I'm sure Nick would have told her."

"Eeeeeee. Eeeeeee."

"Do you think I should mention how many?"

"Eeeeeee. Eeeeeee."

"Alright then, we'll leave it up to Nick."

"Eeeeeee. Eeeeeee."

"Where is he? I think he's picking up the drink from the off licence with Peter Porter."

"Eeeeeee. Eeeeeee."

"What do you mean dad?"

"Eeeeeee. Eeeeeee."

"Your Southern Comfort?"

"Eeeeeee. Eeeeeee."

"Dad, I'm sure he won't touch it. It's not something his friends drink. They've probably never heard of it."

"Eeeeeee. Eeeeeee."

"What do they drink?"

"Eeeeeee. Eeeeeee."

"Beer. I think Nick was getting three or four Pipkins and a few brown and light ales."

"Eeeeee. Eeeeee."

The girls? We'll be drinking vodka and orange or gin and tonic. Plus a few Babychams."

"Eeeeee. Eeeeee."

"What Guinness? Nobody drinks that dad. That's for old people."

"Eeeeee. Eeeeee."

"I'm sure it is dad."

"Eeeeee. Eeeeee."

"How much is it costing? I think Nick said about ten pounds."

"Eeeeee. Eeeeee."

"That sounds a lot?"

"Eeeeee. Eeeeee."

"Well that's inflation for you."

They were joined by mum carrying the Jimmy Young lemon butter bake.

"Would you like a piece with your coffee Stan?"

Dad picked up a piece and inspected it, not sure whether he liked it or not.

"You have eaten it before," said mum.

"Go on dad," said Joanna. "It is nice."

"Eeeeee. Eeeeee."

"Good for you dad."

"Do you want a coffee Joanna?" said mum.

"Yes, please. Dad's concerned his Southern Comfort might get drunk at the party."

"I shouldn't think so Stan. Unless Uncle Ralph's put somebody up to it. You never know with that brother of mine. Take it up to your wardrobe if you're worried."

"Eeeeee. Eeeeee."

"You already have. So what are you worrying about?"

"Eeeeee. Eeeeee."

"Oh Stan, I don't think Nick's friends will be searching through your wardrobe for drinks. They've got better things to do."

"You could put a padlock on the wardrobe," said Joanna sarcastically.

"Eeeeee. Eeeeee."

"Dad, I'm joking."

"Eeeeeee. Eeeeeee."

"Look Stan," said mum. "If your Southern Comfort gets drunk I promise I'll buy you another bottle. Okay?"

Thankfully the generous offer lessened the tension between mum and dad. There were smiles as they drunk their coffees and ate the lemon butter bake. Perhaps the visit to Hainault wouldn't be such a disaster after all.

"Well that cost more than I thought," said Nick when he returned with the drinks and Peter Porter.

"How much?" said Joanna.

"Twelve pounds thirteen and eight."

"Eeeeeee. Eeeeeee."

"Yes, it is a lot dad. Almost a weeks wages."

"Did you get everything you wanted?" said mum.

"I hope so. And at least it was sale or return so I won't waste any."

"What about the Southern Comfort?" said Joanna.

"What about it?"

"Did you get any?"

"No. Nobody drinks that. You know that."

"Eeeeeee. Eeeeeee."

"She's kidding," said Nick. "Peter, do we know anybody that drinks Southern Comfort?"

"I've never heard of Southern Comfort," said Peter. "What is it?"

"Bourbon Whisky. Dad was worried some of his might go missing."

"Oh I see. No, none of our friends drink whisky."

"Eeeeeee. Eeeeeee."

"Yes," said Nick. "I am sure it'll be safe in your wardrobe. Now is it alright to put everything in the kitchen mum? It won't be in the way?"

"No, that's okay. Do you want a hand?"

"No thanks. Peter and I can manage."

"I'll give you a hand," said Joanna. "I can see what you've got then."

"I didn't forget the cream soda."

"Cream soda?"

"Yes, you especially asked for it."

"No, I didn't."

"You did. Cream soda and lemonade."

"Well I don't remember."

"Eeeeeee. Eeeeeee."

"What do you mean dad?" said Joanna.

"Eeeeeee. Eeeeeee."

"What, cream soda?"

"Eeeeeee. Eeeeeee."

"No, sorry dad."

"Eeeeeee. Eeeeeee."

"Surely you don't mean mixing it with Southern Comfort?" said Nick.

"Eeeeeee. Eeeeeee."

"Are you sure?"

"Eeeeeee. Eeeeeee."

"Oh Stan," said mum. "You wouldn't have drunk Southern Comfort with cream soda."

"Eeeeeee. Eeeeeee."

"No, you wouldn't."

"Eeeeeee. Eeeeeee."

"Okay Stan, don't shout. I believe you then."

But she had her doubts and she'd check the facts with Ralph. As a Southern Comfort connoisseur he'd know for sure.

"Eeeeeee. Eeeeeee."

"I said I believe you."

There followed an embarrassed silence. The consensus being that dad's damaged brain was playing tricks. Then Nick suggested to Peter they brought in the drinks. Joanna followed. Dad shrugged his shoulders. Mum smiled. At this particular moment she knew life could be worse. She grabbed hold of his hand and held it tightly.

"I love you Stan," she said. "I always will. I'll always be here for you."

"Your dad looks well," said Peter as they put the drinks away.

"He always does," said Nick. "That's what makes it worse. You'd never guess he'd had a stroke. Well, until he starts talking about adding cream soda to whisky."

# ELEVEN

Mr Talisman overtook Ralph en route from the crematorium. An especially dangerous manoeuvre as the Earlham Road was a busy single carriageway situated in a built up area. But he needed to show his sparing partner that he could drive fast. That given the right circumstances he'd make a competent racing driver. Well, you should have seen the look on Ralph's face as the funeral car shot past with a hoot and a wave moments before the hooting double-decker passed in the opposite direction.

"What are you playing at?" shouted Tommy.

"I want to get you home."

"Yes, and I want to get home in one piece."

"Don't you worry about that, you're as safe as houses."

"If mum could see you driving like this she'd have a heart attack. Look, there's a police station coming up."

But Mr Talisman wasn't about to be deterred by something as insignificant as a police station. It was probably shut anyway. On a roll he shot over the roundabout and continued at a fair pace up Earlham road in the direction of the university. He couldn't wait to drop Tommy off and head for home. It'd been that sort of day.

The majority of mourners returned to mum's after the service. A chance to unwind and catch up with family matters. Not forgetting the little matter of the buffet to digest. Everything from cheese and pineapple on sticks, vol-au-vents, quiche and ham sandwiches followed by trifle and summer pudding. Although the pièce de résistance had to be Jimmy Young's lemon butter bake. The first time mum had made the delicacy since Nick's twenty first. She'd come across the recipe by accident and thought it perfect for the occasion. She hadn't told Nick and Joanna though. She wondered if they would recognize it after all these years. She also wondered what had happened to Jimmy Young's blossoming cookery career. It'd looked so promising back in the sixties. The atmosphere was relaxed – well except for an agitated Ralph that is.

"Did you see the funeral car overtake me?" he said.

"No," said Nick.

"I couldn't believe it. He almost hit a bus."

"Well I suppose he gets fed up driving at a snails pace all day. It's his way of relaxing."

"Relaxing! You are joking. He could have killed someone."

"Anyway, I'm glad you had time to come back."

"Yes, well lucky we made it. I've never seen driving like it. Unbelievable."

"I've got the message Ralph. Where's Joan?"

"She's outside recovering with a cigarette. I'll be joining her in a minute. I need the loo first."

"I think it's engaged."

"What both of them?"

"There's only the one Ralph."

"One?"

"Yes, it's only a bungalow."

"I could have sworn there were two when we stayed at Christmas."

"That must have been the Southern Comfort effect."

They both smiled. That'd been such a good Christmas. Ralph had actually rang mum just a couple of days beforehand and invited himself and Joan. Mum, caught off guard, had agreed and then with fingers crossed sought out dad for his approval. That, thankfully, had been forthcoming.

"We had a really good time," said Ralph.

"So did we Ralph. Your nonchalance charade is still talked about in these parts."

"Very difficult to do, I might tell you."

"You were great."

They started to laugh.

"What are you two laughing at?" said Joanna as she joined them.

"Nonchalance," said Nick. "Do you remember?"

Joanna smiled. "How could I forget? Charades. Whenever the boys get together the topic comes up. It seems funny them reminiscing at their age. You were a great hit Ralph."

"I think dad was laughing as much as anyone," said Nick.

"Yes, he seemed to get it okay," said Ralph.

"Undoubtedly the highlight of Christmas."

"Never to be repeated," said Joanna.

"Well I'm just waiting for the next invite," said Ralph.

"I didn't think you needed too."

"Don't you believe it. I got in so much trouble with Joan the last time. I mean my Joan, not your mum. She thought I'd put your mum in a difficult position. You know, where she couldn't say no when I rang at such short notice."

"I think mum was pleased to see you both."

"Well perhaps you could tell Joan that. Here she comes now. How are you Joan?"

"I'm fine Ralph. Are you up to something?"

"No."

"Well don't forget you're driving. You know what I mean."

"Of course I do."

She turned to Nick and Joanna. "That was a lovely service. You did your dad proud."

"Thank you," said Joanna.

"We were talking about the Christmas you came up," said Nick. "Do you remember?"

"I'll go and see if the bathrooms free," said Ralph.

"I think you'd better," said Joan.

# 1969

Mum had just come in from the garden. She'd had a long conversation with Mrs Watts about dad's state of health six years on from the stroke. What was there to report? Well for starters the Algipan episode had ended. Amazingly overnight dad's back problems had cleared up. Or, rather, his insistence that he couldn't live without that particular ointment smothered over his back daily. The family were relieved although wary of dad doing an about turn in the future. As for the doctor, well strangely he seemed put out. As though the issuing of the prescription somehow alleviated his guilt with regard to dad's stroke.

Besides that development life went on much as before. There were good days and bad. On a good day he might walk to the Bakers Arms and do the shopping. On a bad day he'd just sit in the armchair either staring into space, reading or dozing. When she thought he might be receptive mum suggested he went back to the day centre – arguing that the change of scenery would do him good. But dad wouldn't hear of it. They weren't going to get him to talk so what was the point?

But regardless of his state of mind he shaved daily. Something which mum took heart from. That he'd make the effort however low he might be feeling. Because of that mum had learnt not to criticize his attempt. Whenever he asked for her opinion she'd give the thumbs up. Similarly dad had ceased making a fuss about using the electric razor. Now he realized it was for the best.

Mum, as head of the household, busied herself keeping things ticking over. Paying the bills, serving up the meals, cashiering at Henry Taylor's and holding the peace between Nick and Joanna on the vexed question on whom should have the box room. (Nick continued to stand firm on that particular debate). Sometimes mum and dad were loving towards each other and sometimes just the opposite. Occasionally dad would push mum away in a fit of temper or slam the door in her face. But thankfully he hadn't hit her.

As mum made herself a cup of tea before settling down to her favourite crossword dad came in wearing his sports jacket, flat hat and slippers and carrying a letter.

"Eeeeeee. Eeeeeee."

"I've been talking to Joan next door."

"Eeeeeee. Eeeeeee"

"You're going to post the letter. Well don't forget your shoes Stan."

Dad was most indignant that mum thought he'd venture out in his slippers. His brain wasn't that unreliable.

"Eeeeeee. Eeeeeee."

"Alright Stan, you don't have to shout."

"Eeeeeee. Eeeeeee?"

"Your shoes? They should be next to the hall seat. That's where you normally leave them."

"Eeeeeee. Eeeeee."

"They're not. Well when did you last wear them?"

"Eeeeeee. Eeeeeee."

"I haven't moved them Stan. Let's go and have a look."

Dad accompanied mum up the hall convinced she'd be unable to locate the missing items. But sticking out from under the hall seat were dad's brown shoes.

"Look Stan, can you see them?"

Dad held his hand up apologetically. He couldn't understand how he'd missed them.

"That's okay. Now are you just walking round the block?"

"Eeeeeee. Eeeeee."

"Well make sure you've got your key. I'm off to work soon."

Dad produced the door key from his jacket pocket and gave mum the thumbs up.

"Good. Now have you remembered that Nick's bringing his girlfriend home tonight?"

"Eeeeeee. Eeeeeee."

"The Persian one."

"Eeeeeee. Eeeeeee."

"She's a nurse. She was on your ward when you were in Whipps Cross for your ulcer."

"Eeeeeee. Eeeeeee."

"Nasrin. You liked her. She got you to take the drinks trolley round at night. Do you remember?"

"Eeeeeee. Eeeeeee."

"It is a coincidence. That was five years ago."

"Eeeeeee. Eeeeeee."

"She's at the Charring Cross hospital now."

"Eeeeeee. Eeeeeee."

"No, Nick doesn't remember seeing her back then. Well he says he doesn't but I'm sure she must have been on duty when he visited. She remembers you Stan. You were one of her favourite patients."

"Eeeeeee. Eeeeee."

"She's coming for dinner."

"Eeeeeee. Eeeeeee."

"No, it won't be late Stan. They'll be here by six thirty. Nick's promised. Now don't start worrying about that already. Just be on your best behaviour."

"Eeeeeee. Eeeeeee."

"You know what I mean."

"Eeeeeee. Eeeeeee."

"Joanna? No, she won't be here. That's a shame because they could have compared nursing notes."

"Eeeeeee. Eeeeeee."

"No, she's at Westminster hospital."

"Eeeeeee. Eeceeee."

"You've forgotten Stan. She's always been there."

Dad put on his shoes, gave mum a kiss and set off on his walk. But he wasn't going round the block as mum had been informed but intended heading for Woods the newsagents on the corner of James Lane. He thought it'd make a pleasant change. Mum didn't have to know. He walked in that direction when commuting all those years ago – on route to Leytonstone underground station. And he remembered a pillar box outside the newsagents. Having a letter to post gave dad an incentive to undertake a walk. Although sometimes he thought the letters suspicious. That mum simply put an address on an envelope to encourage him to step outside. But he could cope with that charade.

He reached the top of Nottingham Road and looked back – just to make sure mum wasn't checking up on him. Good, no sign of her. He turned left and set off along Essex Road. He passed the grammar school and reached St Paul's church. Now was that where they'd married? He couldn't be sure. They had already bought the house in Nottingham Road so perhaps they had. He remembered they'd paid £750.00. A lot for a three bedroom terrace in nineteen thirty nine.

Prior to the big day they'd spent time getting the place shipshape. That included mum sowing grass seed in the front garden. Well it should have been grass but lo and behold a few weeks later lettuces sprang up. To say they were astonished was an understatement. Thirty years on and mum still refused to accept the blame – arguing that the packet must have been incorrectly labelled. But whatever, they were the laughing stock of the road. He smiled. They were exciting times. Getting married and then off to war.

Mum definitely attended the church. She met up with her mother every Sunday for evensong. They invariably sat in the same pew – sixth from the back on the left hand side. Dad found that amusing. Joanna had joked that they should put their names on the pew. Mum laughed at the absurd suggestion but was most put out if the occasional worshiper sat in their place. They had no right to be there.

He remembered that the children belonged to the Boys Brigade and Guide groups. Nick had also been headhunted to join the choir. But unfortunately in those days you couldn't belong to both. Which was just as well because Nick couldn't sing.

As he passed the vicarage Mrs King, the vicar's wife, appeared from behind the hedge.

"Hello Stan," she said. "How are you today? Getting some exercise?"

"Eeeeeee. Eeeeeee."

"It's a nice day for a walk. I see you've got a letter to post."

"Eeeeeee. Eeeeeee."

"How's Joan?"

"Eeeeeee. Eeeeeee."

"I'm glad about that. And the children?"

"Eeeeeee. Eeeeeee."

"It's always nice seeing them in church. They're good kids. You must be proud of them?"

"Eeeeeee. Eeeeeee."

"Well cheerio Stan. We're always praying for you and the family."
Dad smiled and nodded. He knew she meant well.

He continued up Essex Road and soon arrived at Woods the newsagents. He thought how shabby the place looked. A tin of paint certainly wouldn't go amiss. He peered in the dirty window. The shop seemed empty except for the unrecognizable assistant. He wouldn't bother going in. He'd just post the letter.

But there wasn't a pillar box. That confused dad. He knew there used to be one. He passed it every day. Well, well, well, definitely a mystery. He thought about asking the shop assistant – but then it was only a pillar box. He'd just have to revert to plan B and return home via the box on the corner of Matlock Road.

"Are you looking for the pillar box mister?" said a kid's voice.

Dad turned to see a young girl on her bicycle. He nodded.

"They moved it the other week. It's near the off licence on the corner of Peterborough road. Do you know where I mean?"

Dad nodded again.

"Would you like me to post the letter? It'll only cost you tuppence."

Dad smiled but shook his head.

"Alright, a penny then."

Dad shook his head again.

"Well alright I'll……No, forget it. I've got to go mum's coming. Don't tell her I asked for money or I'll be in trouble. Please. Do you promise? Bye, bye."

She sped off down James Lane in the direction of her waving mother. Dad smiled. Off course he wouldn't let on about her ingenious money making plans. How could he anyway?

# TWELVE

The lemon butter bake hadn't gone down well with the mourners. To make matters worse Nick and Joanna hadn't recognized it as the hit of his twenty first party twenty two years ago. After being coerced into trying it they offered the opinion that Jimmy Young should stick to singing – although ironically they'd never heard his vocal cords. But mum wasn't giving up that easily. For the third time that afternoon she picked up a plateful of the sixties pièce de résistance and embarked on a hard sell of the dining room. First on the list was dad's brother Alan.

"Hello Alan. Have you tried the lemon butter bake?"

"Hello Joan. No, I haven't. Do you mind if I give it a miss. I'm feeling quite full."

"It's a Jimmy Young recipe."

"Well I definitely won't try it then. What does he know about cooking?"

"In the sixties he was quite popular."

"Yes, singing but not cooking. Miss You, wasn't that his big hit? I've probably got it on a seventy eight."

"Seventy eight! He's not that old."

"I think he is."

"I made it for Nick's twenty first."

"Poor old Nick then, I hope that wasn't his main present."

They smiled and Alan put a supportive arm round his sister-in-law.

"Stan would have appreciated today's turnout," he said.

"I think you're right. I'm glad you could make it."

"I'm sorry I didn't get up to Norwich more often."

"That's okay Alan. You made up for it when you did visit. I've never heard Stan laugh so much. Just what the doctor ordered."

"Thanks Joan. Talking about Stan laughing, do you remember Fred's funeral?"

Mum stared daggers at Alan. "Alan, how could I forget? You and Ron egging on Stan. Making him laugh louder and louder. You never would have thought it's a funeral."

"Yes, things did get a bit out of hand."

"You can say that again. I think the whole street must have heard him. I don't know what the other relatives thought."

"They probably didn't notice."

"Alan, you know that's not true."

They were joined by Uncle Fred's son Peter.

"Hello Auntie Joan, how are you coping?"

"Well so long as it doesn't get as loud as at your dad's funeral I'll be okay."

"What do you mean?"

"The laughter."

"The laughter?"

"Yes, your dad's brothers. Don't you remember?"

"That's brothers for you."

"I've never been so embarrassed," said mum.

"Oh Auntie Joan, it wasn't that bad. In fact it helped to lighten the proceedings. I'm sure nobody took offence. What do you say Alan?"

"No, I'm sure they didn't but perhaps we were a bit too loud."

Mum felt reassured by Peter and pushed the lemon butter bake under his nose.

"Thanks for saying that Peter. Now can I interest you in Jimmy Young's lemon butter bake?"

"Jimmy Young?" said Peter. "What that Jimmy Young?"

"That's right. I was telling Alan I made it for Nick's twenty first."

"It's lasted well then."

They smiled at the thought of mum serving up a twenty two year old speciality.

"Oh go on then" said Peter. "I'll try a bit. What about you uncle?"

Well what could Alan say now except, "That'll be lovely."

But if truth be told neither of them thought it tasted particularly lovely and struggled manfully to finish their portions while mum looked on. After what seemed an age, but happened to be just a couple of minutes, they simultaneously digested the last morsel.

"That wasn't bad," said Alan.

"Yes, quite tasty," said Peter.

"Any seconds?" asked mum hopefully.

"You can have too much of a good thing," said Alan.

"Just what I was thinking," said Peter.

So mum abandoned the hard sell and returned to an empty kitchen pleased to have some time by herself. It was eerily quiet save for the background banter going on elsewhere. Thankfully there were no raised voices or uncontrollable laughter. Though that could quickly change if Alan engaged in conversation with her brother John. Undoubtedly that duo currently possessed the loudest laughs amongst the relations.

She began to tidy up, tipping leftovers into the bin. Unfortunately there seemed to be a disproportionate amount of lemon butter bake left on peoples plates. She couldn't understand it but accepted the probability she wouldn't be calling on the services of Jimmy Young again. Perhaps she'd lost the Midas touch where it was concerned.

She poured herself a cup of tea. She had to admit that after all the years of preparing for Stan's death it had still come as a shock. Probably because he'd survived for such a time – twenty eight years to be precise. She wondered whether that was some sort of record for a stroke sufferer. Thank God he hadn't outlived her – which had occurred to her as the years passed. That didn't bear thinking about. Nick had promised to contact the Hospital for Nervous Diseases, where dad had been admitted in nineteen sixty three, to inform them of the death and inquire whether twenty eight years survival amounted to a unique case.

But would it have been a better option if dad hadn't survived that first stroke? The sixty four thousand dollar question. She thought, perhaps naively, that until the second stroke in seventy five he enjoyed a certain quality of life. His brain functioned to a degree whereby he contributed to family life. He undertook errands and lit the oven at the appropriate time. The second stroke put an end to those activities. That should have been it. As the doctor predicted it would be. (Wrong again).To have lived a further fifteen years served no purpose whatsoever. Extremely confused for the majority of the time he didn't deserve the extra suffering. Death would have been a welcome relief.

And what about Dr Jarvis? How come he continued to be their doctor after that fateful diagnosis in sixty two? It didn't make sense. The times they'd talked about changing surgeries. Family and friends encouraged them to. But they never got round to it. Indeed Dr Jarvis remained their doctor until the move to Norwich in seventy nine. Mum knew that ultimately she took the blame for that decision. She should have made the effort.

Oddly the person most affected by the wrong diagnosis had the least to say on the subject. Whenever the family discussed the stroke and the ramifications of the doctors diagnosis dad shrugged his shoulders as if to say – "Oh well, we all make mistakes." Yes, dad but some mistake.

She imagined their life together if he hadn't suffered the stroke – something she rarely did when he lived. How different would it have been? For sure with the extra income they'd have bought that Singer Vogue. There'd have been more holidays. They might even have ventured abroad. Would they have moved out of London earlier? It's impossible to say. But certainly without the night time interruptions from Stan she'd have slept better. Life would have been less stressful. But besides that, who knows.

She was woken from her daydreaming state by her sister Joyce.

"Are you alright Joan?"

"Yes, I'm fine Joyce. Just having a think, you know."

"Of course I do. Do you know I always admired the way you never moaned about your lot Joan. You just got on with life. You were such a rock for Stan. I'm sure he appreciated it."

"I hope so. But I was short tempered at times Joyce. Only Stan saw that side of me."

"I'm not surprised Joan. Who wouldn't have been?"

"I suppose so."

"But changing the subject, have you any more of that Jimmy Young whatever it's called?"

Mum was caught off guard and stared suspiciously at her sister.

"Are you being serious?"

"Yes, why shouldn't I be? It's very tasty."

"That's what I think, but it hasn't gone down very well this afternoon."

"Well Joan, some people have got no taste."

"No, you're right. But I'm sorry it's all gone."

"Well it couldn't have gone down that bad then. You'll have to give me the recipe."

Mum smiled. No, way could she admit to her elder sister that she'd binned almost half of what she'd baked because of a disappointing take up ratio.

"Okay Joyce, I'll have a look for it."

"Better late than never."

"What do you mean?"

"I asked for the recipe after Nick's twenty first?"

"Did you?"

"Yes, my Richard was at the party and mentioned it. He couldn't decide whether he liked it or not. You were supposed to send me the recipe."

"Was I? I've got no recollection of that."

"Well I'm not leaving without it this time Joan."

# 1970

Mum and Joanna were at the bedroom window trying to ascertain whether it was dad's brother, Ron, walking up and down outside.

"It's definitely him," said mum. "But he knows where we live so why does he keep walking past?"

"Perhaps he's forgotten," said Joanna. "When did he last visit?"

"Not that long ago. He's been here so many times."

"I'll go and get him."

"Look, it's alright he's crossing over. He's coming this way. No, he's gone past again. I think he's going to knock on the Jaycock's. Yes, you'd better go and help him."

Joanna opened the front door just before Uncle Ron knocked on it.

"Hello Joanna," he said. "You wouldn't believe the trouble I've had finding you today."

"Hello uncle. Yes, we thought we saw you walking past."

"There's something different about the house. That's what confused me."

"I don't know what that is."

"Is it the door? It's a different colour."

"I don't think so."

"Yes, it used to be brown."

"That was ages ago. Before dad had his stroke."

"Really. Oh I must be mistaken then. I've had a few as well. That doesn't help. How is your dad?"

"He's quite bright today. He's about to have his Guinness."

"That sounds a great idea. Have you got one for me?"

"I'm sure we have. Come in."

"Thanks. Is your mum in?"

"Yes, she's upstairs."

"Oh good, I thought she might be working."

"Mum," shouted Joanna. "Uncle Ron's here. I'm going to get him a Guinness."

"I thought as much," said mum. "I'll be straight down."

Ron followed Joanna into the back room where dad was reading the Ring Magazine. Unaware of the interruption he continued reading.

"It's your brother Ron," said Joanna.

"Hello Stan, you old devil," said Ron. "What have you been up to lately?"

Dad looked up, smiled and pointed at Ron.

"Eeeeeee. Eeeeeee."

"You want a fight Stan? Come on then. Let's see what you're made of."

He approached dad and proceeded to shadow box. Dad, laughing loudly, stood up and joined in the antics. They circled each other weighing one another up. Throwing a few bogus uppercuts here and there.

"Now let's see who's the heavyweight champ," said Ron.

"Eeeeeee. Eeeeeee."

"Unbeaten! We'll soon see about that."

"Eeeeeee. Eeeeeee."

"You watch out for my right hook Stan."

"I'll get you the Guinness," said Joanna.

"Okay," said Ron. "I'll soon have your dad on the floor."

"Well don't be too rough, mum will never forgive you."

But after a few minutes they tired of their tomfoolery. They were whacked. They hugged, shook hands and sat down. The Guinness that Joanna had brought in would go down a treat. They raised glasses and sipped.

"Eeeeeee. Eeeeeee."

"Yes, that tastes lovely," said Ron.

"Is that your favourite beer?" asked Joanna.

"No, I wouldn't say that. I prefer a bitter. But this will do. What do you say Stan?"

"Eeeeeee. Eeeeeee."

"You used to drink Brown ale in the old days. God, I don't know how you managed it. It's got such a sweet taste."

"Eeeeeee. Eeeeeee."

"What do you mean dad?" said Joanna.

"Eeeeeee. Eeeeeee."

"Oh you mean Nick. Yes, he drinks Brown ale."

"The poor boy," said Ron. "Hopefully he'll progress like you Stan."

They were joined by mum.

"Hello Ron," she said. "We thought we saw you in the road."

Uncle Ron stood up and kissed mum on the cheek.

"Hello Joan. Good to see you. I don't know why I couldn't find the house. Probably the amount of beer. I'd been down our local at lunchtime. It's quite a walk from there."

"You walked?"

"Yes, usually I enjoy the exercise. It's takes about forty minutes.

That's right, that's why I couldn't find the house. I thought you had a red door."

"We have got a red door."

"No, I mean a brown one."

"That was ages ago. Before Stan had his stroke."

"That's what Joanna said. I can't believe it. It must be the beer."

"Eeeeeee. Eeeeeee."

"Yes, Stan always preferred the brown door," said mum.

"Eeeeeee. Eeeeeee."

"I prefer a red one," said Ron. "Brown is too dull. You're outvoted Stan."

With his brother present dad seemed relaxed. Although Ron by his own admission had had a few you wouldn't have guessed from his behaviour. Except that he liked to reminisce when under the influence. To talk about family life when they were growing up in Leslie road, Leyton and then Hainault. And the fact that Fred, the eldest brother, was undoubtedly mum's favourite. By all accounts he got away with murder. Mum looked perplexed. The last time Ron visited he'd made it clear that Stan happened to be the blue eyed boy. Perhaps next time around younger brother Alan would have that honour.

"Have you got another Guinness?" asked Ron.

"I'm sure we have," said mum. "Joanna, could you go and see please?"

"Okay, what about dad?"

"Eeeeeee. Eeeeeee."

"No, Stan," said mum. "You know the hospital said one a day was sufficient."

"Eeeeeee. Eeeeeee."

"It makes you aggressive."

"Eeeeeee. Eeeeeee."

"I'm sorry Stan."

Dad looked really sorry for himself. The atmosphere had changed completely. Now there was a strained silence. Joanna desperately wanted mum to change her mind. Uncle Ron looked uneasy. He probably thought the same but couldn't say anything. Thankfully mum picked up on the Guinness vibes.

"Alright Stan," she said. "Just this once, but drink it slowly."

"Thank God for that," whispered Joanna under her breath as she disappeared to replenish the glasses.

"You look well Stan," said Ron.

"Eeeeeee. Eeeeeee."

"He always does," said mum. "He's probably the same weight as when he had the stroke. He's never lost his appetite."

"Eeeeeee. Eeeeeee."

"We've got steak and kidney pie tonight."

"Our mum cooked some lovely meals," said Ron. "Do you remember Stan?"

"Eeeeeee. Eeeeeee."

"I remember her Yorkshire pudding," said mum. "The first time Stan took me home we had a Sunday roast. I'd never tasted Yorkshire like it. I thought my mum's was good but it didn't compare with yours. I wish I knew the secret."

"Guinness," said Ron.

"Guinness?"

"Yes, the magic ingredient of a Yorkshire pudding. It makes it rise better."

Dad started laughing.

"You're having me on, aren't you?" said mum.

"Now would I do that? The next time you make a Yorkshire add some Guinness."

"I think I've heard that before," said Joanna as she returned with the Guinness.

"See I told you," said Ron.

"Well I think it sounds far fetched," said mum.

"Eeeeeee. Eeeeeee."

"Well that's what we used to do," said Ron. "And what we had over we mixed in with the potato peelings. The chickens loved it."

"Did they really," said mum.

"Yes, they considered it a real treat."

"Eeeeeee. Eeeeeee."

"That's right Stan, chickens can hold their drink."

"I've never heard so much rubbish," said mum.

Dad started laughing which set Joanna off. Mum smiled and shook her head.

"I'm really glad you visited," she said. "It's done Stan the power of good."

"I've got a few more stories yet," said Ron. "Now where shall we start?"

# THIRTEEN

Nicole offered her condolences to mum and moved on. She felt uneasy. It was the first time they'd met since the breakdown of the marriage. She guessed she wouldn't be her most favourite person at the moment. That would be natural, wheelchair issue or no wheelchair issue. She looked for a friendly face and spotted Joanna.

"You must find it difficult being here?" said Joanna.

"Yes, it is strange."

"Well I know mum appreciates you making the effort."

"Did she ever tell you what I said about Nick?"

Joanna looked puzzled and shook her head.

"If he'd had a stroke," continued Nicole.

Joanna shook her head again.

"I said I might have put him in a home."

"Oh I see. No, she never mentioned that."

"I thought I might have been unable to cope."

"Well I know mum should have put dad in a home long before she did. Those last four or five years were really difficult."

"But I didn't really mean what I said," said Nicole. "I was just being argumentative."

"Well I know dad appreciated you taking the time to talk to him."

"I used to wonder what he thought about sitting in his armchair all day. How many years was he ill?"

"Twenty eight."

"That's such a long time."

"Yes, over half their married life. Are you returning to Canada?"

"I don't know. I've been here so long now it feels like home. I am going back for Christmas though."

"Well I wish you all the best Nicole."

"Thank you. I'm going to miss seeing everyone. Especially your boys."

"They'll miss you as well."

They were joined by Joyce.

"Hello Nicole," she said. "It's nice that you could make it. I'm sorry about you and Nick separating."

"That's okay."

"It happens more and more nowadays. You take Ralph's daughter Carol. She's had some really nice husbands. Let's hope its third time lucky for her."

"Yes."

"I imagine she's about your age."

"I think so."

"So you've got plenty of time."

"Not for three husband's hopefully," said Nicole smiling.

"No, of course I didn't mean that. But good luck in the future Nicole. I'm going to see if there's any tea going."

She disappeared into the kitchen.

"I like the way she said Carol's had some nice husbands." said Joanna.

"Yes, but I don't think she was being judgemental," said Nicole.

"No, you're right. But Carol's probably got the distinction of being the first family member to have three husbands."

"I'm sure she won't be the last."

# 1971

The wedding of the year had gone off without a hitch. Okay the weather hadn't been great but then snow could never be ruled out in March. And mum seemed to be the only person unhappy with the roast pork dinner. Everybody questioned on its merits (and mum had questioned everybody at least twice) gave the thumbs up. But mum still didn't seem convinced.

The bride and groom, Joanna and David, had already left for their honeymoon in Ireland while the remaining guests had been rounded up and despatched back to Nottingham Road for the buffet.

At last mum could relax. Her biggest concern leading up to the big day had been dad's role in the proceedings – and primarily that of giving away his daughter. Those concerns increased when he missed the dress rehearsal because of a particularly difficult day and threatened to pull out of the big event altogether. But she needn't have worried. Dad performed his duties to perfection – and with a smile. He looked really smart in his blue serge suit, white shirt with gold cufflinks, Institute of Export tie, black shoes and flat hat.

"Stan," shouted mum. "You can't wear that hat. It's you daughters wedding."

"Eeeeeee. Eeeeeee."

"No, Stan. You wear that when you go shopping. Come on now."

But dad was pulling mum's leg.

"Eeeeeee. Eeeeeee."

"Very funny."

"Eeeeeee. Eeeeee."

"I have got a sense of humour Stan but not at the moment. There's too much to think about."

But he did look a picture of health – a fine figure of a man. You wouldn't have guessed he'd suffered a stroke eight years ago. How appearances could lie.

Joanna felt proud of her father. That he'd been able to perform his duties. Well, except for the speechmaking of course. That responsibility had been given to Ralph. He hadn't disappointed, delivering an amusing well received speech. Naturally he made reference to the warm Southern Comfort welcome whenever he visited Nottingham Road. That got the biggest laugh. If only he knew the half of it though. The continual bickering between host and hostess, the sudden disappearances to the wardrobe, the biro marked level on the bottle after each visit. Obviously it was for the best to be unaware of the facts.

The newlyweds had met at Westminster Hospital. The classic nurse falls for trainee doctor from Grimsby scenario. Or, alternatively, doctor falls for student nurse from the East End. His parents had kindly offered to help with the financing of the wedding, deducing that with the breadwinner unable to work money might be tight. But mum, stubbornly, would hear none of it. Tradition stood and the bride's family footed the bill.

They married at St Paul's Leyton. The church mum and dad married in on the eve of the second world war. The recently enthroned Rev. King took the service. A likeable man but like his predecessor, the Rev. Seago, not renowned for captivating sermons. But notwithstanding that he happily took up the invitation to the evening buffet.

There'd been a good turnout. Besides those invited many neighbours and Girl Guides attended. The sun shone for the photos and then it snowed. Only a few flurries but enough for people to exaggerate in years to come, "Do you remember Joanna and David's wedding? Didn't it snow?"

The reception had been held at a community centre in Lea Bridge Road, Clapton. A venue recommended by mum's work colleague Mrs Walker. That in itself had been a surprise because in all the years they'd worked together she'd never recommended or suggested anything. But on the community centre she'd been most adamant.

"You won't find better, believe me. My sister Harriet had a lovely time with her school reunion. You'd be silly to go anywhere else."

Mum felt so intimidated by her strength of feeling that she had to concur. Though now with her disappointment of the roast pork she wished she'd made further enquiries.

"Nick," said mum. "I want you to be honest with me."

"Mum," interrupted Nick. "I'm telling you for the third time. The pork was okay."

"Only okay?"

"Mum. No, better than okay. Very tender and tasty. Believe me."

"It must be me then."

"Yes, it is you. Now stop worrying. It's been a great day. Look at dad. Who'd have thought he'd get through it without a hiccup."

"You're right. Shame it wasn't a bit warmer though."

"Well it is March, anything's possible. And at least it didn't snow for long. Remember sixty three? Taking the bus to the hospital? Could you imagine if we'd had that sort of weather today?"

"No, that would have been dreadful."

They were joined by an agitated dad and a flustered Kitty.

"I don't know what Stan's on about," said Kitty.

"What is it Stan?" said mum.

"Eeeeeee. Eeeeeee."

Immediately Nick had an idea what dad meant and hoped mum didn't reach the same conclusion. That the pork could have been tenderer.

"Joanna and David?" said mum. "Where have they gone for their honeymoon?"

"Eeeeeee. Eeeeeee. "

"No. My mum? She's gone home."

"Eeeeeee. Eeeeeee."

"I don't know Stan. I'm tired. You must be too. It's been a long day."

But dad wasn't giving up that easily.

"Eeeeeee. Eeeeeee."

He pointed to his mouth – as if eating something. This made Nick even more convinced that dad was concerned about the pork.

"No, I'm sorry Stan," said mum. "Would you like a coffee?"

"Eeeeeee. Eeeeeee."

But dad wouldn't be fobbed off that easily. He stormed away indicating that they should stay right where they were.

"I think he's getting tired," said mum.

"He's done well," said Kitty. "It must have been lovely for Joanna that he was able to give her away."

"Yes, after he refused to go to the rehearsal I'd given up hope. I'd even asked Ralph to be on standby."

"That's when dad decided he'd be up to it no matter what," said Nick.

"He didn't know," said mum. "I certainly didn't tell him. Did you then?"

"No, but he had a sixth sense. He could cope with Ralph making a speech on his behalf but not giving his daughter away as well. Definitely one Southern Comfort step too far."

Mum smiled but Kitty didn't get it and shook her head in bewilderment.

"It's alright Kitty," said mum. "Stan's got this thing about Ralph drinking his spirits."

"Oh I see, so that's what Southern Comfort is. But I've never seen Ralph as a drinker."

"He's not. Stan likes to exaggerate. It annoys me. Do you know we have to hide the drink in his wardrobe when Ralph's expected."

"Really?"

"Yes, but when his brother Ron visits it doesn't matter how much he drinks. Oh no, that's different."

"Well yes, but that's his brother Joan. Of course he's going to treat him differently. As they say, bloods thicker than water."

Mum, annoyed that Kitty had so easily sided against her, changed the subject.

"So you didn't think the pork was tough?" she enquired.

"Joan! I've already told you. No. Stop worrying. It's been a lovely day."

"What about the weather?"

"Well you can't control that. You often get snow in March anyway."

"Mum will ask you again in half an hour," said Nick.

"Okay," said mum. "I won't mention the subject again. Here comes Stan with Iris."

"Eeeceee. Eeeeeee."

"What do you mean Stan?"

"Eeeeeee. Eeeeeee."

"Oh, you want to know where Ted is?" said mum.

Dad sighed with relief and sarcastically clapped his hands.

"I'm afraid he doesn't travel very well these days" said Iris.

Dad looked bewildered and shook his head.

"He doesn't like leaving Middlesbrough," continued Iris. "It's too much effort for him."

"Eeeeeee. Eeeeeee."

"Yes, he used to come down for the cup final every year. He really enjoyed himself then. But not anymore Stan."

"Eeeeeee. Eeeeeee."

"What will he be doing? Let's see, it's six o'clock. He'll be sitting in his chair, smoking, drinking barley wine and listening to his jazz records."

"Eeeeeee. Eeeeeee."

"Yes, unfortunately he still smokes as much as ever. You can tell by the stain on the ceiling. Dark brown when it should be white."

Eeeeeee. Eeeeeee."

"You never tried it Stan?"

"Eeeeeee. Eeeeeee."

"I'm glad you didn't," said mum. "There wouldn't have been so many rations for me during the war."

"I remember you smoking and doing the ironing," said Nick. "I can't believe it now. My mum with a fag in her mouth."

"Quite an art that," said mum. "I mean smoking without dropping ash on the clothes."

"You're right. I don't remember any burnt marks on my shirts."

"Eeeeeee. Eeeeeee."

"What do you mean Stan?"

"Eeeeeee. Eeeeeee."

"You went to work with a singed shirt?"

"Eeeeeee. Eeeeeee."

"Oh come off it Stan."

"Eeeeeee. Eeeeeee."

"And Mr Whitehorn told you to go home and change. That's very funny."

"Eeeeeee. Eeeeeee."

"Yes, of course it's true."

Nick smiled, relieved that dad hadn't been questioning the tenderness of the pork. Sometimes dad's actions when attempting to make himself understood bore no relationship to the real thing. Obviously the brain played tricks when you were a stroke sufferer. Then there were occasions when you could guess what dad meant with no trouble whatsoever. A kind of telepathy took over. But today dad had excelled himself.

There must have been moments when he'd considered his lot –

his role in life since that eventful day in sixty three. Especially at family occasions like these when he couldn't participate as of old. But it hadn't showed. Outwardly he looked happy and proud. And there'd been one particularly poignant moment. After the applause had died down following Ralph's well received speech, dad made a point of walking up to him and shaking his hand warmly. It brought a tear to mum's eye. She smiled, happy that it wasn't all Southern Comfort and family bias.

"Have you enjoyed yourself today Stan?" she asked when everybody had gone.

"Eeeeeee. Eeceeee."

"That's good. I bet Joanna was proud of you."

"Eceeeee. Eeeeeee."

"You're proud of her. Yes, I bet you are Stan."

"Eeeeeee. Eeeeeee."

"Their honeymoon? Killarney in Ireland."

"Eeeeeee. Eeeeeee."

"No, we've never been to Ireland."

"Eeeeeee. Eeeeeee."

"We haven't Stan."

Dad shrugged his shoulders convinced they had visited Ireland. But decided not to pursue the point. He felt tired. It was time for bed.

"Eeeeeec. Eeeeeee."

"Yes goodnight Stan. See you in the morning."

They kissed and smiled at each other. It'd been a good day all round.

# FOURTEEN

As the afternoon wore on the weather deteriorated. By five o'clock the skies were pitch black and the rain incessant. The puddle that invariably appeared by the back door had encroached past the shed. Intrigued onlookers watched from the dining room. Would the water reach the back fence for the first time since mum and dad moved in?

"The path needs levelling," said Ralph.

"Yes," said Joanna. "It's the next job for mum's handyman."

"Handyman, well good for Joan. It must be reassuring having somebody you can rely on in her position. And she probably pays less than in Leyton."

"Yes, he's very reasonable and so far, fingers crossed, reliable. He turns up on time and on the right day."

"That's a plus."

"He likes his tea though, old Mr. Botwood. A cuppa every hour with three sugars and a couple of dad's ginger nuts."

"That's your British workman for you."

"And he likes to natter. According to mum he never stops."

"How did dad get on with having somebody else in the house?"

"He hated it. Besides eating his biscuits dad thought he was lazy. He couldn't relax. Then mum couldn't. Dad would check up on Mr Botwood and mum would check up on dad checking up. I don't know what old Mr Botwood made of it all."

"He was probably checking up on the pair of them. Is he that old?"

"Well I'm not very good at ages but I should think he's way past retirement. Early seventies. Actually he's probably a similar age to your friend the undertaker."

They both smiled.

"I take it he can manage a ladder though," said Ralph.

"Yes, although dad had to hold it steady once because of the strong winds. Mum's idea. That didn't go down well."

"I can imagine."

"Dad hid the ginger nuts until mum gave him a good talking to."

They were joined by Ralph's brother John. He cast an inquisitive eye over the puddle.

"You've got a problem there Joanna."

"You're right. Do you remember that puddle in West End Avenue when it rained? We used to go round in our wellies and play for hours."

"I certainly do. The blooming drains. It took the council twenty five years to sort out. Can you believe that? Twenty five years! Ralph, you were a councillor. Why did it take so long?"

"Sorry John, highways wasn't my department. But it couldn't have been much fun if you lived there,"

"No, that's true," said Joanna. "But when you're a kid you don't think about that. We just wanted to splash about and sail our boats. There were a dozen of us sometimes. The Nottingham Road gang plus all hangers on. The residents got fed up. I don't know why because we weren't interfering with them. Well except for the occasional game of Knock down Ginger and the other one. Now what did we call it? Where we used to tie wire across the pavement to trip up the old people. They threatened to call the police. But they never did."

"Joanna, I'm surprised at you," said John. "Tying wire across the pavement?"

"It wasn't my idea but boys will be boys."

"You could have used string," said Ralph. "That would have been safer."

"That's what we suggested but the boys thought that'd be too obvious."

"I'll have a word with your brother," said John. "I take it he belonged to the gang."

"Yes, chief spy."

"Chief spy! Well, well, well."

In the kitchen, over a cup of tea, mum, Kit and Mary were discussing the possible causes of dad's stroke. Mary convinced that dad's boxing career, although short, had been a contributory factor. Especially with him suffering a knockout on that infamous occasion.

"But Dr. Jarvis never connected the two," said mum.

"Joan," said Mary. "You know that doesn't mean anything. If he'd been on the ball Stan might never have had the stroke."

"I know that. I often think if our previous doctor hadn't died things would have been different. But Stan only had a dozen fights. Surely not enough to cause brain damage."

"But he did get knocked out," said Mary. "That one punch might have done it."

"Didn't the vicar say that Stan was unbeaten?" said Kitty.

Mum put her hand to her mouth and gawped. "Oh no, that must have been me. How did I do that? Of course Stan got knocked out. So why did I tell the vicar he hadn't? I can't believe I said that. What's everyone going to think now?"

"Oh don't worry Joan," said Mary. "You've had a lot on your mind."

"Yes, but what a mistake to make."

"I think we all assumed Stan was unbeaten," said Kitty. Ron and Alan were probably the culprits They wanted to give their brother this air of invincibility. Now don't worry about it Joan."

"Okay, but I can't believe I said that."

"Did you ever see Stan fight?" asked Mary.

"No, it never worked out. I would have done – although reluctantly. I'm not a boxing fan and seeing your husband knocked out must be a bit upsetting."

"I remember Stan had an interest in boxing at school," said Kitty. "He preferred reading the Ring Magazine to doing his homework."

"Yes, he still enjoyed reading the magazine long after the stroke. Not every day mind you. It depended on how the brain was behaving. But until he had the second stroke he kept up the interest. My brother John had it delivered and passed it on to Stan."

"Well I do think the boxing had something to do with his stroke," reiterated Mary.

"Yes, you could be right. Anyway Nick's going to write to the Hospital for Nervous Diseases and inform them of Stan's death. He's going to mention how long he survived after the stroke. I'll ask him to mention the boxing."

"It'd be interesting to know."

"Do you think I should go round and tell everyone that Stan got knocked out?"

"You'll do nothing of the sort," said Mary.

They were joined by a smiling Alan. He put his arm round mum's shoulder and hugged her.

"Hello Joan. Now what's all this about Stan being unbeaten?"

Mum looked crestfallen. She sighed. She'd been found out.

"Yes, and who started those rumours in the first place?" said Kitty.

"What me? No, you've got to blame Ron for that. You know what that brother of ours was like."

"Well it really doesn't matter now, does it?" said Mary.

"I'm sorry Alan," said mum. "I don't know how I came to say that. Of course I knew Stan had been knocked out. He wouldn't have kept that from me."

"Oh don't worry Joan, I'm only messing about. Don't take it seriously."

"A fine time to be messing about" said Mary."

"Oh that's alright," said mum. "Stan would have seen the funny side. Especially where his brothers were concerned."

"We should remember the fights Stan won," said Kitty. "Considering he only lost the once."

"Yes, a great record," said Alan. "I saw Stan box a few times. He had style. He certainly had the ability to turn professional."

"Well I'm glad he wasn't tempted," said mum.

"He never considered it. He might have done if he'd had no commitments. But he had you Joan. What more would he want?"

# 1972

Mum shook her head and tutted. She wasn't happy with the idea of selling off the spirits that family and friends had bought dad. She considered it mercenary. Hadn't the drinks been bought in good faith by those who simply wanted to bring a smile to dad's face? Those who found it difficult coming to terms with his predicament and with this gesture could show their support. But dad wasn't that sentimental and with Nick's encouragement, plus mounting orders from his workplace, MK.Electric, the business had taken off big time.

"I'm not keeping any of the money myself," protested Nick.

"That's not the point," said mum. "I just don't like the idea."

"Oh mum, it'll be nice for dad to have some money. He might give you some."

"He'd better. What does he need it for?"

"I could actually sell double the quantity dad's got. We need more visitors mum. But remember not to let them in unless they've bought a bottle."

"I could actually see Stan doing that."

"That'd be funny, wouldn't it?"

"No, it wouldn't be funny at all. How can you say that? Where is your dad anyway?"

"He's going through his wardrobe again. Just to make doubly sure there aren't any more bottles lying about."

"How many times is that?"

She shook her head in despair – but then smiled. She could see the funny side. Stan forgetting where he'd put the latest bottle and searching high and low. Eventually finding it and reappearing with a big grin on his face. And if he wasn't searching for spirits he'd be counting the proceeds, putting it in his drawer, and then ten minutes later checking that nobody had stolen any. Obviously if money went missing there'd be no guessing who'd be number one suspect. She certainly couldn't rely on his stroke damaged brain failing to notice a discrepancy. A smarter approach would be needed to gain access to the goodies.

At that moment dad walked in carrying a bottle of Bell's Scotch whisky. He smiled and gave Nick the thumbs up.

"Eeeeeee. Eeeeeee."

"Oh that's great dad," said Nick. "Where did you find it?"

"Eeeeeee. Eeeeeee."

"On top of the wardrobe?"

"Eeeeeee. Eeeeeee."

"Oh, on top of mum's wardrobe. Well I never. Mum, what have you been up to?"

"I think your father's getting his wardrobes mixed up," said mum.

"Eeeeeee. Eeeeeee."

"Stan, I've got no idea how it got there."

"Anyway," said Nick. "That's another two pounds for the kitty."

"Eeeeeee. Eeeeeee."

"That's about half price dad."

"Eeeeeee. Eeeeeee."

"No, we don't want to be greedy."

"Oh no," said mum. "God forbid you get that reputation."

"Eeeeeee. Eeeeeee."

"Well I reckon you should have £14.00," said Nick.

"Eeeeeee. Eeeeeee."

"Yes, go and check."

"Before you go," said mum. "What are you going to do with the money?"

Dad immediately went on the defensive knowing that mum thought she deserved a share. But that wasn't going to happen. Okay he didn't need the money, he couldn't remember the last time he'd spent anything. But it felt good having a few pounds stashed away in the sideboard drawer.

"Eeeeeee. Eeeeeee."

"Okay Stan, you don't have to shout. I'm not after the money. I just thought it might be a good idea to buy some Premium Bonds."

Dad shook his head in derision. Premium Bonds! What a Joke. What a complete waste of money that would be. When had their numbers ever come up? To think they'd been buying them since they started in nineteen fifty six. How many years was that? And they hadn't won a penny – not a penny. Mum picked up on dad's negative reaction.

"I know we haven't had much luck in the past," she continued. "But there's got to be a first time."

"Eeeeeee. Eeeeeee."

"It's just an idea."

Dad shook his head again and went off to count his money. What an utterly stupid idea.

"Oh well, worth a try," said mum.

"Yes, you might have better luck another day," said Nick. You never know with dad. But do you have to claim a premium bond win?"

"No, they send it automatically. Of course you let them know if you're moving."

"But we haven't moved so there's no chance of us having a fortune hidden away?"

"I'm afraid not."

"I reckon it'd be a good idea to buy Beatle shares with the money. You know, Northern Songs. Do you remember?"

"You and your Beatle shares, how could I forget? That's something we definitely won't be doing. And don't go suggesting that to dad."

"I already have."

"Nick, you had no right to. What did he say?"

"He thought it too risky. A shame really."

Mum smiled. "Well good for Stan, we're on the same side on that one. I think the best thing is not to mention it again. Perhaps he'll come round later."

"What, to my idea of the Beatle shares?"

"No, Nick, to the much more sensible idea of premium bonds."

Ten minutes later Dad returned clutching a wad of pound notes. He handed them to Nick. He counted them, then again and then for a third time. He looked puzzled.

"I must have miscalculated. You've got sixteen pounds there."

"Eeeeeee. Eeeeeee."

"Yes, good job you checked. Now how many bottles have we left?"

"Eeeeeee. Eeeeeee."

"Two whisky and two brandy?"

126

Dad nodded then disappeared again to return the money to its rightful place.

"I should be able to sell those at the end of the week," said Nick. "It's pay day Thursday. That'll make it twenty four pounds."

"That is good news," said mum sarcastically. "Twenty four pounds, now what could I buy with that?"

"Twenty four premium bonds I suppose."

"No, I was thinking more along the lines of something for the house."

"Oh I see. Well what would you like to buy?"

"You could do with some new bedroom curtains."

Dad reappeared grinning and holding yet another bottle of whisky. This time Dewer's

"I can't believe it," said Nick. "Where did that one come from?"

"Eeeeeee. Eeeecee."

"Under the sideboard?"

"Eeeeeee. Eeeecee."

"No. Behind the tele?"

"Eeeeeee. Eeeeeee."

"Well how did it get there?"

"Eeeeeee. Eeeeeee."

"You were probably hiding it from Ralph when he called in," said mum. "You didn't have time to take it upstairs and panicked."

Dad looked embarrassed and nodded. After a pause he handed her the bottle.

"Eeeeeee. Eeeeeee."

"Is that for me?" said mum.

"Eeeeee. Eeeeeee."

"Oh thank you Stan. I won't drink it all at once."

Mum handed the bottle to Nick.

"Now what can I buy for two pounds?" she said. "I'll have to think of a special treat."

"Eeeeeee. Eeeeee."

"Yes, thank you Stan, I do appreciate it."

With that she gave dad an unexpected kiss on the cheek.

"Eeeeeee. Eeeeeee."

"No, I won't expect any more peace offerings from you."

"Eeeeeee. Eeeeeee."

"And I won't mention the premium bonds again."

"Eeeeeee. Eeeeeee."

As dad disappeared again to search for bottles of whisky the door bell rang.

"Eeeeeee. Eeeeeee."

"Yes, answer it Stan," shouted mum. "But don't go searching whoever it is for spirits. That will never do."

"Eeeeeee. Eeeeeee."

"Or if you do, do it discreetly," shouted Nick. "Especially if it's the vicar."

Dad walked up the hall with a purposeful stride.

# FIFTEEN

Timothy and William were in the lounge discussing the form of Norwich City with their dad present as a silent observer. Opinions were bantered about light-heartedly until, to the boys shock and indignation, dad suggested accompanying them to the next home game. The big one against arch rivals Ipswich. The East Anglia derby.

"But you're not a fan," said William.

"Yes, I am," said David."

"Since when?" said Timothy "You don't like football."

"I do. I followed Grimsby when I was growing up."

"What, you used to watch them play?"

"No, but I followed their results."

"Typical. To be a real fan you have to go to the matches."

"Well I'd like to see Norwich play."

"I always thought mum was a bigger fan than you" said William. "You wait until I tell her."

"I can't believe you're making all this fuss," said David. "It's only a football match."

"Only a football match, you're joking. We're playing Ipswich. Football doesn't come into it. They're the Suffolk scumbags."

"Is that right?"

"Yes," said Timothy "We've got to thrash those tractor boys no matter what."

"That's right," said William. "But if you supported Grimsby what was their nickname?"

"The Mariners of course."

Timothy and William looked surprised and disappointed by their dad's correct answer. They were joined by Joanna and her cousin Jacqueline. It would probably have been the first time the boys and her had met.

"This is my cousin Jacqueline," said Joanna. "Uncle Ron's daughter."

"Uncle Ron was Grandpa's brother?" said William.

"That's right, I don't know if you ever met him."

"I don't think so, but I've heard nana talk about him."

"Did he like a drink like Grandpa?" asked Timothy.

Joanna looked embarrassed but Jacqueline smiled.

"You could say my dad enjoyed a pint or two," she said.

"I think all the brothers liked a drink," said Joanna. "Dad loved his Guinness. A bottle a day at precisely eleven o'clock. A pity it had to stop after the second stroke."

"Why was that?" said Jacqueline.

"The doctor thought it contributed to his aggressiveness. It's true his behaviour did become more and more unpredictable. That was a worry for mum."

"Did he mind giving it up?"

"Not really. Mum had prepared herself for a big argument but he just accepted it. I don't think he ever asked for a Guinness again."

"My dad preferred bitter," said Jacqueline. "I remember as a child waiting outside the pub while he had a quick pint or two."

"That's funny, so did Nick and I on the way home from Leyton swimming baths. We used to get six pennyworth of chips and a pickled onion from the fish shop while dad popped in the Prince of Wales. He took an age sometimes."

"You were lucky. We didn't have a fish shop near dad's local – just another local. Really miserable in the winter."

"Did your mum know?" said Joanna.

"Well I never mentioned it in case she didn't and I got dad in trouble. But she must have done. It went on for years."

"That's just what Nick and I thought. That mum knew dad popped in the pub but best not to say anything."

"Well mum never asked why we'd been so long over the park,"

said Jacqueline. "That was usually dad's excuse to get out – to push me on the swings. I didn't get much pushing though. Actually I preferred him not to push me after a drink. It wasn't safe. I might have landed on the concrete. But I remember your dad as a good swimmer."

"Yes, he had a really good front crawl."

"Did he go swimming after he had the stroke?"

"I don't think so. Do you know I've never thought about that. I'm sure he could have managed it – especially in the early days. The last time I remember dad swimming was at his firms outing in about nineteen sixty. A coach load of employees and family were invited to a big country house near Bletchley. I think one of the directors lived there and they were celebrating opening a factory nearby. It was a really hot summer's day. They had this enormous outdoor pool – probably Olympic size. Dad won the front crawl by a mile. He refused to enter the other races in case it got too one-sided."

"Olympic size?" said William. "Are you sure?"

"Well not one hundred per cent. It's a long time ago. But it was certainly big."

"Did you know dad supported the Canaries?" said Timothy.

"What my dad?"

"No, our dad."

"Your dad a Canary fan. Is that right David?"

"Yes."

"He wants to go to the Ipswich match," said Timothy.

"Really, in that case then we could all go because I'd liked to see my first match."

Timothy and William's faces dropped. Oh dear, the Lower Barclay with their parents. What would their friends say?

"I doubt if we'll be able to get tickets now," said William.

"Any excuse," said Joanna.

"No, he's probably right," said Timothy. "Especially as Ipswich are their opponents."

"Why should that make a difference?"

"Mum!!" said the pair of shouted in unison.

"I remember seeing Charlton beat Norwich six nil," said Jacqueline.

Well you could have cut the atmosphere with a knife. Timothy and William looked gobsmacked.

"It's true," she continued. "I'm a Charlton season ticket holder. I never miss a game."

"Six nil!" said William. "Are you sure?"

"Positive, although the score did flatter us somewhat. It's a few years ago now."

"I don't remember ever losing by six goals," said Timothy.

"Nor do I," said William.

"Well we have," said David. "I can recall the match clearly. Something only a real fan would."

# 1973

Mum brought in the double cream meringues and strawberries. The assembled licked their lips in anticipation. There was something very special and reassuring about a Sunday evening in front of the tele with mouth watering homemade delicacies and a bone china cup of tea. Even more so on a hot summers evening with the sun streaming in through the window.

Mum, nana and Nick had just returned from church while Joanna and David, with their ten months old son Timothy, had called in on the way home to Oxford. Dad, who hadn't had a bad day and for the last couple of hours had been reading the Ring magazine, waited impatiently for the feast to begin. Although with Timothy on his lap he couldn't unfortunately make a lightening swoop for the goodies.

"Eeeeeee. Eeeeeee."

"He's making your arms ache?" said mum. "I know your game Stan. You want to get started on the meringues."

"Eeeeeeeeeeeeeeeeeeeeeee," screamed Timothy.

Dad shrugged his shoulders and looked as helpless as possible.

"Would you like me to take him from you?" said Joanna.

"Eeeeeee. Eeeeeee."

Dad didn't need a second invitation. In a flash he'd handed

Timothy to his daughter and grabbed a couple of meringues.

"Just go easy Stan," said mum. "There are other people here."

Dad nodded, smiled and handed the plate to his mother-in-law.

"Eeeeeee. Eeeeeee."

"Thank you Stan," said nana. "I'll just take one for now."

"Well don't leave it too long for seconds or there won't be any," said mum. "I've got my eye on you Stan."

The sound of munching filled the room as the family tucked into the meringues. They were absolutely delicious, mouth-wateringly sumptuous. Definitely mum's tour de force. Well that's if you didn't include her expertise with cheesecakes. But that's another story, suffice to say that she could produce a cheesecake for every day of the year. Indeed her son-in-laws overriding memory of visiting Nottingham Road during those courtship days with Joanna were the variety of cheesecake served up as a dessert. Mind boggling, he said. It'd been suggested she should collate the recipes and publish them. Or at least hand them on for the attention of Jimmy Young. His cookery career seemed to have stalled lately.

"Are you going out tonight Nick?" asked mum.

"I shouldn't think so," he replied.

"So you're able to give nana a lift home?"

"Of course I can."

"Thank you Nick," said nana. "I do appreciate it."

Never had a truer word been spoken because Nana Bailey was eternally grateful for any favour however small. She took nothing for granted, not even a weekly visit to Nottingham Road after church. She much preferred an invite. Something to look forward to then.

Nick's reason for going out on a Sunday night was to ensure he missed Last of the Summer Wine. A programme he disliked but seemed to be compulsive viewing for the rest of the family. Nana, especially, enjoyed the weekly shenanigans of the Yorkshire folk and whenever she visited mum ensured they watched it. Luckily, because dad also enjoyed the programme, there were no arguments on the matter. In fact you could say that dad and nana bonded over it. And since the stroke that hadn't always been the case. Often dad showed impatience with her. Not that she ever noticed, but mum certainly did and would give dad a good talking to. He'd just shrug his shoulders and plead ignorance.

"Last of the Summer Wine isn't on tonight," said David putting down the Radio Times.

There were looks of disappointment on everybody's face except Nick.

"Are you sure?" said Joanna picking up the Radio Times.

"Well I can't see it," said David.

Joanna studied the magazine closely while those around nervously fidgeted.

"Perhaps it's the end of the series," said Nick.

"You mean you hope it's the end of the series," said mum.

"Well yes, I do actually."

"David," shouted Joanna. "You're looking at yesterday's page."

You could feel the room sigh with relief – except for Nick of course.

"Oh sorry about that," said David. "I should have realized when I couldn't see Songs of Praise."

"Eeeeeee. Eeeeeee."

"Yes, it is on dad," said Joanna. "Everything's fine with the world."

Dad gave nana the thumbs up.

"I would have missed seeing that," said nana. "I look forward to Last of the Summer Wine more than any other programme on the television."

"Eeeeeeeeee," cried Timothy again.

"I think he's tired," said mum.

"Yes, and he probably needs changing," said Joanna. "I'll take him upstairs. I've got time before the programme starts. David, is it okay to watch Last of the Summer Wine before we go?"

David nodded. By the tone of Joanna's voice he knew it pointless to suggest otherwise – especially as he'd been looking on the wrong page in the Radio Times.

"I'll get some more tea," said mum. "Does everybody want seconds?"

Everybody nodded and while Joanna popped upstairs with Timothy mum collected the cups. She stood over dad before leaving the room.

"Right Stan, how many meringues have you had?"

"Eeeeeee. Eeeeeee."

"Two. So can you leave the last one for mum?"

"Oh Joan," said nana. "If Stan wants the last one he can have it."

Dad smiled and prepared to grab the remaining meringue.

"He'll do nothing of the sort," said mum. "Now you have it."

Mum put down the tray of cups, picked up the plate and offered the one remaining meringue to nana – who looked a trifle guilty as she put it on her plate.

"Don't feel bad about it," said mum.

"Perhaps we could have half each," said nana.

"You can't share a meringue."

"Eeeeeee. Eeeeeee."

"Well you would say that Stan."

After mum left the room nana sat and looked at the meringue unsure of what to do for the best. Should she scoff it down or offer it to dad?

"You could share it with dad if you want to," said Nick. "I'll cut it in half."

"Eeeeeee. Eeeeeee."

"Well if you're going to," said David. "Do it before your mum returns."

"What do you say nana?" said Nick.

"Oh I don't know. Oh go on then."

She handed her plate to Nick who carefully sized up the halfway mark on the meringue.

"Is this going to work?" said David.

"I don't see why not," said Nick.

He carefully cut into the meringue. But mum knew best – that you couldn't share a meringue without some kind of mishap. And, alas, as Nick made contact with the meringue it shot into a thousand pieces over the floor. Dad and David started laughing. Nana put her hand to her mouth in shock. Nick got down on his hands and knees and began picking up the pieces. And mum returned with the tea demanding to know what had happened.

"Eeeeeee. Eeeeeee."

"Oh it's your fault, is it Stan?"

"No, don't blame dad, said Nick. "It's my fault, I attempted the impossible."

"What, cutting the meringue in two? I told you it couldn't be done."

"No, sorry mum."

"Well go and get the Hoover and clear it up before Last of the Summer Wine begins."

"I'm sorry Joan," said nana. "I did say Nick could cut it into two."

"It's not your fault. He should have known better."

So Nick went to fetch the Hoover and Joanna returned with a contentedly sleeping Timothy.

"Did you drop your meringue on the floor nana?" she asked jokingly.

"That was Nick's doing," said mum. "He was trying to divide it into two."

"Dividing a meringue into two? But why would you do that?"

"So that your father could have an extra half."

"Eeeeeee. Eeeeeee."

"Dad, I'm surprised at you," said Joanna. How many meringues have you had then?"

"Eeeeeee. Eeeeeee. "

"Two. Oh is that all. I've had two as well."

"You've had two," said mum.

"So have I," said David.

At that moment Nick returned with the Hoover.

"How many meringues have you had?" asked mum.

"Two, the same as everybody else. I have been counting you know."

Mum seemed surprised that dad hadn't been particularly greedy and grabbed more than his share while nana hadn't divulged that she'd already eaten her quota.

"Well I did say Stan could have it," said nana deducing what her daughter was thinking.

But the damage had been done. In future she wouldn't be getting preferential treatment where meringues were concerned.

# CHAPTER SIXTEEN

Mum sat with Iris drinking tea and reminiscing. It continued to rain but because of the darkness they couldn't establish whether the puddle had encroached past the shed or not.

"I take it you'll be going round Joanna's for Christmas?" said Iris.

"Yes, we did that for the last few years. I gave up cooking Christmas dinner. Too stressful with Stan around. He didn't appreciate the effort and got so moody because we ate later than normal. I remember the last time we tried it. God, what a day. Torrential rain and gale force winds. I got soaked just bringing the potatoes in from the shed. Stan was in such a foul mood. He kept shouting and waving his arms about. We were waiting for Nick and Nicole to arrive. They were late. That didn't help."

"So how did Stan get on with going round Joanna's?"

"He didn't. For the first couple of years he'd have dinner and then David would take him home. But even that got too much. He started falling over and shouting. Really showing off. We decided it'd be better if we left him at home."

"So he missed his turkey and Christmas Pudding."

"I'm afraid so. Well the first year we took him home a plateful but he didn't eat it. He preferred his ravioli."

"Ravioli?"

"His usual lunch."

"Poor old Stan."

"There's nothing wrong with ravioli," said mum smiling.

They were interrupted by what sounded to Iris like thunder.

"Did you hear that?" she said. "I'm glad we're not driving back tonight."

"No, that wasn't thunder," said mum. "That's Mrs Bunn shutting her back door. It sticks. It has done for ages. It's about time her son sorted it out."

"What are your neighbours like?"

"Mrs Bunn's okay. She's lived there for sixty years. Born and bred in Norfolk. She's a widow. I don't see a lot of her, especially at this time of year. I did knock to tell her about Stan but couldn't get an answer."

"I read somewhere that Norfolk people take twenty years to accept outsiders."

"Twenty! I should be so lucky. Mrs Bunn said thirty. She complained once about the noise not long after we moved in. I think she thought we were having a party. But it was only the tele. I could have mentioned her banging the back door."

"Talking about parties," said Iris. "Do you remember the Boxing Day parties you and Stan had when the children were small?"

"I do. I've been thinking about those days since Stan died."

"They were great fun Joan. You could tell Stan enjoyed them."

Mum smiled. What lovely memories. As many as twenty sat around the table. Wearing paper hats and blowing plastic whistles. Eating sausages on sticks, cucumber sandwiches and drinking cream soda. Playing Lotto and acting out silly party pieces. Dad on top form, the perfect host, taking everything in his stride. And that wasn't always the case when a family do appeared on the horizon. He could be tense and short tempered. Take that memorable Sunday afternoon trip on the boating lake at Broxbourne.

"I'm not enjoying this at all," he said as he attempted to row back to the boatyard in a force eight gale with the family holding on for dear life.

"Come in number eight, your times up," shouted the bloke with the megaphone.

"What do you think I'm trying to do," shouted dad.

"I've no idea," shouted the bloke with the megaphone. "You're just going round in circles. If you're not back soon you'll be paying extra."

"I bet we miss the train home," said dad when they finally made dry land.

"You can't blame me for that," said the bloke with the megaphone.

"Of course I won't," shouted dad – severely tempted to stuff the megaphone down his throat.

And they did miss the train.

Hosting that number of guests would have been impossible without using the huge wooden form. Redundant in the shed under pots of paint the remainder of the year but indispensable over Christmas. Mum remembered questioning the wisdom of dad buying it soon after they married. "When are we going to use that?" she said scathingly. Dad just shrugged his shoulders and remarked the price had been too good to turn down. "Well how much?" she persevered. "Less than a packet of cigarettes," he countered. End of discussion. He didn't say much about her smoking but when he did he made his point.

But boy did she find a cigarette relaxing in those days. Especially when vacuuming and ironing. Today, twenty years five on since that last drag, she still had the taste. She could imagine lighting up and enjoying the inhalation as much as ever. But of course she wouldn't. She'd made the decision to pack up when dad had his stroke. She smiled at the thought of her grandchildren's reaction to her taking up the habit again. Nonplussed would be an understatement.

"Do you remember when I smoked?" she said.

"I certainly do," said Iris. "I remember the shock on mum's face when she caught you doing it while ironing."

"Quite an art that," said mum.

"Yes, my Ted was very impressed. Something he couldn't have done. Not that he's ever ironed. But he smokes as many as twenty a day. Did Nick and Joanna ever try it?"

"I don't think Joanna did but Nick used to take mine."

"Really?"

"Yes, I tried sellotaping the packets to the mantelpiece."

"That sounded drastic."

"It wasn't much of a deterrent."

"What did Nick say?"

"He always denied it, but I couldn't think of anybody else. He buried the ends in the back garden under the sycamore tree. I don't think it did the tree any harm."

"What did Stan say?"

"I don't think he ever mentioned it. It only went on for six months. He was more concerned with the sellotape damaging the mantelpiece. He said I should have hidden the cigarettes."

"Why didn't you?"

"I've no idea. Obviously that would have been a better solution. Anyway we took the mantelpiece down soon afterwards."

"Why, because of the sellotape damage?"

Mum smiled. "No, Iris. They went out of fashion."

"Oh I see. Yes, you're right there."

"Although I think they're back in now. These fashions seem to come and go."

They were joined by Ralph and Joan.

"We were just discussing mantelpieces," said Iris.

"Were you," said a bemused Ralph.

"Yes, said mum. "I was telling Iris how I used to sellotape the cigarette packets to the mantelpiece to stop Nick helping himself."

"Did you? Why didn't you hide them Joan? It's not a good idea sticking sellotape to a mantelpiece. You ask your handy man."

"I will Ralph."

"Anyway, we're off now. Don't want to be too late home."

"No, well thanks for coming. I'm sure Stan would have appreciated it. Now drive carefully. Watch out for those speeding hearses."

Ralph smiled and hugged his sister. "That's a promise. It's a shame I couldn't have had a Southern Comfort in Stan's memory. I think he would have appreciated that. But I suppose you can't drink and drive."

"No, you certainly can't" said Joan.

As they departed mum wondered whether Stan would have appreciated his brother-in-law having a Southern Comfort in his memory. She smiled. Yes, but only a very small one.

# 1974

Dad sat in his armchair studying the framed certificate from the Institute of Export. Usually it hung inside the front door but mum had removed it for spring cleaning duties.

"Do you remember doing that Stan?" she asked.

He nodded, how could he forget? Two evenings a week studying for three years.Unfortunately failing at the first attempt but successful the second time. Feeling proud for keeping at it and happy to take the platitudes. But then, just three years on, he'd had the stroke. So it'd been a waste of time. No, other way of looking at it.

"Eeeeeee. Eeeeeee."

"Yes, you worked hard for that."

"Eeeeeee. Eeeeeee."

"What do you mean Stan?"

"Eeeeeee. Eeeeeee."

"A waste of time? Oh don't say that Stan."

Mum took the certificate from dad.

"It made me feel so proud when you got that," she said. "It didn't come easy. You really had to apply yourself."

Dad shook his head and started to cry.

"Oh Stan, I'm so sorry. I wish there was something I could do."

She knelt down besides him and put her arm round his shoulder. He put two fingers to his head as though to shoot himself.

"I don't know what to say Stan."

He shrugged his shoulders. Nothing she could say. He wasn't going to kill himself. But there were times when he considered his quality of life had reached rock bottom. Surely it would be better for all concerned if he quietly passed away. Or indeed suffered another stroke, which according to the doctor was always on the cards. But on this occasion a fatal one that would put him out of his misery.

He sobbed while mum tried her best to console him. She didn't make the mistake of reminding him that he could walk and then debating whether losing that capability was preferable to losing your speech. Something she'd done in the early days. Better to say nothing than attempt to find the answer to dad's unsolvable predicament.

After a while dad stopped crying. He took out his handkerchief and rubbed his eyes. Something he did regularly even when he hadn't been crying. One of dad's idiosyncrasies since the stroke. Or perhaps his eyes simply itched.

"Eeeeeee. Eeeeeee."

"You feel better Stan?"

"Eeeeeee. Eeeeeee."

Dad nodded, took the certificate from mum and gave her the thumbs up. The studying had been worthwhile.

"That's better Stan. Now has Nick told you about his accident last night?"

"Eeeeeee. Eeeeeee."

"He knocked over a security guard on a zebra crossing."

"Eeeeeee. Eeeeeee."

"No, he's okay but the guard might have broken his leg. Nick could see it sticking out in an odd position through his trousers."

"Eeeeeee. Eeeeeee."

"Yes, an ambulance took him to hospital."

"Eeeeeee. Eeeeeee."

"Nick said it wasn't his fault."

"Eeeeeee. Eeeeeee."

"Well that's what he said Stan. He'll be back soon. He's replacing his windscreen wipers."

"Eeeeeee. Eeeeeee."

"No, that had nothing to do with the accident. They just needed changing."

"Eeeeeee. Eeeeeee."

"Well you can ask him that. He said the security guard had been drinking and didn't look before he stepped on the crossing."

"Eeeeeee. Eeeeee."

"Nick couldn't see him because of the drizzle and the street lights being out."

"Eeeeeee. Eeeeeee."

"The power workers strike."

Dad shook his head as he tried to digest what mum had told him. Nick had knocked over somebody on a zebra crossing but it wasn't his fault. How could that be?

"Eeeeeee. "Eeeeeee."

"No, Nick said he hadn't been drinking. Well just a pint but he wouldn't have been over the limit."

"Eeeeeee. Eeeeee."

"He wasn't breathalysed. The police either didn't bother or forgot. He said the security guard actually apologised for causing the accident."

"Eeeeeee. Eeeeeee."

"That's what he said."

At that moment Nick walked in carrying a windscreen wiper.

"These things are so fiddly to fit," he said.

"Eeeeeee. Eeeeeee."

"Hello dad. So mum's told you then?"

"Eeeeeee. Eeeeeee."

"I know dad, normally you are to blame if you hit somebody on a crossing. But he didn't look before he stepped on it. He'd been drinking. I probably wouldn't have hit him if there'd been an island halfway. There should have been one, the roads wide enough. I didn't make contact until he was three-quarters of the way across."

That did it for dad. How could Nick say it wasn't his fault, street lights or no street lights, when the security guard had almost reached the other side before being hit?

"Eeeeeee. Eeeeeee."

"I would have seen him if the street lights had been on. Bloody power workers."

"Eeeeeee. Eeeeeee."

"What dad?"

"Eeeeeee. Eeeeeee."

"The police?"

"Eeeeeee. Eeeeeee."

"No, they didn't look at my car. Not that there was anything wrong with it. But you would have thought it normal procedure."

"You were lucky they didn't," said mum. "They'd have noticed the faulty wipers."

"Mum they weren't faulty. I know I've been meaning to replace them but they were perfectly okay"

"But you've changed them now – the day after the accident. That's what I call a coincidence."

"That's all it is."

"And they didn't breathalyse you either."

"No, I did think that was odd. But I was definitely under the limit. I only had one pint."

"Eeeeeee. Eeeeeee."

"The police? They'll be in touch."

"Eeeeeee. Eeeeeee. "

"No, they didn't give me any idea if I'm going to be charged. I suppose I could be because it happened on a crossing. I thought about sending the security guard some flowers, but I'm not sure that's the right thing to do. What do you think mum?"

"I don't think you should. That sends out the wrong message however good your intentions. Wait until the police have been in touch."

"Okay I'll leave it for now. Actually he'd probably prefer a drink. That's right he was carrying a bottle of whisky when I hit him. I forgot that. He took it to the hospital with him."

"Probably in shock," said mum.

"I think we both were." said Nick. "It's not a nice experience knocking somebody over."

"I'm sure it isn't – or to be knocked over come to that Nick. That's far worse. Is it still a good idea taking me out in the car when I start my lessons?"

"Yes, why shouldn't it be?"

"Well you might have lost your confidence."

"I might have done if it'd been my fault."

"Eeeeeee. Eeeeeee."

"Well say fifty, fifty then."

"We'll see what the police have to say," said mum.

"Eeeeeee. Eeeeeee."

"I suppose I'll be fined if I'm guilty," said Nick.

"Well perhaps it'll teach you to be more careful," said mum.

"Point taken – and points on my licence as well. I'd forgotten that."

"Eeeeeee. Eeeeeee."

"Yes, I will be more careful in future dad."

"I must say I'm not looking forward to driving," said mum. "Especially going round roundabouts. But I know it'll be handy."

"You'll be okay once you get started. Just remember to go round them the right way."

"And what's the right way?"

"Clockwise."

"Oh that should be easy to remember."

"It will be."

"Eeeeeee. Eeeeeee."

"What Stan?" said mum.

"Eeeeeee. Eeeeeee."

"You can't imagine me driving?"

"Eeeeeee. Eeeeeee."

"You wait and see. I might be a natural. Nick, did you say clockwise or anti-clockwise?"

"Mum!"

# CHAPTER SEVENTEEN

Dad's old army friend, Ted, sat in the mustard coloured moquette armchair in the lounge. The armchair that dad had spent most of his life since the stroke marooned in. He had to admit it was comfy, that it wouldn't take long to nod off. Especially as there were no mourners present. He shut his eyes and thought of those war years with Stan on Canvey Island. Did they really fail to down a single enemy plane between them throughout the entire campaign? It didn't make sense when you considered their natural ack-ack ability. Then he dozed off.

"Hello Ted," said Joanna. "Oh sorry, did I wake you up?"

Ted looked embarrassed at being caught cat napping.

"I must have dosed off. Sorry about that."

"That's okay. I don't envy you driving back tonight."

"No, it's not a nice evening."

"How long will it take?"

"Well it took two and a half hours coming up but the undertaker thought it should be quicker. He's got relatives down our way. But then I watched him pull out of the crematorium. More like a Grand Prix driver the way he overtook your Uncle Ralph. I'm a bit more cautious."

"Yes, he's speedy for an octogenarian."

"Was he that old?"

"Well I might be exaggerating but he's certainly past retirement age."

"Oh yes, definitely."

"I got the impression he had a wooden leg."

"A wooden leg! Why do you say that?"

"Well, when we were making the funeral arrangements he hit his leg against a filing cabinet. It made a wooden sound. But could you drive with a wooden leg?"

Ted looked sceptical about her wooden leg theory.

"Oh well, perhaps I've been mistaken then," said Joanna.

They were joined by mum and Kitty.

"Oh hello Ted," said mum. "I thought you must have gone home."

"No, Joanna caught me napping in Stan's armchair. It's very comfortable."

"Well Stan certainly thought so. He probably spent more time in it than he did in bed. I think it cost quite a lot."

"Where did you buy it?" said Kitty.

"Now you've got me there. I've probably got the receipt somewhere. I bought it just after Stan had his stroke. It could have been Harrison's and Gibson's."

Ted got up and beckoned Kitty to try the armchair. She succumbed gratefully.

"Yes, it is comfortable. It's got good support across the shoulders and the small of the back."

"It's lasted well," said mum. "You think of the wear it's had over the years."

"It probably is a Harrison's and Gibson then," said Kitty.

"Are they still going?"

"They certainly are," said Ted. "Gwen and I were in there just a month ago. We were looking for a suite. What are you going to do with the chair?"

"I'm using it. It's much more comfortable than my old one. Sorry Ted."

"No, I didn't mean that."

"You can have my old one though."

Ted smiled. "No, I couldn't get anything without Gwen's approval."

"How is Gwen?" said Joanna.

"Her legs are still a problem. She can't walk very far. I think she needs a second opinion. Our doctor's not a lot of cop."

"You know something about substandard doctors, don't you Joan?" said Kitty.

"Yes, but I've had no complaints since we moved here. We've got the same one as Joanna."

"I've thought about changing ours," said Ted. "It's such a lot of palaver though."

"Ted, if you're not happy you change," said mum. "Something I should have done years ago. I've always regretted it."

"I'll have a word with Gwen about it."

"Well make sure you do."

# 1975

"You won't believe what the doctor said," shouted an exasperated Nick when he came off the phone.

"Go on," said mum.

"He said he couldn't call in after surgery because being Wednesday his wife had cooked him his favourite steak and kidney pie. So he couldn't afford to be late home. Can you believe that mum?"

Mum shrugged her shoulders. Nothing would surprise her where the doctor was concerned.

"So what did you say?"

"I told him he had to pass the bottom of our road and we'd appreciate a visit. That we thought dad might have slipped into a coma."

"Did it work?"

"I think so. He said he'd do his best."

"Good for you. Let's just hope his steak and kidney pie isn't spoilt."

"God forbid."

That was the second time that day the doctor had been contacted. Dad had woken up agitated and complaining of a severe headache. So severe he'd missed breakfast and his regular shave. With mum's help he just about made it to his armchair – where he remained all day. Dr Jarvis called in after morning surgery and diagnosed nothing more sinister than a run of the mill headache. But during the day dad's condition deteriorated and by the evening he appeared to be drifting in and out of consciousness. When Nick returned from work they thought it best to phone the doctor again – although they realized he wouldn't be happy about it.

"I think dad could have had another stroke," said mum.

"Oh mum, do you really think so?"

"Yes, I do."

"Well let's hope the doctor isn't too long."

"He'll be quicker because of the thought of the steak and kidney pie getting cold."

"I wouldn't have put him down as a steak and kidney person."

"Neither would I. I bet he cuts it up into little pieces before he eats it."

"Then he has spotted dick for afters, sorry mum, dessert, which he also cuts up neatly."

"No, I can't see him eating spotted dick. That's taking it too far. He's more of a crumble man."

"You're probably right."

"But I wish I'd changed doctors all those years ago. That's one of my biggest regrets."

"That's in the past now mum."

"I know, but life might have been so different."

Dad's funny turn had come out of the blue. The last few weeks he'd been quite well. He'd even returned to the fish shop in Boundary road with a reluctant Nick. They discovered that Ron no longer owned it. The new husband and wife team divulged that Ron had retired because of ill health more than ten years ago. But that couldn't have been true because dad had visited since then. The place was now called 'This Is The Plaice Sole Put Your Skates On'. Which Nick thought sounded too clever by half. But then they weren't likely to visit the premises again because a couple of months earlier they'd returned their allegiance to Harry's Bar. Yes, still trading under that name although Harry had passed away years ago. Importantly though mum had faith in the new owner, Clifford, and the amount of batter he used. When mum asked if he'd be changing the name Clifford replied that reputation mattered more than a name and Harry had a good reputation. Mum looked perplexed. A good reputation! What Harry? Were they talking about the same person?

They returned to the dining room to check on dad. He continued to snore loudly. Actually he looked quite peaceful in his favourite armchair. He had a healthy colour and his breathing seemed less laboured and uneven. Then he opened his eyes. He showed no sign of recognition. He just looked around the room and closed them again.

"Has he eaten anything?" said Nick.

"No. No food and nothing to drink."

"Do you remember when dad had his stroke? How he kept looking at his watch."

"Yes, every couple of minutes until the ambulance came."

"I wonder what was going through his mind then. Whether he realized he'd had a stroke."

"I don't know," said mum. "That's it, isn't it? You never know what dad's thinking about."

"It's funny how sometimes you can guess immediately what's on his mind and other times you have to give up. What time does surgery end?"

"Five thirty."

"So the doctor could be here by six then," said Nick.

"I think that's a little optimistic steak and kidney or no steak and kidney."

"Okay seven then."

"It wouldn't surprise me if he decides to admit dad to hospital."

"Well that would be preferable to a wrong diagnosis. Have you phoned Joanna?"

"No, I thought I'd leave it until the doctors been. They should be up at the weekend. Have you remembered its dad's birthday on Sunday?"

"Yes, I've got a card."

"What about a present?"

"I'm working on it. I did think about a boxing book."

"That's a good idea," said mum. "I never know what to buy. If it wasn't for us reminding him he'd never realize it was his birthday."

"I think he would. He always moves the date on his magnetic calendar."

"Yes, but he wouldn't connect the twenty seventh of September with it being his birthday."

"Well, we could try it one year. Ignore the date and see if he says anything."

"Nick, we couldn't do that. That wouldn't be fair."

"No, I suppose not."

"Perhaps I'll get him another cardigan. He can't have too many of those."

"A Henry Taylor's classic?"

"No, I think Marks and Spencer's is the shop for cardigans."

"Really. Would you like a cup of tea?"

While they waited for the doctor they watched the early evening news. It ended with a typical heart rendering story. It concerned an eighty five year old pensioner who'd won a fortune on the horses with his very first bet.

"That's something your dad never did," said mum. "I can't remember him ever having a bet. Well except for the football pools of course. Strange when you consider how much granddad gambled."

"Did he ever win?"

"Yes, occasionally but only small amounts."

"On the horses?"

"That's right. I think Kitty had the biggest win."

"My aunt Kitty! I still find it hard to believe she did the horses."

"Yes, she won fifteen pounds. About two week's wages back in those days."

"What did she do with it?"

"She had to give it to granddad."

"That wasn't fair."

"She had no choice. He probably wanted it for his next bet."

"Poor old Kitty."

At that moment the doorbell rang. They checked the time.

"Six forty five," said mum. "That's not bad going."

"No, obviously the steak and kidney must be a real incentive."

This time the doctor was concerned about dad's health to the extent that he immediately phoned for an ambulance. He thought it possible dad had suffered another stroke and if so that he probably wouldn't survive. The damaged brain would be unable to take a further battering. Nick just about stopped himself from saying, "Excuse me doctor but with your track record what would you know about a correct diagnosis?"

"I'm sure dad will be alright," said Nick after the doctor had left.

"We'll see," said mum. "I just hope the ambulance doesn't take long. Anyway I wished the doctor a pleasant dinner. I said I hoped his steak and kidney wasn't overcooked."

"Did you? What did he say?"

"He looked really embarrassed. I'll give Joanna a ring."

The ambulance arrived at eight thirty. Dad's condition remained unchanged. He drifted in and out of consciousness, occasionally opening his eyes to look around him, but showing no sign of recognition.

"Stan," said mum. "Can you hear me? You're going into hospital. You're not very well. They'll look after you in there."

They were at the hospital until ten thirty waiting for dad's admittance to Nightingale ward. According to Nick the same ward that dad had been admitted to for his ulcer investigation. But mum disagreed. It hadn't been Nightingale but something similar – possibly Curie or Pasteur. They agreed to disagree.

They watched as the nurses made dad comfortable. His eyes were open but he appeared unaware of his surroundings.

"Hello Stan," said mum. "How do you feel?"

"Eeeeeee. Eeeeeee."

"Can you hear me?"

"Eeeeeee. Eeeeeee."

"Oh that's good Stan."

"Eeeeeee. Eeeeeee."

"You're in hospital. You haven't been well all day. You had a bad headache when you got up this morning."

"Eeeeeee. Eeeeeee."

"Can you remember?"

153

"Eeeeee. Eeeeee."

"You even missed your shave so you must have felt bad."

"Eeeeee. Eeeeee."

"Whipps Cross."

"Eeeeee. Eeeeee."

"You probably won't see a doctor until tomorrow. It's very late."

"Eeeeee. Eeeeee."

"Yes, we'll be going now Stan. We'll see you tomorrow."

Mum gave dad a kiss and Nick shook his hand.

"That's a relief," said mum as they left the ward. "At least he seems more with it. Perhaps it's not so serious after all."

"Let's hope not."

They walked through the deserted corridor towards the exit – their feet clomping loudly on the solid flooring.

"It sounds like a hospital, doesn't it?" said Nick. "The unmistakable clomp, clomp, clomp."

"Yes, I think I read that this is the longest hospital corridor in the country."

"That's right, over a mile."

"A mile? No, it can't be that long."

"I think it is. It feels quite spooky at this time of night. I wonder if they still have as many Irish nurses working here?"

"I don't know. Perhaps they can earn as much back home these days."

"I bet there aren't many Persians though. Well its Iran now, isn't it?"

"Yes. Did you ever hear from Nasrin?"

"No, I haven't done for years. I wonder how she coped with the revolution. It sounds like a completely different country today."

"Dad liked her."

"So did I mum."

Although it was almost midnight when they arrived home mum phoned Joanna while Nick put the kettle on.

"They should be here by midday on Saturday," said mum. "Joanna couldn't believe what the doctor said about his steak and kidney pie."

"No, it sounds made up, doesn't it? "I wonder how often he uses that excuse?"

"Presumably every Wednesday."

"Perhaps he's got similar excuses for the rest of the week."

"Well if he has, Monday would obviously be Shepherds Pie."

They went through the week thinking up different dinner excuses for Dr Jarvis. It gave them light relief after a difficult day. Hopefully tomorrow dad's condition would be improved and the diagnosis of a second stroke prove unfounded.

# EIGHTEEN

The Rev. Turner felt full. He enjoyed his food and had appreciated the buffet. That included the lemon butter bake. He could easily have put away two or three portions of the delicacy. His face dropped when mum divulged the earth shattering news. It had all gone. But he quickly pulled himself together and tucked into the alternative cheesecake and trifle.

"It's good to see somebody enjoying their food," said Joyce. "I've been watching him for the past fifteen minutes. Backwards and forwards for second helpings. I don't know where he puts it all."

"No, he's not particularly large," said Joanna. "Although I suppose it's difficult to tell under his gown."

"Joan was saying he liked the Jimmy Young."

"Yes, she regretted throwing the remainder away."

"Why did she do that?"

"The negative response. She won't be making it again."

"Well I enjoyed it. Its funny, Richard went to Nick's twenty first all those years ago and came back talking about this particular delicacy. I asked Joan to send me the recipe. She never did. But now, twenty years later, I've tasted it."

The Rev. Turner made his way to the kitchen to thank mum for her hospitality. He'd decided to leave before he really spoilt his dinner – and got on the wrong side of his wife.

"Thanks for what you said vicar," said mum.

"That's okay Mrs Wisbey. Thank you for inviting me back. I enjoyed meeting the family. And the buffet of course. An excellent spread."

"I'm glad you liked the lemon butter bake. Unfortunately you're in a minority there."

"Well some people have got no taste then."

"No, you're right."

"I've forgotten the singer."

"Jimmy Young."

"That's right Jimmy Young. I must try and remember and inform my wife. I keep thinking of David Jacobs."

"Does he cook then?"

"Not that I know of but he's also a presenter on Radio two."

"Oh I see what you mean. I usually listen to Radio four."

"My wife's a big fan of Delia Smith."

"Yes, I've got a couple of her books."

"Is she big on the lemon butter bake?"

"I don't think anybody's big on lemon butter bake these days. The worlds moved on since I made it for my son's twenty first."

"That's a few years ago then?"

"Twenty two, I think."

"Good Lord. Oh, sorry about that. Slip of the tongue. Not what you expect from your vicar."

"Oh don't worry about that," said mum. "I've heard a lot worse from the clergy."

He looked puzzled. Had she? He hoped not. He turned on his heels and departed.

"Goodbye vicar," she shouted after him. "Thanks again for all you said."

But the vicar was already out of earshot – or had chosen not to respond.

# 1976

Spirits had reached rock bottom in the Wisbey household. Dad had suffered another stroke but, and contrary to what the doctor predicted, had beaten the odds and survived. But it had left him more confused and belligerent than ever. Unable to be left alone for any length of time mum had packed up work. A decision she hadn't taken lightly. Henry Taylor's had given her a life outside of home. Cashiering had relieved the pressure of constantly being at dad's beckon and call. But now that escape route had disappeared. His deteriorating brain ensured he required her constant attention.

The worse aspect of dad's deterioration was the peeing in the bedroom. Invariably in-between Mum's wardrobe and the window. The family were totally out of their depth when dealing with the problem. Did they chastise dad, encourage him to use the bathroom or just ignore the indiscretion and hope things improved? It all came down to one important detail. Did dad realize his misdemeanour? The family had been prepared to give him the benefit of the doubt. Accepting that the second stroke had caused this distressing behaviour. But the doctor saw things differently. In his view dad knew exactly what he was doing and should be castigated. So even though the doctor wasn't renowned for his correct diagnoses it had sown the seed of doubt in the families mind.

When mum pointed out the wet patch dad would shrug his shoulders as if to say, "What are you showing me for? I wouldn't wee on the floor," in either a resigned "I want to die," mode or an aggressive "You'd better be careful what you're suggesting," manner. But, whatever, on a regular basis there'd be a wet patch and the smell of urine.

Mum alternated between the softly, softly approach and the badgering depending on dad's mood. It worked to a degree. He hadn't yet hit her. Although on a couple of occasions it'd come mighty close.

But neither approach made a difference. Sometimes there'd be a week without a rogue peeing and the family would hold their breath in anticipation. Had the problem dissipated? But then they'd be brought back to earth with a fresh patch of damp carpet and that distinctive smell.

"I wonder why it's always next to the wardrobe?" said Joanna.

"I don't know," said mum. "But I suppose that's better than half a dozen different places."

"So what about if we left a bucket in the corner then?"

"I did think about that."

"It couldn't do any harm."

"I'm not so sure. It depends whether dad knows he's doing it. I still think he's unaware – no matter what the doctor says. So he wouldn't use a bucket."

"Wouldn't he?"

"No, because he doesn't realize he's peeing. So it could go in the bucket or next to it."

"I suppose so."

"And if he's doing it on purpose he wouldn't use the bucket anyway. He'd be cussed and pee next to it."

"Complicated, isn't it?"

"You can say that again. I mean he still uses the toilet."

"That's true."

"Yesterday he peed on the floor at midday and then a couple of hours later went in the toilet. It's so difficult to work out."

Joanna had come up for the day from Oxford with her new son William. The first time he'd met the family. And while mum pruned the roses and Nick cut the grass she introduced him to his grandfather. Dad looked relaxed as he sat him on his lap, then held him above his head, then rocked him on his knee. But it didn't last. After five minutes he sighed, puffed his cheeks and handed William back to Joanna.

"Eeeeeee. Eeeeeee."

"William dad."

"Eeeeeee. Eeeeeee."

"You like the name?"

"Eeeeeee. Eeeeeee."

"You don't like it?"

Dad smiled and held up three fingers.

"Oh I see. You mean I've got three boys now."

"Eeeeeee. Eeeeeee."

"Would I have liked a girl?"

"Eeeeeee. Eeeeeee."

"Well I thought the chances were it might have been a girl this time. But I'm very happy with another boy. Tim and Duncan haven't been any problem."

"Eeeeeee. "Eeeeeee."

"Next time?"

"Eeeeeee. Eeeeeee."

"You never know dad."

Dad held up four fingers.

"Yes, that would make it four."

"Eeeeeee. Eeeeeee."

"No, what do you mean dad?"

He held up four fingers again.

"Oh, you and mum planned for four."

"Eeeeeee. Eeeeeee."

"Yes, I remember her telling me. Philip died after five days and then mum had a miscarriage climbing over the Jaycock's fence."

"Eeeeeee. Eeeeeee."

"Philip would have been two years younger than me."

"Eeeeeee. Eeeeeee."

"The hospitals fault. That's what mum said. They didn't make him cry."

"Eeeeeee. Eeeeeee."

"But with the miscarriage, what was mum doing climbing over the Jaycock's fence?"

Dad shrugged his shoulders. He couldn't recall the reason.

"Had the ball gone over?"

Dad shook his head. It was such a long time ago.

"Eeeeeee. Eeeeeee."

"Yes, I'll have to ask her. Anyway, how have you been dad?"

Dad sighed and held his hands out in front of him. He hadn't been good at all. By all accounts he'd been peeing in the bedroom – although he couldn't remember. I mean why would he do that? He knew the proper place to pee. But mum had shown him the evidence – the wet carpet. It looked conclusive. Obviously his brain had deteriorated further.

"Oh dad," said Joanna. "I'm sorry you feel like that."

"Eeeeeee. Eeeeeee."

160

"You'd rather be dead."

"Eeeeeee. Eeeeeee."

"You must have had such a strong constitution to survive the second stroke. The doctor said you wouldn't."

That actually brought a smile to dad's face.

"Eeeeeee. Eeeeeee."

"No, you're right. It's no surprise he got that wrong. He's not a lot of cop. Still tearing up prescriptions I suppose."

"Eeeeeee. Eeeeeee."

"Are you managing your walks?"

"Eeeeeee. Eeeeeee."

"You got lost. Yes, mum told me. Mrs Pond brought you home."

"Eeeeeee. Eeeeeee."

"You carry your name and address with you. That's a good idea dad. I bet that impressed Mrs Pond. She's a funny one."

"Eeeeeee. Eeeeeee."

"Why? Well besides being nosey, when we were selling the firewood all those years ago she wouldn't buy any. She actually shouted at us to go away."

"Eeeeeee. Eeeeeee."

"You don't remember us selling firewood. The Nottingham Road gang. We collected orange boxes from Godlontons and chopped them up into bundles of firewood. Then we went round the houses selling them at a penny a bundle."

"Eeeeee. Eeeeeee."

"We made about ten pounds. But then the boys had this stupid idea of buying a walkie-talkie with the proceeds. Ann Porter and I were livid. We wanted to share the money. But they wouldn't listen. The walkie-talkies never worked. Ten pounds down the drain. We left the gang in protest. They couldn't manage without us and the gang split up."

"Eeeeeee. Eeeeeee."

"Mrs Pond? She said you shouldn't go knocking on doors selling things. That we had to get a licence. But we were only kids. The fuss she made."

"Eeeeeee. Eeeeeee."

"Nick? Yes, he was chief spy. I can't remember the other spy. I wouldn't have thought you needed more than one in a gang of six."

William looked sleepy so Joanna decided to put him down for a snooze. She went upstairs and laid him in the cot in the box room. God, how small her old bedroom looked. She never had managed to persuade Nick to change. She'd moaned endlessly to him and to mum and dad. Indeed to anybody prepared to listen. But to no avail. She heard somebody moving about downstairs.

"Is that you mum?" she called out.

"No, it's me" replied Nick. "Mum's talking to Auntie Ruth next door."

"Do we still call her Auntie?" said Joanna.

"Well I do."

"Oh I see. I thought we were too old for that now."

"I've never really thought about it."

"I wonder why it's always been Uncle Vic and Auntie Ruth on one side but Mr & Mrs Watts on the other?"

"I don't know. What are you doing?"

"Putting William to bed."

"I'll come up then."

"I don't think there's enough room for two adults in my old bedroom. How did I manage for all those years?"

"You're not still going on about that, are you?" said Nick climbing the stairs. "The lovely view you had over the playing fields more than compensated for its size. Well, until they built the school extension on the tennis courts. I would have preferred your room."

"Nick, how can you say that?"

"Easy."

He joined his sister in the box room. As he squeezed by to sit at the foot of the bed he lost his balance and accidentally elbowed her in the face.

"Be careful," she shouted.

"Sorry about that."

"A good job we never had a cat to swing."

"No, I suppose not. Is William walking yet?"

"Don't be silly, there's not enough room in here."

162

"He does look lovely though."

"Yes, with his head squashed against one wall and his feet against another. The room isn't even the size of a box."

"Oh you do go on," said Nick. "How's dad?"

"Not too bad. I made him laugh talking about our gang. When we sold the firewood then wasted the proceeds on that walkie-talkie. Do you remember?"

"Yes, that wasn't the best of ideas. I blame Peter Porter."

"And why did we have two spies?"

"We didn't."

"Well you were chief spy so I assumed there must have been another one."

"No, just me. What did you do in the gang?"

"I can't remember. There weren't many roles for female gang members in the fifties."

"No, but I remember you and Ann were good at knock down ginger. Well you never got caught"

"No. We knocked on Mrs Pond's door regularly."

"Well she deserved it. You should have put some firewood though her letterbox at the same time. That would have shown her."

They smiled at the thought of Mrs Pond picking up the firewood from her doormat.

"Do you think dad knows he's peeing in the bedroom?" said Joanna.

"I really don't know. Actually I think I'll check whether he's peed there recently."

"I'll come with you."

First impressions were good. There didn't seem to be a fresh patch of urine in dad's favourite spot. But unfortunately Nick then discovered a wet patch on the opposite side of the wardrobe. Their spirits dropped.

"Would you believe it," said Joanna. "Don't say he's going to start peeing in a different place. That is depressing. What's mum going to say?"

"Do we have to tell her?"

"Well she's bound to find out."

"Not if we clean it up straightaway. If she does notice we'll pretend we didn't know. I'll go and get the dishcloth."

"Not the one mum uses for washing up I hope."

"No, of course not."

So while Nick went downstairs Joanna, with bated breath and fingers crossed, inspected every inch of the bedroom for further damp patches.

Unfortunately as Nick searched under the sink for a suitable dishcloth mum came in from the garden to collect a rubbish bag.

"What are you looking for?" she said.

Nick didn't know whether to come clean or make up a story. He chose the latter.

"My old cricket ball."

"What would that be doing under there?"

"I don't know, but I can't think of anywhere else to look."

"Dad's got it."

"Dad! Are you sure?"

"Yes, you give it to him to practice his grip on his bad hand. Don't you remember?"

"That's right, of course I did. I'll go and have a look. Joanna's upstairs with William."

"Okay, I'm coming in now. I want to check whether dad's peed in the bedroom today. He's been worse than ever lately."

"Okay."

So while mum got a rubbish bag from the pantry Nick checked whether dad had the cricket ball. Then ran back upstairs, without the dishcloth but with the cricket ball, to inform Joanna of the sequence of events.

"That's very interesting," she said. "But what are we going to do with a cricket ball?"

"Oh gawd, I forgot what I went downstairs for. The dishcloth."

"Well go and get it."

"I don't think there's time. Mum's coming in from the garden."

"Be quick then."

But it was too late. They heard mum at the foot of the stairs.

"Are you two still upstairs?" she shouted.

164

"Yes," shouted Nick as he panicked and threw Joanna the cricket ball.

"That's typical," whispered Joanna as she threw the ball back.

"What are you two up to?" shouted mum as the cricket ball whizzed past her on the stairs.

"Don't ask," said Joanna.

"I'm coming up to investigate," said mum.

# NINETEEN

"Is that right grandpa had three kidneys?" asked Robert.

"Yes," said mum.

"That's what William said. I didn't know you could have more than two."

"It is unusual."

"Did he always have three?"

Mum smiled but refrained from stating the obvious. That the extra kidney didn't appear overnight.

"As far as I know," she said. "Although we didn't realize until grandpa had an x-ray for an ulcer."

"So could you have four kidneys?"

"I don't know about that. There must be a limit."

"I wonder if it tells you in the Guinness Book of Records."

Mum smiled again. Would that be the sort of information gleaned from that prestigious publication?

"You could have a look Robert. Do you know where it is?"

"Yes, in granddad's drawer. The extra kidney didn't help him though. He couldn't talk."

"No, you're right Robert."

"Can you remember what grandpa's voice sounded like?"

"Not really, it's such a long time ago. Nick thought he recorded him on the tape recorder. That would have been the year before his stroke. But he hasn't been able to find it. Perhaps he recorded over it."

"That's a shame. I'll go and look in the Guinness Book of Records."

"Okay, tell me what you find out."

Mum felt tired. It'd been a long day. Hopefully she'd get a good night's sleep. She hadn't had one of those for ages. Dad had been so unsettled during his latter years – primarily because of this wet feeling he experienced in bed. He could disturb her up to a dozen times complaining of his bed being wet. She'd have to get up and run her hands over the sheets in an attempt to reassure him that it wasn't. He'd eye her suspiciously before reluctantly returning to bed. And so it went on through the night. In the morning she'd feel terrible. So what were the chances of returning to a regular sleep pattern? Unfortunately the doctor had warned it might not be that straightforward. That the body would take time to adjust to a different clock.

She was joined by John and Eileen.

"Hello Joan," said John. "We'll be off shortly."

"Okay then. Be careful in the rain."

"I will," said Eileen.

"Oh you're driving."

"Yes, we brought my mini. I really enjoyed the journey. It's the furthest I've driven."

"I'm glad you enjoyed it," said John sarcastically.

"What do you mean?" said Eileen. "There's nothing wrong with my driving."

"If you say so my dear."

"I do say so."

"Don't listen to him," said mum. "I wish I'd learnt all those years ago. It would have been so handy with the grandchildren."

"I'm sure it would have" said Eileen. "I love my car."

"How many lessons did you have?"

"Twenty five."

"That's very good."

"Yes, but I took you out as well," interrupted John. "That's what got you through."

"I probably would have passed in twenty if I hadn't picked up your bad habits."

"Thank you very much Eileen."

"Did you know I had forty lessons," said mum. "And I never put in for a test."

"Why not?" said Eileen.

"The instructor said I wasn't ready."

"Perhaps you should have tried a different one."

"I did. I think I tried three. I just couldn't seem to concentrate."

"Oh that is a shame Joan."

They were joined by a solemn looking Robert clutching The Guinness Book of Records.

"Well did you discover anything?" asked mum.

"No, there's nothing about kidneys. I also checked for the appendix and liver."

"No, you've definitely only got one liver," said mum. "I'm not sure about the appendix though. I think you could have more than one."

John and Eileen looked mystified.

"I told Robert about Stan having three kidneys," said mum. "He thought it might get a mention in the Guinness Book of Records. No, not Stan but the record number of kidneys in the human body."

Uncle John and Auntie Eileen continued to look mystified.

"But there isn't a world record," said Robert.

"Never mind," said mum.

"How are you getting on at school?" asked Eileen.

"It's alright."

"It's the same middle school that his brothers went to," said mum.

"That must be good fun," said Eileen.

"I suppose so, but I wish the teachers wouldn't keep going on about my brothers. About how clever they were. It's really boring. I think I'll read the book."

"Okay Robert," said mum.

They watched him trudge off to find a quiet corner in which to check up on other unusual world records.

"How's he been today?" enquired Eileen.

"Okay. I did feel apprehensive about him coming but Joanna said he wanted to. I'm sure I didn't go to my first funeral until a lot older."

"Yes, that would probably have been our sister Marjorie," said John.

"You're right. Dear Marjorie. So I must have been twenty two. Anyway it's been really good to see you both."

"And you Joan," said John.

"Well you drive safely Eileen. And make sure you're a good passenger John."

"I always am," said John.

"I can see your nose growing," said Eileen.

"She's right," said mum. "I can imagine some of the sarcastic comments you make."

"You women certainly stick together" said John.

# 1977

Things had improved since the previous year. Dad's habit of peeing in the bedroom had all but stopped. His brain less muddled and his aggressiveness restrained. The result? He could be left alone for a while. Long enough for a relieved mum to return to Henry Taylor's and the comraderie that afforded.

"Any gossip today?" asked Nick when mum arrived home from work.

"No, Mrs Walker had a day's holiday and Miss Warner had a stinking cold. She hardly spoke all day."

"That must have been boring."

"Actually it was quite unnerving. How's dad?"

"He seems okay. He's reading the Ring magazine."

"That's a good sign then."

"He did ask what we were having for dinner though."

"That's not so good then. He'll be out checking up in a minute."

"Probably. You know that girl I've met,"

"Yes."

"Can I bring her home for dinner?"

"Of course you can. Let's just hope dad's on good form. I suppose you've told her about his stroke."

"I have."

"Where did you say she came from?"

"Canada. Well Quebec, she's French Canadian."

"What's her English like?"

"Better than my French."

"We're lazy when it comes to languages. I don't remember learning any when I was at school."

"Nor did I. Although I had a go at French."

"What was the name of your teacher at Barclay? The one that made a big thing about you being left handed."

"Mrs Bradshaw. God, didn't she make a fuss. I think there were three of us. We had to stand at the front of the class some days. We felt like freaks. It wouldn't matter today."

"It shouldn't have mattered when you were at school. I mean it wasn't the Victorian times. We're talking about the late fifties."

"She reminded me of your lovely Mrs Saunders."

"No, that's impossible. Nobody compared with her. Did Mrs Bradshaw make you stand in the corner for three hours because you'd missed a days schooling looking after your younger brother because mum was up the hospital with elder brother Bill having his polio assessed? The word tyrant was invented for her."

"Let's hope she met an unpleasant end."

"You can say that again. But you know what really annoyed her? Because I had time off the class never won the best attendance record. She couldn't come to terms with that and took it out on me."

"Just be thankful you weren't left handed as well then."

They were joined by an agitated dad pointing at his watch.

"Eeeeeee. Eeeeeee."

"It isn't late Stan," said mum. "Dinner's always at six thirty."

"Eeeeeee. Eeeeeee."

"What have we got? It's your favourite, liver and bacon."

"Eeeeeee. Eeeeeee."

"You like liver and bacon Stan."

"Eeeeeee. Eeeeeee."

"Well you can leave it then."

"Eeeeeee. Eeeeeee."

"You don't have to shout Stan."

"Eeeeeee. Eeeeeee."

With that dad flapped his hands in front of him and went back to the comfort of his armchair and the Ring magazine.

"Oh dear," said mum. "He's been fairly good tempered lately."

"Yes, things are definitely better than this time last year."

"Perhaps you could go and sit with him. Keep him under control."

So Nick joined dad in the dining room. He didn't look up as Nick sat in the other armchair and picked up the Radio Times.

"Is it alright if I put the tele on dad?"

Dad shrugged his shoulders then pointed at his watch.

"Dinner isn't late dad."

"Eeeeeee. Eeeeeee."

"Mum doesn't get home from work until just before six."

"Eeeeeee. Eeeeeee."

"I'm sorry that's how you feel."

He put the tele on and dad buried his head in the Ring Magazine. The six o'clock news had just started. The headlines were tragic. There'd been a plane crash in Tenerife killing five hundred and eighty three passengers. The worlds worse air disaster.

"Oh that's awful," said Nick. "Look at that dad. A plane crash killing over five hundred people."

Dad looked up and digested the news – then started laughing aloud.

"Dad, it's not funny."

But dad continued to laugh and point at the screen. Unfortunately that happened to be a peculiar side effect of the stroke. In company it could be somewhat disconcerting – although not for dad who seemed oblivious to the reaction. When questioned about his behaviour he shrugged his shoulders as though he didn't grasp the enormity of the catastrophe. Mum had read an article that described the condition perfectly. The "laughing at the inappropriate time" syndrome when part of the brain has been damaged by a stroke. It had given her solace to think that other stroke victims suffered similarly. That they might find a plane crash as amusing as the Morecambe & Wise show.

After a few minutes dad stopped laughing and put his hand up in a mark of apology. Not for the laughing but for his impatience where dinner was concerned.

"Eeeeeee. Eeeeeee."

"That's okay dad. Just let mum know as well."

"Eeeeeee. Eeeeeee."

"Liver and bacon."

Dad gave the thumbs up.

"That's right. It's your favourite."

"Eeeeeee. Eeeeeee."

"I'm bringing my girlfriend home on Thursday."

"Eeeeeee. Eeeeeee."

"Nicole. She's French Canadian. She's been here on a month's holiday. She's going home at the weekend."

"Eeeeeee. Eeeeeee."

"No, I won't see her after that."

"Eeeeeee. Eeeeeee."

"What visit her? Well she did suggest that but it probably won't happen. It's a long way to go."

"Eeeeeee. Eeeeeee."

"What do you mean?"

"Eeeeeee. Eeeeeee."

"What, when you met mum?"

"Eeeeeee. Eeeeeee."

"At the Drill Hall."

"Eeeeeee. Eeeeeee."

"Yes, Leyton's not quite so far as Canada."

"Eeeeeee. Eeeeeee."

"You would have gone to Canada to see mum again?"

"Eeeeeee. Eeeeeee."

They were joined by mum who informed dad that dinner would be on the table at six thirty sharp. Dad held up his hand in apology for his impatience.

"That's alright Stan," said mum.

"Dad said he would have gone as far as Canada to see you again when you first met."

"Is that right Stan?"

"Eeeeee. Eeeeeee."

"That's lovely."

She went over and gave him a kiss on the cheek.

"Have you heard about the plane crash?" enquired Nick.

"No," said mum."

"Five hundred and eighty three killed. The worlds worse air disaster."

"Oh that's dreadful. Isn't it Stan? Or did you find it amusing?"

Dad shrugged his shoulders as though he had no idea what she was talking about.

"Unfortunately he did," said Nick.

"Oh Stan," said mum. "That's so difficult to understand."

Dad shrugged his shoulders again and attempted to change the subject.

"Eeeeee. Eeeeeee."

"What do you mean Stan?"

"Eeeeee. Eeeeeee."

"No, sorry Stan."

"I think he means when you first met," said Nick.

"Eeeeee. Eeeeeee."

"At the drill hall," said mum.

"Eeeeee. Eeeeeee."

"Of course I remember. I was there with my friend Helen and her husband Bert. You asked me to waltz."

"Eeeeee. Eeeeeee."

"Did you say yes mum?" said Nick.

"I did but it wasn't a waltz."

"Eeeeee. Eeeeee."

"No, Stan it was a foxtrot."

Dad took umbrage and pointed at mum aggressively.

"Eeeeee. Eeeeeee."

"Does it matter now?" said Nick.

"Eeeeee. Eeeeee."

"Alright Stan," said mum. "Perhaps I'm mistaken. It might have been a waltz."

"Eeeeeee. Eeeeeee."

"That is easier than the foxtrot."

"Can't you improvise and do whatever step you like to the same music?" asked Nick.

"No, of course you can't. It's a different tempo. It's not like the modern dances where anything goes."

"Eeeeeee. Eeeeeee."

"Yes, we danced well together Stan. Not as good as Helen and Bert but better than average."

"I did ballroom dancing at school, said Nick. "I think we did it in the lunch hour. It seems a funny thing to learn as a teenager. Still I got on better with that than woodwork and metalwork."

"We still use your poker," said mum.

"Oh yes, I did make something useful."

"Eeeeeee. Eeeeeee."

"What do you mean dad?"

"Eeeeeee. Eeeeeee."

"Something else I made?"

"Eeeeeee. Eeeeeee."

Dad got up and disappeared out of the room.

"I can't think of anything else," said Nick.

"Nor can I," said mum.

Dad reappeared a few minutes later clutching a centre punch.

"Of course," said Nick. "I'd forgotten about my deluxe centre punch."

"Eeeeeee. Eeeeeee."

"If you like we could show them to Nicole when she comes," said mum.

"No, please don't," said Nick. "That would be embarrassing."

"Eeeeeee. Eeeeeee."

"What do you mean dad?" said Nick.

"Eeeeeee. Eeeeeee."

"My girlfriend?"

"Eeeeeee. Eeeeeee."

"I told you she's coming for dinner on Thursday."

"Eeeeeee. Eeeeeee."

"No, dinner won't be late," said mum. "Don't start worrying about that already."

"Eeeeeee. Eeeeeee."

"I'll make sure we're in good time dad," said Nick.

"Eeeeeee. Eeeeeee."

"Stan," said mum. "What have I just said?"

But it was to no avail. Dad had already decided that dinner would be late on Thursday and nothing would persuade him otherwise.

# TWENTY

At seven thirty the proceedings were interrupted by a loud knock on the front door. The knock associated with a neighbour who isn't impressed with your loud music. Certainly not the knock associated with a wake. A delay occurred while everyone waited for mum to open the door.

"Can somebody get that?" she shouted. "I'm in the bathroom."

At least half a dozen mourners shaped up to do just that but paused in case somebody jumped in before them. Eventually David took the bull by the horns and strode purposefully up the hall.

He didn't recognize the smartly dressed elderly woman standing before him with her umbrella caught up in the porch stanchion. He attempted to free the umbrella but in the process knocked her beret off. He made a valiant, but unsuccessful attempt, to catch it before it landed slow motion like in the puddle.

"Sorry about that," he said, picking up the beret, shaking it, and handing it back. "What a dreadful night. Can I help you?"

"That's alright," she said in the broadest and most attractive Norfolk accent. "I'm Mrs Bunn from next door. I wanted to offer my condolences to Mrs Wisbey."

"Oh thank you," said David. "Come in."

"No, I'd rather wait here if you don't mind."

"Who is it?" shouted mum.

"It's Mrs Bunn. She wanted to offer her condolences."

"Well invite her in."

"I have, but she'd rather wait on the step."

"If that's alright?" said Mrs Bunn.

"That's okay," shouted mum. "I'll be straight out."

There followed an embarrassed silence while the pair of them waited patiently for mum to appear, neither choosing to indulge in small talk.

"Do you want me to dry your beret on the radiator?" said David.

"No, it's alright."

"I'm sorry about that."

"Oh don't worry. I always have problems with the umbrella. It's about time I replaced it."

David nodded. In his opinion the umbrella had seen much better days. He wondered whether she'd go for the multicoloured golfing type next time around.

"You can buy lots of different colours nowadays," continued Mrs Bunn "But you can't beat a good old fashioned black one."

David nodded again. No multicoloured one then. To their relief mum then appeared giving David the excuse to disappear.

"Hello Mrs Bunn," said mum. "What a night."

"Yes, Mrs Wisbey. It's dreadful. I just wanted to offer you my condolences."

"Oh, thank you very much. I do appreciate that."

"I think we started out on the wrong foot when you moved in. I do regret that."

"Yes, perhaps we did. Are you sure you don't want to come in?"

"No, I'd better be going now. I've got dinner to cook."

"Well thank you again Mrs Bunn."

"That's alright Mrs Wisbey. Your husband was a fine looking man. He always looked cheery although I knew he wasn't well. It must have been very difficult for both of you."

"Thank you Mrs Bunn."

"And I will get the back door fixed."

Mum shut the door and for the first time that day started to cry. Now who would have thought that Mrs Bunn's kind words could have been responsible for that emotion? The same Mrs Bunn who'd informed mum the day they moved in about the thirty years residency apprenticeship before acceptance by the locals. She wiped her tears and smiled. Who knows, perhaps in the summer they'd be chatting like normal neighbours over the garden fence. So long as she didn't inadvertently trim Mrs Bunn's beloved Victoria rose bush and Mrs Bunn didn't interfere with her equally beloved magnolia tree.

"Are you alright mum?" said Joanna.

"Yes, your dad was a fine looking man."

"Oh mum, it seemed so unfair. All those years he suffered."

She started to cry and mum put her arm around her shoulder.

"I know Joanna. It went on too long. He should have died after the second stroke. What quality of life did he have the last fifteen years?"

"I wonder if he's talking now. Wherever he is?"

"Yes, I'm sure he's making up for all those years of silence."

"He's probably laughing to."

"Laughing? So long as it's not at a funeral. I'll never forget that day."

"Do they have funerals up there?" said Joanna.

"No, they wouldn't, would they?"

"Well that's not my idea of the afterlife – attending funerals."

"I fancy another cup of tea, what about you?"

"That sounds an excellent idea."

# 1978

Mrs Tanner from next door had upset mum big time. She'd knocked in "turn that ruddy music down," mode and accused her of shouting at the eldest, by ten minutes, of her twin sons. She'd ranted and raved at the top of her voice using some really choice language. For mum this doorstep confrontation had been totally alien but for Mrs Tanner obviously all in a days work. Like her friendship with the Kray and Richardson gangs no doubt.

Granted mum had shouted at Terry but only because he deserved it. He'd almost knocked her over riding his bike on the pavement. And that hadn't been the first time. He was undoubtedly a ten out of ten teenage tearaway. He showed no respect to his elders and had gained the unenviable reputation of child public enemy number one down Nottingham Road. His twin brother Freddy wasn't much better.

Since the Watts had moved out and the Tanners in there'd been tension. Anything from anonymous phone calls to bad mouthing. Although when you looked at their mum's behaviour what did one expect from the children? She dreaded to think how they'd turn out. She sighed, she recalled Mrs Watts telling her about this nice couple with cute ten year old twin boys moving into their house. That would have suited mum. She liked the idea of children living next door. Obviously they were on exemplary behaviour when they viewed the property. As for Mr Tanner, well he always seemed pleasant enough, but obviously he didn't wear the trousers. He certainly wouldn't have been aware of their bad behaviour and unpopularity in the street.

Mum didn't need this added strife with a sick husband to contend with and similarly dad would have been happier without regularly witnessing their blatant rudeness. It made him even more edgy and anxious. It seemed the neighbours tried their hardest to make life as unpleasant as possible.

So when Joanna announced the family were moving to Norwich because of David's new hospital post mum's hopes rose. She saw a way out. A natural wish to be with her family coupled with a chance to escape the stress of un-neighbourly love. But exactly when would depend on the health of nana who'd recently developed gangrene on top of her other ailments. Her long term prospects weren't good. Mum decided she needn't know about the move. She'd be here for her mother as long as necessary. And likewise until the inevitable happened she wouldn't mention anything to dad. She guessed he'd be positive about it, his natural reluctance to change overridden by the neighbours from hell, but once aware of the plan he'd be on at her night and day.

She returned with the bread from Robertson's to be greeted by an excitable dad.

"Eeeeeee. Eeeeeee."

"What do you mean Stan?"

"Eeeeeee. Eeeeeee."

"Nick. What has he done?"

"Eeeeeee. Eeeeeee."

179

"Next door. What next door?"

"Eeeeeee. Eeeeeee."

"I'm sorry Stan."

"Eeeeeee. Eeeeeee."

"He climbed over their fence?"

"Eeeeeee. Eeeeeee."

"He went in their house? I hope not Stan."

But dad nodded, smiled and gave the thumbs up.

"Stan, he shouldn't have done that."

"Eeeeeee. Eeeeeee."

"They kept phoning and knocking on the door. Yes, okay but you can't walk into peoples houses just like that. That's trespassing. That's just the excuse their mum needs to go to court again. You know what she's like."

"Eeeeeee. Eeeeeee."

"She wasn't there. No, I realize that. I didn't think Nick would have been that foolhardy. But she'll soon hear about it. I hope he didn't hit them."

"Eeeeeee. Eeeeeee."

Dad got up and started shadow boxing.

"You'd have knocked the pair of them out. I'm sure you would have Stan. Then the police would have been involved."

"Eeeeeee. Eeeeeee."

"You'd have knocked them out as well."

"Eeeeeee. Eeeeeee."

"I don't know Stan. It's such a shame Harold and Joan moved. They were really good neighbours. I just hope Ruth and Vic aren't thinking of going. That would be awful."

"Eeeeeee. Eeeeeee."

"Where is Nick? Is he still next door?"

Dad shook his head.

"I hope he hasn't left for football. He said he'd cut the grass before he went."

"Eeeeeee. Eeeeeee."

"Leyton Orient of course. They're playing Arsenal in the semi-final of the F.A. Cup."

"Eeeeeee. Eeeeeee."

"It's true Stan. It's the biggest day in their history."

Dad laughed and shook his head.

"Don't let Nick catch you laughing. I'll go and see if he's in the garden."

"Eeeeeee. Eeeeeee."

"Yes, I know its coffee time. Just give me a few minutes."

But Nick wasn't in the garden and the grass hadn't been cut. She wondered if he'd taken up residency next door. Perhaps dad was sworn to secrecy. She listened for evidence of an altercation. It seemed eerily quiet. Something wasn't right. She called out.

"Nick. Nick, can you hear me?"

She waited for a reply.

"Hello Joan," said Ruth emerging from their shed. "I saw Nick climbing over the fence about five minutes ago."

"What, next doors fence?"

"I'm afraid so. Is everything okay?"

"Not really. The kids were playing up so Nick thought he'd teach them a lesson. Well that's what Stan said."

"Oh Joan, is that a good idea? You know what she's like. It'll be another court case."

"That's just what I said Ruth. I'll have a word with him."

"He had his cricket bat with him."

"Oh he didn't, did he?"

"I'm afraid so."

"I hope he didn't do anything silly."

"No, don't worry Joan. Your Nick's got more sense then that."

"I hope so Ruth. I'd better go and make Stan's coffee."

"How's he been lately?"

"Not too bad. Well during the day but he's so unsettled at night. Did I tell you he gets this feeling that the bed is wet?"

"You did Joan."

"He's continually waking me up and badgering me to check his bed. It isn't wet but he's convinced. You should see the aggressive look on his face when I tell him it's dry."

"Oh Joan, that must be awful. You need your sleep. Then you've got those blessed kids to put up with."

"Yes, we could have done without them moving in. I hope you're not thinking of moving."

"Well not immediately," said Ruth. "But we'd like to move down to Kent in the next couple of years. Vic's always fancied the Tonbridge Wells area."

Mum's face dropped. She wished she hadn't asked. She imagined a second family from hell moving in. How would she cope with that? Ruth picked up on mum's negative vibes and wondered why she'd let on about their plans at this early stage. It wasn't necessary. She attempted to repair the damage.

"It's just an idea," she added. "It probably won't happen. You know what Vic's like. He's always changing his mind. No, you're stuck with us for a few more years yet."

But the damage had been done. Mum went indoors even more convinced that a move to Norwich would be on the cards once things fell into place.

"Eeeeeee. Eeeeeee."

"Yes, I'll do you a coffee now."

"Eeeeeee. Eeeeeee."

"Nick? No, he's not in the garden. You didn't tell me he had his cricket bat with him."

Dad shrugged his shoulders.

"Well I just hope he didn't use it."

Just then the front door opened and in walked Nick carrying his trusty twenty five year old cricket bat.

"Oh there you are," said mum. "I was beginning to think you'd left for football without doing the grass. Don't tell me you hit them with your bat?"

"Mum, would I do that?"

"Yes, I think you might. Why have you been so long?"

"I've been chasing the tearaways of course."

"All this time?"

"Yes, when I went in the back way they disappeared out the front. I've been half way round Leyton."

"Eeeeeee. Eeeeeee."

"No, they were too quick for me dad. I didn't get the chance to whack them with the bat."

"And what good would that have done?" said mum.

"Well personal satisfaction for one thing. They kept ringing up and knocking on the door. Dad was getting really upset. I wanted to teach them a lesson."

"I take it she wasn't in?"

"Mum, do you think I'd have trespassed if she'd been there? I wouldn't have stood a chance. She'd have used the thumbscrews."

Dad started laughing.

"It's alright for you to laugh Stan," said mum. "We'll just wait for her to knock again."

"Eeeeeee. Eeeeeee."

"Yes, she'll probably contact the police."

"They won't be interested," said Nick. "They know she's a troublemaker. That's why she lost the court case."

"Look, if she makes a complaint they'll have to investigate."

"Oh don't worry mum. I'd better cut the grass now. I haven't got long."

"Yes, you'd better Nick."

"Eeeeeee. Eeeeeee."

"You want to do it Dad?"

Dad shook his head. He could mow the lawn on a good day but that wasn't today. He'd stick to his armchair and the Ring Magazine.

They were interrupted by a knock on the door – a very recognizable aggressive knock. It had to be Mrs Tanner. There were frowns all round.

"I'll go," said Nick.

"Well try not to get into an argument," said mum.

"I'll do my best."

Nick walked up the hall unsure of what to expect from the redoubtable Mrs Tanner.

"Hello," said Nick.

"Hello," said Mrs Tanner. "Now before you say anything I just wanted to apologise for earlier. I was a bit over the top. Mind you, your mum had no right to talk to Terry like that. He's not a bad lad. Neither of them are. But I admit I could have been out of order. So let's just leave it, shall we?"

"Okay," said Nick.

She turned to go but then stopped.

"By the way, have you seen the twins lately?"

Nick had a choice of telling the truth or keeping stumm.

"No, why is something up?"

"Something up. Why do you say that?"

"No reason."

"I just thought they'd be indoors. Cheerio."

"Cheerio."

Nick walked back up the hall with a smile on his face.

"So what did she want?" said mum.

"Well you won't believe this, but she wanted to apologise."

"Apologise?"

"Yes, she thought she was a bit hard on you."

"Well, well, well," said mum. "So she didn't say anything about you going into their house?"

"She doesn't know yet. The twins are still out."

"Eeeeeee. Eeeeeee."

"Oh dear, let's wait for the next knock then."

"I'll go and cut the grass, keep out the way. I'll leave the cricket bat just in case you need it for protection."

"It's not funny Nick."

"Eeeeeee. Eeeeeee."

"It's not Stan."

# TWENTY ONE

Mum and Kitty were sitting on the sofa watching Nick and Nicole chatting. From their out of earshot vantage point it was difficult to tell how amicable the couple were.

"At least they're talking," said Kitty.

"Yes, I think they get on okay," said mum.

"Do you think Nick will move to Norwich?"

"He has mentioned it but he'll probably sort out the divorce first."

"Is that straightforward?"

"I think so. They've just got to wait the two years."

"It's so much easier when solicitors aren't involved."

"Yes, and cheaper. I'm pleased Nicole came to the funeral. She was fond of Stan. She always made an effort to talk to him. She must find it difficult being here. I mean seeing the family again. I haven't spoken to her yet. Well, except to say hello."

"Did you get on well?"

Mum thought long and hard about the question. "Well we got on but we weren't particularly close. I think Nicole would say the same. Just one of those things I suppose."

They were joined by Mary and Alan.

"I think it's time we made a move," said Alan. "I was hoping the rain would stop but it looks as though it's set in for the night."

"Okay," said Kitty. "I'll get my coat."

"Well it was good to see you," said mum. "Stan would have appreciated you making the effort."

"I'm sure he would have," said Alan. "Now let's get this straight once and for all Joan. Did Stan remain unbeaten throughout his boxing career or did he get knocked out? I'm a bit confused."

Mum looked really embarrassed. "Yes, fancy me telling the vicar that."

"It doesn't matter," said Mary. "You're a real trouble maker Alan."

"What me?" protested Alan.

"Yes, you."

"Okay point taken. But can you remember the name of the bloke who knocked out Stan?"

"I've got no idea," said mum. "He never talked about his opponents."

"Jack Dempsey," said Alan. "That's right, Jack Dempsey."

"Is that supposed to mean something?" said mum.

"Yes, Jack Dempsey was one of the greatest heavyweights of all time."

"No, wonder he knocked Stan out then," said Mary.

"That was a miss match," said mum. "It shouldn't have been allowed."

"No, it wasn't that Jack Dempsey," said Alan. "What would he be doing fighting in the British army? He was an American."

"Well I didn't know that," said Mary.

"You didn't say he was an American," said mum.

Alan looked exasperated and shook his head. They were rejoined by Kitty.

"Kitty," said Alan. "Have you heard of Jack Dempsey?"

"No," said Kitty. "Should I have done?"

Alan looked forlorn. "No, it doesn't matter. I think it's time to go."

"Jack Dempsey was the name of the bloke who knocked out Stan," said mum.

"Oh, I see," said Kitty.

"But not the Jack Dempsey who happened to be the world heavyweight champion," said Mary.

"Well I think I see," said Kitty. Anyway according to Stan he was a really obnoxious person."

"Is that right?" said mum.

"Yes, because of that his knockout of Stan didn't go down well. You know, beating the good guy. A group of them wanted to take revenge by dumping their pooh in his locker."

"Do you have to Kitty?" said Mary.

Mum smiled. "I've heard about that type of escapade before. They actually did that to their commanding officer."

"Oh Joan," said Mary. "What, our brother Stan?"

"Yes, there were four of them involved."

"Quite a lot of the stuff then," said Alan.

"I suppose so. But they got caught and had to clear the mess up. Although Stan always argued it was worthwhile because they'd made their point."

"Yes, but what a way to make it," said Alan.

"But they didn't do it to Jack Dempsey?" said mum.

"No, they changed their mind for some reason," said Kitty.

"Probably just as well," said Alan. "If they'd got caught the second time they'd have been court marshalled. That wouldn't have gone down well with mum and dad."

"I wonder if he went to any of the reunions," said mum. "I'll have to ask Nick. He accompanied Stan to a few."

"Being that unpopular he probably wouldn't have," said Alan.

"No, although Nick did mention a couple of people Stan shadow boxed with in a sarcastic aggressive manner. You know the way he did."

"I certainly do. He did that with me when we were kids. Well let us know if you discover anything Joan. Right, are we ready to leave ladies?"

# 1979

Mum and dad moved to Norwich in the February. There were no farewell tears from the neighbours at sixty five. Actually they kept a low profile, which in itself was a godsend because they could have chosen to stand on the doorstep shouting obscenities or riding their bikes along the pavement knocking over anybody carrying a piece of furniture. Perhaps they'd been deterred by the sight of Nick's three friends, Gerry, Ray and Keith, helping with the move and more than a match for those pathetic pipsqueaks. Or, alternatively, no nonsense Auntie Iris from the north had put the fear of God into them.

However from Ruth and Vic at sixty one and the Hick's and the Coventry's further up the road there'd been genuine sadness. They'd been neighbours for forty years. As a young married couple at the outbreak of the second world war mum and dad had moved in. Their hopes and dreams ahead of them. Things hadn't turned out as expected but until that February morning in sixty three they'd been very happy. They'd made some good friends – and definitely friends more than neighbours.

Mum thought about the challenge that lay ahead. She hoped dad would quickly settle in Norwich. But who knows, perhaps he wouldn't be around much longer. Dr. Jarvis had warned about the possibility of a third stroke. But then he'd forecast his demise after the last one. At least their new doctor should be an improvement. Joanna had nothing but praise for the medical centre. They had strict guidelines. The most important being the patients well being ahead of the doctors steak and kidney pie on a Wednesday. She smiled. One thing for sure, it'd be great living near Joanna and the kids.

On the negative side she regretted not learning to drive. What an advantage that would have been moving to a new city. To think she'd had forty lessons with nothing to show for it. Well, except for the money spent and going round the Green Man roundabout the wrong way. She should be more positive. Perhaps it wasn't too late to start up again. She'd definitely have more time now she wasn't working. She smiled, she wondered how much she'd miss the comraderie of Henry Taylor's.

The week before the big move Uncle John had taken an advanced transit load of belongings to Norwich. Up until departure the trip had been in jeopardy. The country had been experiencing its worse snow fall since sixty three. (What memories that brought back.) The A11 had been blocked for three days. The odds didn't look good. But on the morning they announced the snow had thawed sufficiently to allow one lane of traffic through. That's all an overconfident John needed to get the show on the road. He made it in four and a half hours but admitted the journey had been scary.

The following week Iris came down to help with the main move and dad went to stay with Kit and Mary. At first he'd protested but then realized that a better option than staying in the house surrounded by boxes and the possibility of trouble from the neighbours.

Considering they'd lived there for forty years mum was pleasantly surprised by the lack of junk they'd collected. The three ton truck Nick borrowed from work, which mum had convinced herself would be too small, provided ample space and a worthwhile saving in removal fees.

The move had been possible because Nana Bailey had died the previous December. Her funeral took place on the same day as her sister Winn. So those, like Nick and Joanna, who were attending their first funeral ended up attending their first two. Luckily the churches were only a couple of miles apart.

Nick didn't make the move to Norwich. It hadn't been an option. For the moment he preferred to stay in London. He bought a flat in Leyton and while waiting for the constantly changing completion date stayed with Ralph and Joan. There he enjoyed three of the happiest weeks of his life. Initially he found this feeling hard to comprehend. But then the penny dropped. His euphoria was a result of living apart from mum and dad. Away from the trials and tribulations of a stroke victim and his wife (and also carer) a weight had been lifted. Though at home he'd never seen his life as particularly stressful (I mean wasn't mum the one that had dad's depression and aggressiveness to contend with?) the sixteen years since the stroke had been eventful to say the least.

Mum decided immediately that life in Norwich beat London. The overriding factor being the nearness of Joanna and the three boys. She regularly babysat, met them from school, had them stay over, and took them for treats. All the normal things a grandmother did. And she did them well.

She liked Norwich itself. From her bungalow she could either walk or take the bus into the fine city. She enjoyed spending time in the garden, her magnolia tree being second to none. Okay the neighbours weren't too friendly, but she could cope with that. She'd been warned that Norfolk people were genuinely reserved but that once she'd been resident thirty years the neighbours would come running with good wishes, pots of tea and homemade scones.

But what about dad – had it been a good move for him? Well as ever there were good days and bad. There was the frustration of being unable to talk, the impatience with mum and the sleepless nights because of the wet feeling. But at least he wasn't peeing on the floor or demanding his back be smothered with Algipan. Thankfully his condition hadn't deteriorated further since the second stroke. He managed the occasional walk around the Larkman Estate and visited Joanna and David at weekends.

So life went on much as before but in a different city. That included his meals routine, which mum found easier to keep to since she wasn't working. And breakfast in bed served in a bungalow was certainly less tiring than in a three up and three down.

He continued to shave religiously after his morning shower. Something to be commended. Whether he felt fine or miserable he attempted it. On a bad day it could take up to forty five minutes. Then he'd apply Henry Cooper's favourite Old Spice aftershave. Mum had learnt her lesson and didn't criticise his shaving attempt. When he asked for her opinion she felt his face and always gave the thumbs up.

"Eeeeeee. Eeeeeee."

"That feels fine Stan. Very nice and smooth."

"Eeeeeee. Eeeeeee."

"A coffee? Yes, I'll be doing that next. Have you been following the election news?"

"Eeeeeee. Eeeeeee."

"It's likely we're going to have our first woman prime minister."

Dad looked disbelievingly at her and shook his head.

"You can shake your head all you want but its true."

"Eeeeeee. Eeeeeee."

"What's her name?"

"Eeeeeee. Eeeeeee."

"Margaret Thatcher. She's a long way ahead in the polls."

"Eeeeeee. Eeeeeee."

"Of course I'll be voting Stan. Are you up to it?"

Dad looked aggrieved that mum had questioned his commitment to support the Labour Party.

"Eeeeeee. Eeeeeee."

"Alright Stan, you don't have to shout."

"Eeeeeee. Eeeeeee."

"Where do we vote?"

"Eeeeeee. Eeeeeee."

"At Timothy's school. Joanna said she'll give us a lift if you don't feel like walking. But it's not far."

"Eeeeeee. Eeeeeee."

"You don't feel like walking? Well how do you know now Stan? We've got another three days yet."

"Eeeeeee. Eeeeeee."

"Alright, I'll ask her when we go shopping this afternoon."

"Eeeeeee. Eeeeeee."

"No, what do you mean Stan?"

"Eeeeeee. Eeeeeee. "

"Joanna?"

"Eeeeeee. Eeeeeee."

"Who does she vote for?"

"Eeeeeee. Eeeeeee."

"Well I assume it's Labour but I don't really know."

"Eeeeeee. Eeeeeee."

"Nick? I think he's usually Labour but he has voted for all three. He should be coming up this weekend."

"Eeeeeee. Eeeeeee."

"Where does he live?"

"Eeeeeee. Eeeeeee."

"No, he's not with Ralph now. He's got his own flat in Leyton. We've been invited down."

Dad shook his head and sighed.

"You don't think you're up to it? Well I'm sure Nick won't mind."

"Eeeeeee. Eeeeeee."

191

"I could go on my own? Yes, I probably will. If Joanna can pop in and make sure you're okay."

"Eeeeeee. Eeeeeee."

"No, I haven't decided when I'm going. I'll have to check with Nick first."

"Eeeeeee. Eeeeeee."

"Now don't start worrying about it already. Are you going for a walk today?"

"Eeeeeee. Eeeeeee."

"No, I haven't got a letter to post."

"Eeeeeee. Eeeeeee."

"I can't think when the next birthday is. Where are we now?"

"Eeeeeee. Eeeeeee."

"It's a quiet time of year for birthdays."

Having a letter to post gave dad the incentive to set foot outside – but today he decided to go anyway.

"Eeeeeee. Eeeeeee."

"It'll do you good Stan. Would you like me to come with you?"

Dad stared at mum in horror. She never accompanied him on a walk so why should she offer today? It sounded suspicious.

"Eeeeeee. Eeeeeee."

"Well it's obvious you're not keen on the idea," said mum.

"Eeeeeee. Eeeeeee."

"No, that's okay Stan. I'll go and do the coffee."

Dad felt a little chastened and gave mum a hug. But he still didn't want her joining him on the walk. Definitely off limits that.

"Or would you prefer the coffee when you get back?"

"Eeeeeee. Eeeeeee."

"Alright Stan, I'll do it now."

"Eeeeeee. Eeeeeee."

"Yes, of course you can have a ginger nut."

"Eeeeeee. Eeeeeee."

"Oh, you don't want one."

"Eeeeeee. Eeeeeee."

"No, it doesn't matter – it's just that you always have one."

"Eeeeeee. Eeeeeee."

Mum went to make the coffee thinking it odd that dad didn't want a ginger nut – while dad wondered why ginger nuts were invariably the only biscuit on offer. Surely there must be an alternative available?

When mum returned with the coffee dad was asleep. She toyed with the idea of waking him but decided against it. He looked so peaceful with the sun shining in through the dining room window. She smiled. She might as well join him for a snooze.

# TWENTY TWO

Shortly after Alan, Mary and Kitty departed it stopped raining. So those that had delayed their journey with that hope in mind were vindicated.

"You were right about the weather," said Jacqueline.

"Yes, I did say that to Uncle Alan," said Peter. "But he wouldn't listen. If it's okay with you we'll leave in half an hour?"

"That suits me."

They were joined by Joanna's friend Dot carrying the umpteenth tray-full of piping hot tea.

"Anybody interested?" she asked.

"Yes, I'll have another cuppa," said Jacqueline.

"I'd like to," said Peter. "But I'm afraid I'd be stopping in a lay-by on the way home."

"That's okay for a man," said Dot.

"It isn't if they're with me," said Jacqueline.

"Well at least I know where I stand," said Peter. "I'll have a double whisky then. Spirits don't have the same effect."

Dot assumed Peter was joking and didn't continue down that avenue in case it provoked an argument.

"Have you far to go?" she asked.

"Well I'm dropping Jacqueline off in Kent and then back to Essex," replied Peter.

"That sounds a long way."

"It's not that bad. I should be home by midnight. I take it you live locally?"

"Yes, a fifteen minutes walk."

"And you're a friend of Joanna's?"

"That's right. We met at Amnesty International ten years ago. Our kids grew up together and now we do aerobics together."

"Did you know her dad very well?" said Jacqueline.

"Actually I never met him."

"Didn't you?"

"No, I was only thinking about that the other day. I never saw him round Joanna's and I can't remember ever coming round here. Well there'd be no reason to."

"I'm sure he didn't visit Joanna's very often. Well I think Auntie Joan gave up trying to persuade him."

"That's what Joanna said. She's talked a lot about her dad since his death. His stroke at the age of forty nine. I can't comprehend what it must have been like unable to talk for all that time. It just seems unbelievable."

"I know," said Peter. "You're talking about thirty years. Can you imagine the frustration?"

"I'm sure Auntie Joan was the reason he survived that long," said Jacqueline. "The way she looked after him."

"Yes," said Dot. "Joanna said his general health was good. I mean from the time of his stroke until his death he didn't have much else wrong with him. He rarely had a cold. He suffered from hay fever but he did prior to the stroke. He actually had a strong constitution."

"I always thought how well he looked," said Peter. "He never lost that fine physique. You'd never have guessed from looking at him that he'd had a stroke."

They were joined by Dot's husband John.

"Can you remember meeting Joanna's dad?" said Dot.

"No, but then I can't remember meeting her mum before today."

"Oh John, of course you can. What about on Boxing Day round Joanna's? How many times have we been round there?"

John thought long and hard. "Well you might be right. I definitely remember playing charades with an uncle one year. He did a great impersonation of nonchalance."

"Nonchalance?" queried Dot.

"The boys thought it hilarious. You ask Joanna."

"No, I'll take your word for it. But I do want to see her before we go. I'll leave you to take the tea round."

She handed John the tray and went off in search of Joanna.

"Thank you Dot," shouted John.

"I'll take that from you," said Jacqueline.

"Are you sure?"

"Yes, it'll give me a chance to say cheerio. We're off shortly."

"Okay then," said John handing over the tray. "Much appreciated."

"That's alright. I'll make sure I'm back in half an hour Peter."

She followed Dot into the kitchen.

"It's like musical chairs," said John.

"That's right," said Peter. "But nonchalance does sound a difficult charade to do."

"It would be for most people but not Joanna's uncle."

"One of Auntie Joan's brothers?"

"That's right, the one that attempted to reverse over the undertaker."

"Oh you mean Ralph?"

"Yes, Ralph. I missed that incident."

"I tell you it was close."

"I bet he played it in a nonchalant manner," said John.

"Well, he made a big thing about checking his car for walking stick damage," said Peter. "Implying the undertaker shouldn't have been walking behind it. That didn't go down well."

"That sounds like my man. I think every family needs an Uncle Ralph."

"You're right. Anyway nice to meet you John, I'd better start saying my goodbyes."

"Yes, I hope you have a good journey home."

"You too."

"I'm sure ours will be uneventful. We'll be home before you've reached the A11. And that's walking nonchalantly."

"Just like my driving."

# 1980

Mum and dad had arrived at Joanna's for Sunday lunch. They were late because dad had been at his belligerent worse. Initially refusing to entertain the idea of visiting his daughter when mum could quite easily prepare dinner in the comfort of his home. Was that too much to ask? Had she forgotten he'd suffered a stroke? That his life had been turned upside down not hers. She could go on her own, after she'd served dinner of course. That wasn't a problem. He'd enjoy spending the afternoon by himself.

But mum saw it differently, that a monthly visit to Joanna's not too much to ask. That he should make the effort. Although when he made so much fuss perhaps that argument didn't stand up. She admitted she'd been on the offensive from the start today. She thought that dad had peed in the spare bedroom. Something she'd feared since the move. She couldn't be sure but the carpet definitely felt wet. And the thought of dad slipping into those ways again depressed her, especially as things hadn't been too bad lately. Well, on an even keel anyway.

She felt more at home in Norwich each day that passed. It really was a fine city. Besides the splendid array of shops there were the cobbled streets, the Roman wall, a couple of cathedrals and a castle. Not forgetting a pub for every day of the year and a church for every week. (Though she hadn't checked either of those facts out) And if she needed the supermarket she could walk to Sainsbury's in fifteen minutes.

She continued to enjoy her garden and the grandchildren. She'd already taken them by rail to Cromer, Yarmouth and Lowestoft. They were invariably well behaved. The special treat of playing Newmarket saw to that. Even Mrs Bunn from next door had said hello on a couple of occasions. Although she hadn't yet offered any local delicacies.

Whether dad would say the same about the move was debatable. Okay he didn't have those awful neighbours to contend with but she'd noticed a deterioration in his condition. He seemed more impatient and aggressive. One minute he'd be okay and then the next flying off the handle. She had to be very careful not to antagonize him. As in Leyton he spent the majority of the time ensconced in his armchair either watching the tele or reading – but the National Geographic rather than the Ring Magazine. Uncle John wasn't on hand to pass on the latter and dad wasn't bothered about buying it. The National Geographic had been Nick's idea. Dad seemed to enjoy the articles and photos.

He occasionally exercised. He had a preferred route and kept to it religiously. It took him twenty minutes. His name and address were written on a piece of paper just in case. And that proved invaluable on the occasion he got lost and the police were on hand to return him safe and sound in a squad car. To say mum felt embarrassed was an understatement. Especially as Mrs. Bunn happened to be waiting at the bus stop outside when the police drew up.

Of course there could be another possibility regarding the wet patch in the spare bedroom. That one of the grandchildren had spilt water when they'd slept over on the Friday. She'd have to question them before accusing Stan of the dastardly deed. Fingers crossed.

Accordingly mum and dad were both uptight as they sat at the table. Negative vibes enveloped the dining room. There was silence save for the dishing up of food. The three boys (Tim eight, Duncan six and William four) looked at their granddad with trepidation. Just because they were present didn't mean he wouldn't show off. They'd seen that side of him before. They were wary and kept their heads down – as did son-in-law David.

"Have you heard from Nick?" said Joanna.

"Not this weekend," said mum. "He usually rings on Sunday night."

"Eeeeeee. Eeeeeee."

Dad sounded agitated. That meant it more crucial than ever to ascertain what was on his mind, to be correct the first time around. Everybody looked at dad but said nothing, hoping against hope that another member of the family would grasp the nettle.

"Eeeeeee. Eeeeeee."

"Do you mean Nick?" said Joanna.

Dad nodded and clapped his hands sarcastically.

"Coming up to visit?" said Joanna.

Dad nodded again.

"He usually comes every three weeks," said mum. "So he should be here next week."

Dad shook his head and grinned sarcastically.

"What do you mean Stan?" said mum.

"Eeeeee. Eeeeeee."

"He doesn't come up enough."

Dad nodded and pointed at mum.

"It's nothing to do with me how often he comes up."

"Eeeeeee. Eeeeeee."

"I think every three weeks is fine."

"Eeeeee. Eeeeeee."

"What do you mean Stan?"

"Eeeeeee. Eeeeeee."

"What, go down and visit him?"

As mum suggested that she knew it wasn't viable. I mean, how would he cope with a two hour train journey? Or more importantly – how would she cope with him on a two hour train journey? She prayed that wasn't what he had in mind.

"Eeeeeee. Eeeeeee."

"You don't mean that?"

Dad nodded and mum sighed with relief.

"Eeeeeee. Eeeeeee."

"When I speak to Nick I'll ask him when he's coming up."

That seemed to placate dad and he got up and went to the toilet. Mum refrained from reminding him he'd been just before they left home. And then she spotted it. Her face dropped and she pointed to the mantelpiece.

"Where did that photo come from?" she asked.

"Last Christmas," replied Joanna.

"I don't remember seeing it before."

"No, we've only just had them developed. It's a good one of both of you."

"I don't like it."

And with that she walked across to the mantelpiece and laid the picture on its face.

"Mum," said Joanna. "It's a nice photo."

"I'm sorry Joanna but I can't bear to look at a photo of Stan taken after his stroke. It's too painful. It makes me think of the man he used to be. You can stand it up again when we're gone."

"Well okay mum. I didn't realize it affected you like that."

"Well I have mentioned it before. Nick's got a picture of us in his bedroom. He's learnt to put it away when I visit."

"But you can look at a photo of dad taken before his stroke?" said Joanna.

"Yes, because he was normal then."

"Isn't that more difficult?"

"No."

"What about dad, can he look at photos of himself?"

"Yes, it doesn't seem to bother him. Nick's photo was taken not long after the stroke. Stan's wearing that rust coloured cardigan. He looks awful. Like somebody who's not quite the ticket. But he just smiled and gave the thumbs up when Nick showed him."

"What's happened to that cardigan? I haven't seen dad wearing it lately."

"I threw it out."

"I thought it was dad's favourite."

"It might have been but it had holes in it."

"What did dad say?"

"I didn't tell him and he didn't ask. I got him that nice striped one from Selfridges."

"I thought he didn't like that one."

"Well it's the only one he's got so he's got no choice."

"Well try not to throw that one out then."

Mum smiled as so did her grandchildren and son-in-law. But then Dad reappeared and the subject quickly changed.

"What about Peter Sellers?" said Joanna.

"Yes, he was only in his fifties," said mum.

"I think he'd had a heart attack before," said David.

"He had," said mum. "The same year that Stan had his stroke."

"Eeeeeee. Eeeeeee."

"Peter Sellers," said Joanna. "He's died of a heart attack."

"Eeeeeee. Eeeeeee."

"What do you mean Stan?"

"Eeeeeee. Eeeeeee."

"The Goon Show?"

"Eeeeeee. Eeeeeee."

"Yes I remember listening to that in Nottingham Road."

"Eeeeeee. Eeeeeee."

"Funny? Well it wasn't bad but I preferred Tony Hancock."

"So did I," said mum."

Dad look aggrieved that the family had opted for Tony Hancock rather than Peter Sellers. He shrugged his shoulders and got on with his Sunday Roast.

"I've seen the blood donor episode," said Timothy. "That is funny. An armful of blood. That's the best bit."

The family looked at Tim in disbelief. How could an eight year old have memories of that classic episode?

"Are you sure?" said Joanna.

"Yes, I watched it at Ben's. They had a video. They were the first family in the street."

"No, they weren't," said Duncan.

"Yes, they were."

"No, they weren't."

"Alright you two," said Joanna. "Just get on with your dinner."

The disagreement between two of his grandchildren tickled dad and he started laughing.

"Alright Stan, don't encourage them," said mum.

But dad just laughed and laughed. It reminded mum of that time at Fred's funeral. Soon everybody was laughing. Oh well, at least the atmosphere had lightened.

# TWENTY THREE

Joanna and Nick were peering out of the window watching the rain fall. It was absolutely chucking it down. The thirty minute cessation had been a false dawn. Now you'd get soaked walking to the car – let alone walking home.

"Dot and John will get soaked," said Joanna.

"Well I did offer to run them home," said Nick. "But they said they wanted the exercise."

"I think John wanted the exercise. You wait until I see Dot. She'll have something to say on the matter."

"When it rains like this it reminds me of Nottingham Road," said Nick. "Looking out of my bedroom window with mum. That's before dad had his stroke. He would have been at work. There's thunder and lightening and a depressing drabness about everything. But there's also the comforting fact that you're inside with mum all safe and sound. With the sash cord windows, the shiny green lino and the yellow painted chest of drawers. And this classical piece of music by Eric Satie comes to mind. I don't know whether it's from that time or just my imagination. But whenever I hear the tune I'm back in that bedroom. It gives me the shivers."

"Eric Satie?" said Joanna. "Are you sure you don't mean Eric Sykes?"

"Of course I do. Eric Sykes the famous composer."

"But seriously Nick, you were lucky you had a window that size"

"Oh Joanna, you're not still going on about the size of your bedroom."

They laughed as they recalled the battles of the box room. Who deserved the biggest bedroom when growing up? Obviously opinions were divided and always would be.

"You had a better view than me," said Nick. "Lush green playing fields and tennis courts."

"Yes, it wasn't bad until they built the extension. But a good job we didn't have a cat."

"What do you mean? Oh, very funny. Not enough room to swing one."

"That's right. But we never had any pets, did we?"

"No. Yes, we did – the budgerigar. I suppose you would call that a pet."

"But it never talked?" said Joanna.

"It never did anything," said Nick. "I can't remember it ever flying round the room."

"Perhaps it wasn't allowed out. I remember coming down one morning and finding it dead on its perch. Really surreal that. You thought it would have fallen off."

"Wasn't it a Christmas present from Ralph and Joan?"

"Yes, that's why we called it that silly name. In memory of Ralph's favourite opera singer. Benjimeno or something? We had one of his records on seventy eight."

"Wasn't it a she?"

"I don't think so."

"A strange name for an opera singer anyway – male or female."

"I think they were Italian."

"They usually are."

"I didn't miss having a cat or dog," said Joanna.

"Neither did I," said Nick. "Anyway I made up for it living with Nicole. We had as many as four cats at one time."

"Four?"

"Yes, plus the neighbours two. They used to come in through the cat flap and nick food from the fridge."

"How did they manage that?"

"They're very clever animals."

"Do you think mum will get a dog?"

"I don't know. I think it'd be good company but whether she'll ever get round to it. She couldn't have considered it with dad around."

"I'm not so sure that would have been a bad idea. I know that's what mum said but perhaps dad would have enjoyed taking it for walks. You know, instead of having a letter to post. Get him out the house."

"Yes," said Nick. "But could you imagine it barking when dad was having an off day? Mum would really have suffered. And he might have lost it on his walk."

"You might be right," said Joanna. "Do you remember Kit and Mary's dogs?"

"Yes, well behaved Muffet and uncontrollable Candy. Talk about chalk and cheese."

"That's because they spoilt Candy. She got away with murder. I remember how she used to jump up on the table when we were having dinner. She never got told off."

"And what a loud annoying bark."

"Yes, that was dreadful. I suppose she died."

"I can't remember what happened to her," said Joanna. "We should have asked Kit and Mary."

"I'm glad they made it today. They don't travel far these days."

"No, a good job that Alan offered to pick them up."

"He's always got a good story."

"All our uncles have a good story. I think that's a requirement for an uncle. I hope you're keeping up the tradition with my four boys."

"Of course, that applies to me, doesn't it? I'm an uncle. I do my best."

"I've heard some good reports."

# 1981

Dad wasn't interested in watching the Royal Wedding on the tele. It meant nothing to him. He much preferred to read the National Geographic sat in his favourite armchair behind the lounge door. Furthermore he didn't see why he should be shunted off to the dining room just because mum, Joanna, David, Tim, Duncan, William and Nick wanted to indulge themselves in front of the box. Wasn't it his room? They were the guests. He had an idea – a compromise of sorts. He'd take the armchair with him. What could be simpler?

"No, that's not a good idea Stan," said mum.

"Eeeeeee. Eeeeeee."

"Well for a start we won't get it though the door."

But dad knew that wasn't true. I mean how did they manage when they moved in? Quite easily if he recalled. One removal man with the chair balanced on his back. No, problem whatsoever. Mum obviously recalled that and quickly changed her line of attack.

"Even if we could get it through the door we need the chair. There'll be seven of us watching the wedding."

Dad shook his head in anger and pointed aggressively at mum. That just wasn't good enough. He wanted the chair moved or he'd stay put.

"Eeeeeee. Eeeeeee."

"Don't shout Stan."

"Eeeeeee. Eeeeeee."

But dad shouted again. This time flaying his arms about in an exaggerated aggressive manner. Mum felt quite intimidated. Thankfully they were saved by a knock on the door.

"That'll be Nick. We'll see what he has to say."

"Eeeeeee. Eeeeeee."

Dad couldn't care less what Nick had to say. It's what he wanted that mattered and he wouldn't give up on this one.

"You always take sides with him," said mum when Nick agreed to dad's suggestion of moving the chair.

"No, I don't," said Nick. "It just seems the best thing to do."

"Where's everyone going to sit without the armchair?"

"We'll manage, it's only one chair. The kids can sit on the floor."

"Well see if you can get it though the door then. And I don't want the paint work scratched."

"I'll be careful."

Mum, feeling aggrieved, stormed out leaving Nick to seek out dad and suss out the tricky operation.

"Hello dad."

"Eeeeeee. Eeeeeee."

"I'm okay. How are you?"

"Eeeeeee. Eeeeeee."

"I take it you're not interested in the wedding."

Dad dismissed the idea with a wave of his hand.

"No, I'm not that bothered either. Do you remember the Coronation in fifty three?"

"Eeeeeee. Eeeeeee."

"We didn't have a television then. I think we watched it on the Forrest's."

"Eeeeeee. Eeeeeee."

"What mum? Yes, she went up town to watch it with her friend from America. I think it rained all day. I wonder what happened to her. Can you remember her name?"

"Eeeeeee. Eeeeeee."

Dad had had enough of this small talk. He wanted the armchair sorted out.

"The armchair?" said Nick. "Well it must go through the door because the removal men managed it when you moved in. Although, granted, they were experts. There's not going to be much room. Let's think about it."

"Eeeeeee. Eeeeeee."

"What, take the door off?"

"Eeeeeee. Eeeeeee."

"You don't mean that. No, but it might help."

Dad stood up and attempted to convey in a mime that the removal man had balanced the chair on his back.

"Somebody wearing a hat?" queried Nick.

Dad shook his head angrily and tried again.

"Eeeeeee. Eeeeeee."

"With a cloak?"

"Eeeeeee. Eeeeeee."

"Somebody in the family?"

"Eeeeeee. Eeeeeee."

"No, I'm sorry dad. I don't get it."

Dad sat down frustrated and left Nick to fathom out for himself the best way forward. As he pondered the rest of the family arrived.

Before long everybody had gathered round the chair offering all sorts of advice. Except for mum that is, she hadn't yet forgiven Nick for taking dad's side. She said hello then disappeared again on the pretext of preparing sandwiches for the big event.

"Lay it on its side," said David. "I'm sure that will work."

"Wouldn't it be easier taking the door off," said Joanna.

"That's what I said," said Nick. "I'm sure that'll be the best way. I'll go and get a screwdriver."

But before he could depart dad decided to act out his mime one more time.

"Eeeeeee. Eeeeeee."

"Okay dad," said Joanna. "We're watching."

Dad got up and lent forward. He walked through the doorway as though carrying a heavy load on his back. He waited for a reaction. That wasn't forthcoming so he walked back again. There were more puzzled looks so he walked through the doorway again. Then back again.

"You look like the coalman," said Nick.

"Eeeeeee. Eeeeeee."

To say dad felt frustrated underestimated his feelings. He sat down with a shake of the head and angrily pointed his hand at everyone.

"I'm sorry dad," said Joanna.

"Do you mean the removal man carried the chair on his back?" said Duncan.

"Eeeeeee. Eeeeeee."

Dad smiled with relief and gave Duncan the thumbs up.

"Well done Duncan," said Joanna.

"Oh I see what you were getting up to now," said Nick. "Right, so shall we try it that way or shall I get the screwdriver?"

"If you want to carry it go ahead," said David. "I wouldn't like to support that weight."

"Well I'll give it a go."

"Eeeeeee. Eeeeeee."

"No, I'll be alright dad. If it's too heavy I'll put it down. But I can't do it with you sitting in the chair. That would be too much weight."

There was laughter as dad stood up with an apologetic wave. At the same time mum reappeared and watched as Nick prepared to balance the chair on his back.

"Is that going to work?" she asked.

"I don't see why not," said Nick.

"Well remember what I said, I don't want the paintwork scratched. Surely it would have been easier removing the door?"

But Nick had travelled too far down this particular road and with David's help positioned the chair comfortably on his back. He then proceeded to slowly manoeuvre the chair through the doorway.

But unfortunately every time he attempted the tricky manoeuvre the chair became wedged. After half a dozen attempts he reluctantly conceded defeat.

"Well there's something I'm not doing right," he said. "Anyone got any ideas?"

"No, you might as well get the screwdriver," said Joanna.

"What do you think David?"

"I think the screwdriver is the best option."

"Eeeeeee. Eeeeeee."

"And you do dad? Okay then I'll go and get one."

"You've scratched the paintwork," said mum pointing to scratch marks on the door frame.

"No, I haven't. They were there beforehand."

"Are you sure?"

"Yes, because I did it bringing in the step ladders. Don't you remember?"

Mum smiled. Yes, she did remember the occasion. The same day he'd dropped a tin of white emulsion all over the carpet.

"Okay I'll let you off this time. You'd better get that screwdriver."

Nick heeded the advice and went off to the shed in search of a suitable screwdriver.

He returned with a choice of three to discover the said armchair blocking the hall.

"You've done it," he said. "How did you manage that?"

There were condescending smiles all round.

"It's easy if you know how?" said Joanna. "We just laid the chair on its side and slowly swivelled its back around the door frame."

"That's great. So we can try the same method in the dining room?"

"I don't see why not."

The three boys were given the responsibility of pushing the armchair up the hall towards the dining room.

"Can we keep going?" said William when they reached the dining room.

"Yes, please mum," said Tim.

"Well okay then," said Joanna. "But take it slowly."

The three boys carefully manoeuvred the armchair around the door frame. Well not that carefully because they managed to collide with the door frame and send a large piece of paintwork hurtling through the air. There was a hush as the family looked to mum for the next move. Timothy, Duncan and William looked suitably chastened.

"Oh dear," said Nick. "That is a shame. Did you see that mum?"

"Of course I did. But I suppose if you can have a mishap we shouldn't make a big thing about the boys bad luck. And they haven't spilt any emulsion."

"Not yet they haven't."

But except for that mishap the boys were successful. Soon the armchair stood safe and sound by the window in the dining room. Dad gave the thumbs up, ruffled his three grandchildren's hair in a mark of affection and sat down with the National Geographic.

"Eeeeeee. Eeeeeee."

"That's right dad," said Joanna. "They're clever boys."

But that's not what dad meant. He'd moved on. He wanted to convey to those present that he wished to be left on his own now he'd been reunited with his armchair.

"Eeeeeee. Eeeeeee."

"Well we'll leave you to it Stan," said mum.

Dad nodded then indicated he'd like a coffee and a biscuit.

"I'll do that shortly Stan. You have had a coffee this morning."

"Eeeeeee. Eeeeee."

"You've forgotten. Less than an hour ago."

"Eeeeeee. Eeeeeee."

"I won't forget."

The family left dad reading the National Geographic and returned to the lounge and the Royal Wedding.

"Who is it getting married?" enquired William.

"Oh William, you couldn't have forgotten again," said Joanna.

"I can nearly remember."

"Prince Charles and Lady Diana."

"I think I'd rather play cricket," said Timothy.

"Yes, so would I," said Duncan.

"And me," said William.

Mum and Joanna looked to Nick for some sort of sign regarding his willingness to take charge of a game of cricket in the back garden.

"Oh go on Nick," said Timothy.

"Yes, please," said Duncan. "You can bat first."

Nick thought about his options. He didn't fancy either. So what was the lesser of two evils? Well if they were going to let him bat first it had to be...

"Okay kids," he said. "We'll play cricket."

"Well just be careful with the windows," said mum.

"I think I've learnt my lesson."

"I hope you have," said Joanna.

"That was really funny," said William.

As they reminisced about the occasion Nick walloped a ball through Joanna and David's kitchen window dad walked in carrying the National Geographic.

"Eeeeeee. Eeeeeee."

"I'll do it in a minute," said mum.

But coffee wasn't the only reason for dad's reappearance. He wanted to show everybody the article about the spectacular wildlife in the Galapagos Islands.

"Eeeeeee. Eeeeeee."

"Yes, they're amazing turtles," said Joanna.

"They're so huge," said Timothy.

"Like the tortoise we had," said Duncan.

Everybody laughed.

"Eeeeeee. Eeeeeee."

"Yes, I'll do your coffee now Stan," said mum.

Dad nodded and gave the thumbs up. He returned to the dining room safe in the knowledge that reading the National Geographic gave more satisfaction than watching the Royal Wedding. He just hoped they'd leave him alone all day. Well, except for serving up food and drinks at regular intervals.

# TWENTY FOUR

Mum decided to make the effort to talk to Nicole. After all she had travelled from Birmingham to attend the funeral. Nobody would have raised an eyebrow if she hadn't bothered. But she'd always made a point of chatting to dad and he always seemed pleased to see her.

"Hello Nicole. I'm pleased you were able to make it today."

"So am I," said Nicole. "And I apologise for what I said about the wheelchair. That must have sounded awful."

"Wheelchair?" said mum – puzzled.

"Yes, I think I said I couldn't have guaranteed to push Nick in a wheelchair if he had a stroke."

Mum continued to look puzzled.

"That's what Nick said anyway. He reminded me today. Evidently we'd been talking about how you looked after Stan. I said in similar circumstances I couldn't have been so devoted. Well I might have been, but I just didn't know. Perhaps I wouldn't have coped and put him in a home. I know it sounds terrible. I'm sorry."

Mum shook her head. "I didn't consciously make a decision to look after Stan. Remember the vows, for better for worse. I suppose you could have called it my duty but I didn't see it like that. I never have done."

Nicole wished she'd never brought up the matter. She didn't know what to say.

"Anyway Nicole, the wheelchair situation's not going to happen now. I mean with you and Nick separating ."

"No, that's true but I would have pushed him. I probably said that to start an argument. I did that when I felt insecure. I'm sure I didn't mean it."

Mum smiled. "That's reassuring. But I do know that Stan appreciated you taking the time to talk to him."

"Oh thank you. It must have been so difficult for both of you."

"Well yes, but at least I didn't have to push Stan in a wheelchair."

Nicole wasn't sure whether that was sarcasm or not.

"No, I'm being serious Nicole. I've often wondered whether it would have been easier if Stan had been physically disabled but able to talk. Would that have been less frustrating for him? I don't know. I think it might have been easier for me. Being able to converse would have been such a blessing. The time I spent trying to guess what Stan wanted to say. But for Stan confined to a wheelchair, how would he have coped for all those years? Obviously being his weight we'd have needed help to dress and undress him. Then there's the business of taking a shower and going to the loo. There would have been so many things to take into consideration."

She paused and thought about dad being wheelchair bound but able to converse. She looked sad. But then her mood changed.

"Anyway Nicole, have you any plans to go home?"

"Not at present," said Nicole. "Because I've been here for so long it seems more like home than Quebec. But I know I'll end up there eventually. I'd like to die there."

"Oh Nicole, don't talk about dying."

# 1982

It was eleven thirty and mum had just turned out the light. She invariably went to bed at that time while dad retired an hour earlier. She wondered how long it would be before he came in requesting her to check whether his bed felt wet. Lately he'd been disrupting her sleep more than ever. Sometimes the interruptions reached double figures. In the morning she'd feel dreadful and take out her irritability on dad. Well he deserved it.

She tried to think positive, to count the plusses in her life. And of course Nick and Nicole's impending wedding was a big plus. She hoped Stan would be alright for the big day in his role as a witness. Fingers crossed his signature would bear some resemblance to S.P. Wisbey. Some days it did, some days it didn't.

The bedroom door opened and in walked dad.

"I wonder who this is?" she whispered sarcastically.

"Eeeeeee. Eeeeeee."

"What is it Stan?"

"Eeeeeee. Eeeeeee."

"The beds wet? Okay I'll have a look."

She followed dad back to his bedroom and felt the sheets. No, of course they weren't wet. They never were.

"No, it feels dry to me Stan."

"Eeeeeee. Eeeeeee."

"Yes, it must be just a feeling. Try and get some sleep."

She walked back to her room and checked the time. It was almost midnight. She felt more awake now then when she went to bed. Her thoughts returned to the wedding. She counted the number of guests expected. She made it forty two. Unfortunately that included nobody from Nicole's side. Nick had divulged they planned to have a blessing in Canada in the new year. That would be some consolation but mum did feel sorry for Nicole having no family present for her big day. She must be disappointed.

Then she dozed off.

The bedroom door opened again.

"Eeeeeee. Eeeeeee."

"What is it Stan?"

"Eeeeeee. Eeeeeee."

"The bed's wet? I'll come and have a look."

She checked the time. Twelve thirty. So she'd probably had fifteen minutes sleep. She followed Stan back to his room. He stood over her as she felt the sheets again.

"No, I'm sorry Stan they feel dry to me."

Dad looked agitated and disbelieving so mum felt the sheets again.

"They're definitely dry. Try and get some sleep Stan."

She went back to her room and climbed into bed. She felt wide awake now. She thought back to Joanna's wedding eleven years ago.

Stan had definitely deteriorated since then. As well as being more aggressive and irrational he'd picked up some irritating habits. Besides the wet feeling he'd started to fall over at inopportune moments and to wee on the bathroom floor. Not as regularly as in Leyton but a worry nonetheless. Usually it occurred next to the linen basket. Whenever she showed him the proof he shrugged his shoulders. As for the falling over, well mum thought that was for attention because it invariably occurred in company. Usually round Joanna's when he thought it time to go home.

The door opened again and in walked dad.

"Eeeeeee. Eeeeeee."

"Hello Stan, what is it?"

"Eeeceee. Eeeeeee."

"The bed's wet? I'd better come and have a look then."

She felt the bed for the third time that night.

"No, it feels okay to me Stan. Try and get some sleep."

This time Stan didn't dispute the truth and got back into bed.

Because mum wasn't feeling tired she decided to make a cup of tea. She took it to bed with a ginger nut and attempted to finish the Daily Mail crossword. Today had been one of those frustrating occasions when she'd been unable to complete it over morning coffee. Now she finished it within five minutes and wondered why she'd had so much difficulty earlier. She turned out the light at one forty five.

At one fifty the door opened and in walked dad.

"Eeeeeee. Eeeeeee."

"What is it Stan?"

"Eeeeeee. Eeeeeee."

"The bed feels wet. I'd better have a look then."

She followed dad down the hall making faces behind his back and clenching her fist in anger. She felt the sheets again.

"No, they feel dry to me Stan. Now try and get some sleep. It's nearly two o'clock."

Dad rubbed his hand across the sheets and pointed towards the foot of the bed.

"Eeeeeee. Eeeeeee."

"It feels wet there? Let me have a look."

She felt the foot of the bed.

"No, it's not wet Stan. It must be just a feeling."

Dad looked at mum suspiciously and shook his head. But, thankfully, after a few seconds got back into bed.

This time when mum returned to her room she felt tired but unable to sleep because of the certainty that dad would soon be interrupting. She thought again about the impending wedding and tried to recall where the couple were heading for their honeymoon. Nick had informed her just a couple of days ago. Yes, somewhere in the West Country. She had a feeling that she and Stan had visited the resort when they were courting. Now what was the name? Then she dozed off.

At two forty five dad walked in for the fifth time that night.

"Eeeeeee. Eeeeeee."

"What is it this time Stan?"

"Eeeeeee. Eeeeeee."

"The bed's wet? Stan, it's just a feeling. It's not wet."

"Eeeeeee. Eeeeeee."

"I had a look half an hour ago."

But dad wasn't taking no for an answer. He stood at the foot of the bed glaring at mum.

"Eeeeeee. Eeeeeee."

"Alright Stan, I'll come and have a look."

She followed him up the hall again. This time she clenched her fist in anger then pretended to punch him hard in the back. She smiled. The thought of it gave her great satisfaction.

"No, the bed's not wet," said mum after a really thorough going over. "It must be just a feeling."

Dad stared at her with hands on hips. He felt the bed himself.

"Eeeeeee. Eeeeeee."

He pointed to the pillow.

"The pillow feels wet? Okay, let me have a look."

"Eeeeeee. Eeeeeee."

He watched suspiciously as mum felt the pillow.

"No, it not wet Stan."

As she removed her hand dad grabbed it and put it back on the pillow.

"Don't be so rough Stan."

"Eeeeeee. Eeeeeee."

"I'm telling you it's not wet," shouted mum. "Now get back into bed."

She didn't wait for the abuse and stormed out before dad slammed the door.

When dad interrupted proceedings for the sixth time that night it woke mum. So at least she'd managed to doze off. But with the time at three thirty it hadn't been for long.

"Eeeeeee. Eeeeeee."

Dad held his hands up in apology for his recent outburst.

"That's alright Stan. But when I say the bed isn't wet, it isn't. I know you're convinced otherwise but it's just a feeling. Okay Stan?"

Dad held up his hand in agreement.

"Eeeeeee. Eeeeeee."

"What is it now Stan?"

"Eeeeeee. Eeeeeee."

"The bed feels wet. What have I just said Stan?"

"Eeeeeee. Eeeeeee."

"Don't you believe me?"

"Eeeeeee. Eeeeeee."

"Alright, I'll come and have a look."

So once again she followed him up the hall.

"Now where does it feel wet Stan?"

Dad slowly moved his hands backwards and forwards across the sheets half a dozen times then shrugged his shoulders.

"Eeeeeee. Eeeeeee."

"It doesn't feel wet now?"

"Eeeeeee. Eeeeeee."

"Well that is a relief. Now try and get some sleep."

What a turn up for the books thought mum. Dad deciding the bed wasn't wet. That must have been a first. Now would that be it for the night? She closed her eyes.

At four o'clock dad walked in again. Mum continued to sleep so dad tugged at her arm.

"Eeeeeee. Eeeeeee."

"What is it now Stan?"

"Eeeeeee. Eeeeeee."

"The bed feels wet?"

"Eeeeeee. Eeeeeee."

"Stan, can't you remember? You felt the bed yourself and said it wasn't wet."

Dad stared disbelievingly at mum.

"You did Stan."

"Eeeeeee. Eeeeeee."

"Okay, I'll come and have a look."

How many times is that she thought as she walked down the hall? She felt the bed sheets once more.

"No, they're not wet Stan."

On this occasion dad accepted mum's word and got back into bed.

"Eeeeeee. Eeeeeee."

"Now try and get some sleep."

She got back to bed at four thirty. Another two and a half hours and it'd be time to get up. She couldn't go on like this for much longer. She needed her sleep. Okay not a regular eight hours but four would be a blessing. It was a vicious circle. When she didn't get sufficient sleep she took it out on dad. Then he started the day on the wrong foot and they'd be at each others throats for the remainder of the day.

She dozed off again – but not for long.

"Eeeeeee. Eeeeeee."

"What is it this time Stan?"

"Eeeeeee. Eeeeeee."

"The bed feels wet?"

"Eeeeeee. Eeeeeee."

"Do you know it's nearly morning," shouted mum. "I haven't had any sleep because you keep coming in and waking me up. Stan, your bed isn't wet. It's just a feeling. Can't you understand that? Now go back to bed."

Dad said nothing. He stood at the foot of the bed looking dejected. Unable to understand why mum shouted at him just because he said the bed felt wet.

"Eeeeeee. Eeeeeee."

He sat on the bed and took mum's hand. He began to cry and mum's anger evaporated. She put her arm round him. He couldn't help this wet feeling. It was something out of his control.

"Okay Stan," she said. "I'll come and see if your bed is wet."

"No, Stan," she said after running her hands over the sheets. "It doesn't feel wet to me."

Dad held up his hands in apology for wasting her time and got back into bed.

"That's okay Stan. Now you try and get some sleep."

She kissed him on the cheek and returned to bed convinced that would be it for the night.

But it wasn't, ten minutes later the door opened and in walked dad. Mum took a deep breath. This could be a record night for interruptions. But what was the record? She'd have to refer to her diary in the morning. She smiled sarcastically. It was the morning.

"What is it Stan?"

"Eeeeeee. Eeeeeee."

"The bed feels wet?"

"Eeeeeee. Eeeeeee."

"Okay I'll have a look."

So at a quarter past five once more she followed Stan down the hall.

"No, the bed's not wet Stan. It must be just a feeling."

Dad looked resigned to the fact that mum would say that whatever the truth. He dismissed her with an aggressive wave of the hand and climbed into bed. Mum pondered over returning to bed or making another cuppa. She decided on the former in the hope it might be possible to nick a couple of hours sleep.

But alas at five forty five the door opened once more. Before dad could say anything mum got up. She'd had enough for one night.

"Would you like a cup of tea Stan? I'm just making myself one."

Without waiting for a reply, or a request to check his bed, she barged past him into the kitchen and put the kettle on. So much for a good nights sleep, she thought. Perhaps tomorrow she'd have better luck.

"Eeeeeee. Eeeeeee."

"Yes, I'm sure it is wet Stan. But I couldn't care less."

# TWENTY FIVE

"Would you like me to make some more tea Auntie Joan?" asked Lyn.

"Oh that would be nice," said mum. "Or coffee if people prefer it."

"Okay. Did the umm, now what was it called? The Jimmy Young special. Did it all go?"

"I'm afraid so. Why, did you want some?"

"I wouldn't have minded. I missed out first time around."

"Oh, that's a shame."

Mum then had a mischievous thought. Would it be possible to retrieve what she'd thrown away? And, more importantly, without being caught.

"I'll go round and take orders," said Lyn.

"Okay, I'll be in the kitchen," said mum.

She returned to the kitchen relieved to find nobody present. She made for the pedal bin and started rummaging through it. She'd wrapped the thrown away lemon butter bake in foil paper so if located there shouldn't be a problem with its edibility. But unfortunately because she'd discarded it much earlier other leftovers, plus teabags and used kitchen roll had been thrown on top. The task was proving more difficult then she imagined. She took a break then delved again.

"What are you up to?" said Joanna when she bought in some empty cups.

"Oh, I thought I'd dropped a knife in the bin," said mum, trying hard not to appear flustered. "I must have been mistaken."

"Do you want me to have a look?"

"No, that's okay."

"Do you feel tired mum? All of a sudden I feel really weary."

"Yes, I know what you mean. It's been a long day. Hopefully I'll get a good night's sleep."

"I hope you do, but remember what the doctor said. That it might take time to get back to a regular sleep pattern because you've had so many interrupted nights."

"I know, but it would be nice."

Mum waited for Joanna to leave so she could resume delving but her daughter seemed quite content to wile away the time staring into space.

"I'm glad we haven't far to go," said Joanna.

"No."

"I couldn't imagine driving back to London in these conditions."

"No."

"Dot and John must have got soaked walking home."

"Yes. Would you like another cup of tea?"

"I think I've had enough for one day."

"What about a coffee then?"

"Yes, I wouldn't mind a coffee."

"And a ginger nut to go with it?"

"Why not."

"Well go and find Lyn. She's collecting orders."

"Okay mum."

As soon as Joanna departed mum continued rummaging. Delving further and further into the pedal bin. Touching all sorts of unsavoury objects but not the one thing she craved. She realized the lemon butter bake must have dropped to the bottom and that without tipping the contents out she'd be unable to retrieve it. She pondered over the idea of picking the bin up and emptying its contents into the sink. She decided to go down that avenue and had the bin tipped and ready to empty when Lyn returned.

"Do you need a hand Auntie?" she enquired.

Mum tried once more to appear unflustered as she put down the bin.

"No, its okay Lyn. I know it sounds silly but I was going to give the bin a wipe down. They get so greasy. One of my pet hates I'm afraid."

"Yes. Right, well I've got orders for four teas and two coffees."

"Does that include Joanna?"

"Yes."

"I'll put the kettle on. I'll tell you when it's boiled."

"That's okay. I'll dry up why I'm waiting."

"Are you sure? You don't have to."

"No, I'd like to."

Mum's hopes of retrieving the lemon butter bake seemed dashed as she watched Lyn pick up a tea towel and start on the pile of plates, cups and saucers. She realized the delicacy would be lost forever. History would judge whether it'd been a success or otherwise.

# 1983

Ted had come up for the day to visit his old army friend Stan. The first time they'd got together for an age. Indeed while dad shaved mum and Ted tried to recall the last occasion.

"It might have been at the reunion," said Ted. "When Nick came along."

"No, you've visited since then," said mum.

"Well I know I haven't been up here. How long have you been in Norwich?"

"Four years now."

"Good Lord, doesn't time fly. Has it been a good move?"

"Yes, definitely for me. I really like Norwich. It's a fine city as they say."

"They certainly push that one, don't they? Every half a mile they're reminding you."

"It's great being near Joanna and the kids. I get to baby sit, meet them from school and take them to the seaside."

"What about Stan? He looks well."

Mum thought long and hard about that question.

"That's the trouble Ted, he always looks well. But that's no consolation. The fact is he's deteriorated since being up here. He's more aggressive these days. Well he'll be alright with you, but I have to be very careful what I say. Then he gets this wet feeling in bed. He's forever waking me and pestering to check whether the bed sheets are wet. Of course they never are."

"I'm sorry Joan," said Ted. "It must be difficult."

Mum nodded and shrugged her shoulders. But then she smiled.

"No, there are good days," she continued. "He enjoys seeing the grandchildren. He's probably better off here than in Leyton. At least we haven't got awful neighbours to contend with. Anyway he spends most of the time sitting in his armchair so he could be anywhere. No, to be fair he does go for the occasional walk."

"So have you been accepted?" said Ted smiling. "I hear the Norfolk people are quite reserved when it comes to welcoming strangers."

"Yes, that's true. We're on thirty years probation."

"Thirty years! I didn't realize they were that reserved. Does Stan still read the Ring Magazine?"

"No, it's the National Geographic now."

Ted looked surprised. "The National Geographic? That doesn't sound like the Stan I know."

At that moment dad walked in carrying a copy of the magazine.

"What are you doing reading that?" said Ted.

Dad opened the magazine and showed Ted an article about the Antarctic and its wildlife.

"Eeeeeee. Eeeeeee."

"I'm sure it is interesting Stan but what happened to the Ring Magazine?"

Dad shook his head. He looked puzzled. At that moment he couldn't recall reading such a magazine.

"Eeeeeee. Eeeeeee."

"Some days he remembers," said mum. "But when we moved up here my brother John wasn't around to pass on the magazine so Nick suggested the National Geographic. You find it interesting, don't you Stan?"

"Eeeeeee. Eeeeeee."

"I don't know how much of it he understands though."

Dad took umbrage at that assertion.

"Eeeeeee. Eeeeeee."

And mum realized she shouldn't have said that in front of visitors.

"Sorry Stan, I didn't mean that."

"Eeeeeee. Eeeeeee."

Dad presented himself in front of mum for the inspection of his shave. A routine unchanged since he'd suffered the stroke twenty years previous.

"Eeeeeee. Eeeeeee."

"Yes, that feels okay Stan."

Mum invariably complimented dad on his shave whatever the standard. She was proud of him for making the effort. How could she be critical?

"Can I have a feel Stan?" said Ted.

Dad walked over to Ted for his seal of approval.

"Yes, that feels fine. Right, are you ready for a pint down the local?"

Mum shook her head in the knowledge that dad would decline. She recalled the number of times Nick had tried unsuccessfully to tempt him with a pint down the Fiveways. But surprise, surprise dad couldn't have been more enthusiastic.

"Eeeeeee. Eeeeeee."

"Oh that's good," said Ted. "What's your local like?"

"Eeeeeee. Eeeeeee."

"Not that inviting according to Nick" said mum.

"Well as long as they sell Guinness we'll be okay. Is that right Stan?"

Dad gave the thumbs up.

"Well just take it easy Stan," said mum.

"Eeeeeee. Eeeeeee."

"Don't worry Joan," said Ted. "I'll make sure he doesn't overdo it."

Mum nodded. Of course she could trust Ted. She smiled. She wondered how Nick would react to the fact that Ted had been able to persuade his father into a pub.

"Eeeeee. Eeeeeee."

As Dad stood up to get his jacket he stumbled forward in spectacular fashion and fell on the floor.

"Eeeeee. Eeeeeee."

"Are you alright Stan," shouted an alarmed Ted going to his aid.

"Eeeeee. Eeeeeee."

"Yes, he's alright," said Mum exasperated. "I'm afraid this happens quite often."

Ted helped dad to his feet and sat him down in his armchair. Dad was annoyed that mum hadn't shown more sympathy.

"Eeeeee. Eeeeeee."

"I'm sorry Stan but that's getting to be a habit."

"Eeeeee. Eeeeee."

Dad growled at mum, stuck two fingers up, and went to get his jacket. Ted didn't know what to say.

"I'm sorry Ted but that gets tiresome after a while. He's always falling over like that. He doesn't hurt himself."

"Oh I see."

"I don't like to say it but he does it for attention. Anyway, how's Gwen?"

"Not too bad. Her legs are improving. She sends her love."

"That's good. Well I think I'll disappear before Stan returns. Probably for the best if you know what I mean. You have a good time down the pub."

"Okay Joan, don't worry about Stan. We won't go on a pub crawl."

"No, I'm sure you won't."

But although she sounded laidback she wouldn't relax until they returned. She headed for the bathroom where she intended staying until the pair of them had departed. No, point in aggravating Stan more than necessary.

Ted wasn't particularly impressed with The Fiveways Public House. He thought it lacked character. It certainly wouldn't win the pub of the year award. But there again it probably knew its limitations and wouldn't bother entering. It also lacked customers. They being the only two present. But it sold Guinness and the barmaid, although loud in both voice and dress, was pleasant enough.

"I haven't seen you in here before," she said.

"No," said Ted. "I'm up from Essex for the day visiting my old army pal."

"Essex," she cried. "That's a long way to come for a day. I've got relations down there. "

"Whereabouts?"

"I was hoping you wouldn't ask me that. Oh dear. No, I can't remember."

He gave it a few minutes while she desperately tried to think of the place in Essex, then picked up the beer and joined dad near the silent jukebox.

"Well the upholstery's okay," said Ted.

"Eeeeeee. Eeeeeee."

"It looks like it's been recovered lately. I can't stand pubs where there's cigarette burns and chewing gum on the seats."

"Eeeeeee. Eeeeeee."

"Well cheers Stan. Good to see you."

They clinked glasses and took that first expectant mouthful. They waited for the taste buds to click into action. They nodded appreciatively.

"Yes, not bad at all," said Ted.

"Eeeeeee. Eeeeeee."

"When was the last time you had a drink Stan?"

"Eeeeeee. Eeeeeee."

"You can't remember?"

"Eeeeeee. Eeeeeee."

"Me. I go down the Conservative club with Gwen most weekends. The beers half price. Unfortunately I have to play bingo though. I suppose that's the sacrifice for enjoying a cheap pint."

"Eeeeeee. Eeeeeee."

"Yes, like the army reunions. It's a shame they changed the location."

"Eeeeeee. Eeeeeee."

"I wonder why they did that."

226

"Eeeeeee. Eeeeeee."

"You don't get to know who's passed away when you miss the reunion. For all we know we might be the only two remaining."

They laughed at that possibility.

"Can you remember the war years Stan? On the ack-ack at Canvey."

Dad smiled and nodded.

"They were some of the happiest days of my life? I mean the comradeship. Something special."

"Eeeeeee. Eeeeeee."

"We never hit anything, did we?"

"Eeeeeee. Eeeeeee."

"Yes, we were getting closer by the day. We just needed a bit more time. The war didn't last long enough."

"Eeeeeee. Eeeeeee."

They laughed aloud as they reminisced.

"The worlds changed since then Stan. There won't be another war like that. Did you have an air raid shelter in the garden?"

"Eeeeeee. Eeeeeee."

"We did too. I often wondered what would have happened if a bomb had landed right on top."

"Eeeeeee. Eeeeee."

"Yes, that would have been it."

"Eeeeeee. Eeeeeee."

"What do you mean Stan?"

"Eeeeeee. Eeeeeee."

"A bomb landed right outside your house?"

"Eeeeeee. Eeeeeee."

"Somebody else's house?"

"Eeeeeee. Eeeeeee."

"Where Joan was living. That must have been frightening."

"Eeeeeee. Eeeeeee."

"Sorry Stan, I don't understand."

"Eeeeeee. Eeeeeee."

Dad picked up his empty glass.

"Oh you want another drink. Of course you can. Is it a pint?"

Dad nodded and Ted went off to buy another round.

"Same again, is it?" said the barmaid.

"Yes, please," said Ted. "It's very quiet in here."

"It always is at lunchtime. It gets busy at the weekend though. I've thought of the place where my relations live. Canvey Island."

"Really, now that's a coincidence. That's where we were stationed in the war."

The barmaid looked puzzled. "The war?"

"Yes, the second world war."

"What were you doing there?"

"Shooting down the enemy planes."

"What in Canvey Island?"

"Yes, as they flew across from Germany."

"Germany! That seems strange. How many did you get?"

"Oh I can't remember now. It's such a long time ago."

"The next time it'll be nuclear."

"That's hope there isn't a next time then."

Dad and Ted enjoyed another hour reminiscing over the war years. Ted had a third pint but dad refrained. He'd enjoyed the two but thought that sufficient. He didn't want to give mum the impression he couldn't be trusted.


"So did you have a good time?" said mum when they returned home.

"Eeeeeee. Eeeeeee."

Dad gave mum a big hug and kissed her on the cheek.

"Oh I am pleased Stan," said mum. "That's just what you needed. What did you think of the pub Ted?"

"Not a lot, but it did a good pint of Guinness."

"Were there many in there?"

"No, just us and the barmaid. She was friendly. She's got relations in Canvey Island."

"Perhaps Nick will be able to persuade you to go to the pub?" said mum.

Dad didn't look too sure about that.

"Do you ever have a Guinness at home Stan?" asked Ted.

Mum cringed. Now why had Ted asked that? Having a drink at home wasn't on the agenda because of dad's unpredictability. It hadn't been for years.

"Eeeeeee. Eeeeeee."

"You don't enjoy a drink at home?" said Ted.

Dad nodded in agreement and mum sighed with relief.

"No, it never tastes the same," said Ted.

"Are you staying for dinner?" asked mum.

"You bet I am. I wouldn't miss your home cooking."

"Actually it's fish and chips tonight. We've got a good local shop."

"That's even better then."

Dad smiled happy in the knowledge that Ted would be staying for dinner. He passed him the National Geographic to read while they waited.

"I think that's taking a good time too far Stan," said Ted. "I'm happy with the tele."

"Eeeeeee. Eeeeeee."

"Yes, the sooner you get back to the Ring Magazine the better."

# TWENTY SIX

Mum, Joyce, Iris and David were disputing the year of the long hot summer. There were two votes for nineteen seventy five and two for seventy six. They called on Nick to adjudicate.

"They were both scorchers," he said.

"No, they weren't," said mum. "We didn't have two consecutive hot years."

"No, he might be right," said Joyce. "That does ring a bell."

"Well I'm still going for seventy six," said David.

"So am I," said mum.

They were joined by Joanna and Lyn who were immediately press ganged into giving their considered opinion.

"Definitely seventy five," said Joanna. "I remember how uncomfortable dad found it."

"Yes," said mum. "Stan found it uncomfortable but in seventy six."

"I think it was seventy six as well," said Lyn. "I'd just changed schools."

"You changed schools in seventy five," said Iris.

"Well whatever year it happened to be," said mum. "Dad didn't enjoy the heat. Even before the stroke he wasn't one for sitting in the sun."

"What about when we used to go to Chalkwell for the day?" said Joanna.

"He'd sit in the shade with a hankie on his head."

"I don't remember that," said Nick. "My dad with a hankie

on his head? Ex army boxing champ Stan Wisbey?"

"Well it's true," said mum. "He enjoyed swimming in the sea but wouldn't sunbath."

"It was certainly convenient getting the train from Leyton?" said Joanna. "Door to door in under the hour. You couldn't do that nowadays."

"Where is Chalkwell?" asked Iris.

"Next door to Southend," said mum.

Iris shook her head. The name didn't ring a bell. But she did have a memory of Southend.

"I remember going to Southend with Sue to see Alan Price. Not really my cup of tea."

"Did you," said Nick. "Well that's a coincidence. Mum, can you remember dad's favourite record?"

"Favourite record? I didn't know dad had a favourite."

"Yes, he did. One particular song appealed to him. I'm talking about a pop tune. There's a clue in Alan Price."

"I remember," said Joanna, "Simon Smith and the Amazing Dancing Bear."

"That's right," said Nick.

"I do vaguely remember now," said mum. "But I wonder why that song?"

"I've no idea," said Nick. "You think of all the pop tunes there's been over the years. All the Beatles hits for a start. But dad always recognised that one particular song. It always brought a smile to his face. He'd sort of hum along with it."

"Well it was catchy," said Joanna.

"No, more than a hundred others," said Nick.

"Oh no, the Amazing Dancing Bear was different. More of a novelty tune. I think we bought him the single for his birthday."

"In that case then we should have played it at the funeral. That would have been a first."

There were smiles as they imagined the congregation's reaction to Alan Price's classic reverberating round the chapel.

# 1984

Mum had spent the weekend with Nick and Nicole. While there she'd had a surprise seventieth birthday meal with her brothers at an Italian restaurant. The break had done her the power of good and she'd returned to Norwich invigorated. Dad, meanwhile, had had a weekend like any other. Most of the time sat in the armchair staring into space, reading or watching the tele. He hadn't fancied a walk or going round Joanna's. Instead she'd called in regularly to check up and provide him with meals and drinks. And that was about it. So when mum returned full of the joys of spring it put dad's back up. He wasn't interested in her news about the brother-in-laws. Not even the surprising divulgence that Ralph and Joan had enquired about coming up for Christmas.

"And I've got some more news," she said.

Dad feigned interest.

"Nick and Nicole are looking after a Nigerian girl until the end of the year."

"Eeeeeee. Eeeeeee."

"Her father's friendly with the head teacher at Nicole's school."

"Eeeeeee. Eeeeeee."

"She's three years old."

"Eeeeeee. Eeeeeee."

"That's all I know Stan."

"Eeeeeee. Eeeeeee."

"Actually she was born in London but her parents are Nigerian. You'll meet her when they next visit. Shall I put the tele on for the news?"

Dad nodded, that sounded a good idea. Especially as the article in the National Geographic about Australia wasn't very interesting. Today he pined for the good old days of the Ring Magazine. Unfortunately he'd lost touch with the boxing world and all its glamour.

The news lead story remained the same. The I.R.A bomb blast at the Grand Hotel in Brighton where the Tory Party were holding their conference. Two had been killed and many injured. The Prime Minister, Margaret Thatcher, had narrowly escaped injury.

"I actually feel sorry for her," said mum. "I didn't think that day would ever come. It's just awful."

She expected dad to start laughing, as he often did when presented with loss of life. But on this occasion he didn't. Indeed he couldn't have been more sympathetic.

"Eeeeeee. Eeeeeee."

"You feel sorry for her as well?"

Dad nodded, but then anger took over and he stuck two fingers up at the screen. Then he faked to shoot the culprits.

"Eeeeeee. Eeeeeee."

"I know," said mum. It's the I.R.A."

"Eeeeeee. Eeeeeee."

"What hang them?"

"Eeeeeee. Eeeeeee."

"Would that make any difference?"

"Eeeeeee. Eeeeeee."

Dad didn't care if it did or didn't. He wanted them hung.

They watched the rest of the news in silence while mum drummed up the courage to ask dad if he minded going round Joanna's for dinner – seeing as they'd been invited. She realized the idea might not go down well. She couldn't remember the last time he'd visited his daughter. Although to be fair she'd given up asking. But on this occasion, returning from London revived, she felt determined to pursue her powers of persuasion.

"Now don't shout at me Stan, but Joanna's invited us round for dinner tonight."

"Eeeeeee. Eeeeeee."

Dad shouted at mum. That made no sense whatsoever. Why couldn't she cook him a meal seeing as she'd been away enjoying herself? Was that too much to ask? He had no wish to visit Joanna's. Yes, he enjoyed seeing his daughter and family but in his own surroundings where he felt comfortable. She should know that by now.

"Oh Stan, why do you have to make such a fuss?"

"Eeeeeee. Eeeeeee."

"Can't you make the effort just this once?"

"Eeeeeee. Eeeeeee."

"Okay, stop shouting. I've got the message."

Now mum had to decide whether to go on her own or stay with dad. Normally leaving him didn't create a problem but this time because she had been away she thought it best to forgo dinner with her daughter. She looked forlorn.

"Eeeeeee. Eeeeeee."

"I said stop shouting. We'll have dinner here then. Although I don't know what we've got in the fridge. It might have to be fish and chips."

Dad thought that an excellent idea and gave the thumbs up.

"You want fish and chips?"

"Eeeeeee. Eeeeeee."

"Well let's hope they're open today."

"Eeeeeee. Eeeeeee."

"I don't know. They might not open on a Monday."

Dad checked his magnetic calendar to confirm it was Monday. So would the fish and chip shop be open? He couldn't think of a reason why not. He'd better offer to walk down there himself in case her intentions were less than honourable.

"Eeeeeee. Eeeeeee."

"You'll go and get it? Okay Stan, that isn't a problem. The exercise will do you good."

"Eeeeeee. Eeeeeee."

"The usual time, six thirty."

"Eeeeeee. Eeeeeee."

"Stan, it's always that time. I'd better phone Joanna and tell her not to expect us."

"Eeeeeee. Eeeeeee."

"What is it Stan?"

"Eeeeeee. Eeeeeee"

"You've had your lunch."

"Eeeeeee. Eeeeeee."

"Ravioli. It's always Ravioli."

"Eeeeeee. Eeeeeee."

"You like Ravioli."

"Eeeeee. Eeeeee."

"A cup of tea? I'll make you one after I've phoned Joanna."

Mum went off and dad picked up the National Geographic again. Perhaps Australia would be more interesting the second time around. Then it dawned on him what mum had said about Ralph and Joan visiting over Christmas. Or had he been mistaken? They'd never been up at Christmas before. Or perhaps they had but he'd forgotten? When mum returned he'd have a word.

"Eeceeee. Eeeeeee."

"What do you mean Stan?"

"Eeeeeee. Eeeeeee."

"Joanna?"

"Eeeeeee. Eeeeeee."

"Fish and Chips?"

"Eeeeeee. Eeceeee."

"Nick?"

"Eeeeeee. Eeeeeee."

"Oh I know what you're going on about. Ralph and Joan coming up over Christmas. I thought you hadn't taken that in."

"Eeeeeee. Eeeeeee."

"They'd like to stay for a couple of nights."

"Eeeeeee. Eeeeeee."

"Where would they sleep? Well in my bedroom and I'd share with you."

"Eeeeeee. Eeeeeee."

"It's only for two nights Stan."

"Eeeeeee. Eeeeee."

"Oh, don't be like that."

The phone rang and an exasperated mum went to answer it while an equally exasperated dad sighed and picked up the National Geographic again. They'd continue the conversation when she returned.

"Guess what?" said mum on her return.

"Eeeeeee. Eeeeeee."

"That was Ralph. They won't be coming up for Christmas after all. They've had a better offer from their daughter Carol up in Northumberland."

Dad tried to conceal his pleasure.

"Eeeeeee. Eeeeeee."

"Yes, you look disappointed Stan. But anyway I said they'd be welcome in the New Year."

"Eeeeeee. Eeeeeee."

"No, they'll probably just come for the day. Is that okay?"

"Eeeeeee. Eeeeeee."

"I said you had a bottle of Southern Comfort waiting."

"Eeeeeee. Eeeeeee."

"It's a joke Stan. When did you last have a bottle of Southern Comfort in the house?"

"Eeeeeee. Eeeeeee."

"Exactly."

The phone rang again.

"Now who is it?" said mum.

She went out again and dad closed his eyes. He'd return to the National Geographic tomorrow.

"That was Nick," said mum. "Checking up I got home okay. He'll probably be coming up at the weekend with Abiodun. That's the name of the three year old they're looking after."

"Eeeeeee. Eeeeeee."

"Stan, I told you. Nick and Nicole are looking after a Nigerian girl until the end of the term."

But dad had forgotten that conversation. He shook his head in puzzlement.

"I'll make you that cup of tea Stan."

Dad nodded. He could do with a cuppa. He closed his eyes while he waited.

"Here you are Stan," said mum. "I think I'll pop round Joanna's this afternoon as we're not going for dinner. Is that okay?"

"Eeeeeee. Eeeeeee."

"You won't go out until I get back, will you?"

Dad nodded again.

"Cheerio."

"Eeeeeee. Eeeeeee."

"What is it now Stan?"

Dad pointed to his cheek.

"I don't think you deserve a kiss."

"Eeeeeee. Eeeeeee."

"Okay then, but try not to shout so much."

He held up his hand in apology as she walked across and planted not the most affectionate of kisses on his cheek. But it seemed to satisfy him and he smiled as she left for Joanna's.

When dad woke from his snooze he decided he would go for a walk. A reconnaissance trip to the fish shop. Then if mum returned with negative news regarding its opening hours he'd know the truth. Granted he didn't normally venture out when mum wasn't there but he'd be okay As long as he remembered to take the piece of paper with his address on it and, more importantly, to lock up.

He made his way up Cadge Road trying to remember whether he'd locked up. He couldn't be sure but he wouldn't be out long so it didn't really matter. But he had remembered to bring the piece of paper with his name and address on it. So far so good, he thought as he reached the crossroads.

But a few minutes later it all went horribly wrong. He reached the bottom of the road and couldn't decide whether to turn left or right. Nothing looked familiar. He couldn't believe it, the times he'd walked this way since the move. Oh dear, he had to reach home before mum returned or he'd be trouble. But no, he mustn't panic. Give it a few minutes then if need be knock on a door and show the occupier the piece of paper.

He stood at the junction contemplating which way to continue. He hadn't a clue. It was the youth club in front of him that threw him. Where had that sprung from? It definitely wasn't there on his last walk. Perhaps he'd taken a wrong turning. Oh dear, he'd have to seek help.

At the third door he knocked on he got a reply. But unfortunately the very elderly lady immediately phoned the police for assistance.

Dad hadn't considered that possibility. He assumed they'd point him in the right direction or accompany him until he recognised his surroundings.

She didn't invite him in, which was fair enough, but provided him with a stool, the Mirror newspaper, which he'd never read in his life, and a glass of orange. Then she informed him the police would be there within ten minutes. Dad nodded, grateful for her assistance. Now if only he could fathom out which way to continue before they arrived. That would save such a lot of bother.

The young policeman who arrived couldn't have been more helpful. He checked dad's piece of paper, spoke sympathetically then helped him into the back of the car. As they set off dad realized the reason for his confusion. He should have turned off Cadge road earlier. Oh dear, never mind. We all make mistakes.

Within a couple of minutes they were drawing up outside the bungalow – unfortunately just as mum appeared from around the corner. Dad's face dropped.

"If I'm not mistaken I would say that's Mrs. Wisbey," said the policeman observing the groan from dad and the shock on mum's face.

"Eeeeeee. Eeeeeee."

"I thought so. Yes, looks like you're in trouble. Well good luck."

"Eeeeeee. Eeeeeee."

"I'll put in a good word for you."

"Eeeeeee. Eeeeeee."

"All part of the service Mr. Wisbey."

# TWENTY SEVEN

The grandchildren were having a heated discussion about the talents, or otherwise, of Phil Collins. Opinions couldn't have been more divided. In the right-hand corner, and number one fan, Timothy pronounced his latest offering 'Another Day in Paradise' a masterpiece unlikely to be bettered in modern times. While in the left-hand corner his two younger brothers were equally adamant the new release was simply wishy-washy self-indulgent rubbish.

"Have you listened to M.C. Hammer?" enquired Duncan. "Now that's what you call music."

"You must be joking," said Timothy.

"I think Mariah Carey tops both of them," said William. "She's got a great voice."

"Yes, better than Phil Collins anyway," said Duncan.

"Did you know Phil Collins was the only Live Aid artist to appear in both the U.K and the States," declared an exuberant Timothy. "Doesn't that tell you something?"

"Yes, he likes his gimmicks," said Duncan.

"That's pulling power," said Timothy.

"That's pretentiousness," said William.

And so the banter went on until mum came through to check on the raised voices.

"Sorry," said Timothy. "Are we making a lot of noise?"

"Not compared to your granddad at his brother's funeral."

"What do you think of Phil Collins?" asked Duncan, hoping for a negative response.

Mum looked puzzled. "I don't think I've heard of Phil Collins. Should I have done?"

"See," said William. "Nana hasn't heard of him."

Timothy looked concerned but wasn't giving up that easily. "What about the group Genesis. Have you heard of them?"

"Yes."

"Well Phil Collins used to sing with them."

"Oh I see, like Alan Price."

"Alan Price?"

"Yes, he sang with the Animals before going solo."

"I've heard of the Animals," said Duncan. "House of the Rising Sun."

"That's right," said mum.

"What did Alan Price sing?" asked William.

"His biggest hit was 'Simon Smith and the Amazing Dancing Bear'. Grandpa's favourite."

"I didn't know grandpa had a favourite song," said Timothy.

"No, I'd forgotten until Nick reminded me."

"But he couldn't sing it."

"I think he tried to hum it."

"When did grandpa have his stroke?" asked Duncan.

"Nineteen sixty three. Your mum was thirteen. He survived twenty eight years. That's the surprising thing. It's a pity all you boys can remember is Eeeeeee."

"He could say coffee and tea."

"That's true."

"He made me laugh sometimes," said Duncan.

"Did he?" said mum, surprised.

"Yes, when he boxed with us. He used to take guard and then move his hands in slow motion as though preparing to punch us in the stomach. But then he'd suddenly slap us around the face. We fell for it every time."

"Nick used to fall for the same trick. And that's going back to his teenage days before grandpa had his stroke."

"Did you see grandpa box?" asked Tim.

"No, it never worked out. Not that I really wanted to. See my Stan get hurt?"

"Mum said he had a good record."

"He did."

She thought it best to change the subject before somebody brought up the vexed question of the authenticity of his unbeaten record.

"I'm really glad you're all here today. Grandpa would have appreciated it."

Her three grandchildren smiled respectfully, looked at each other and nodded. It had been quite a day for all of them.

# 1985

While mum spent a week with her sister Iris in Middlesbrough dad spent a week's respite in St Andrews hospital. Nick would never forget that first sighting when he visited on the day of the fete. Dear dad sitting alone in the gardens. Akin to being put out to graze. Surrounded by fete activity, sideshows, raffles, cup cakes and the local celebrity drumming up support for the hospital charity. But impervious to it all, looking sad and vulnerable. Rooted to the spot. He'd have been much happier inside away from the hustle and bustle. So why couldn't they have let him be? Well, misguidedly the staff assumed he'd appreciate the hot sunny weather and no amount of arguing would convince them otherwise. But he didn't concede without a fight. Not ex army boxing champ Captain Stan Wisbey.

"Hello dad," said Nick. "How are you?"

Dad looked surprised at seeing Nick.

"Eeeeeee. Eeeeeee."

"Did you forget I was coming?"

"Eeeeeee. Eeeeeee."

"It's only a two hour drive."

"Eeeeeee. Eeeeeee."

"No, I'm going straight back. We've got friends coming round this evening."

"Eeeeeee. Eeeeeee."

"Nicole. Yes, she's okay. Are they looking after you?"

Dad looked agitated and firmly shook Nick's hand.

"Eeeeeee. Eeeeeee."

"What is it dad?"

"Eeeeeee. Eeeeeee."

"I don't know what you mean."

"Eeeeeee. Eeeeeee"

Dad pointed inside the hospital and then clenched his fist and pretended to punch somebody.

"Somebody you don't like?"

Dad shook his head and pointed to one of the staff taking round refreshments.

"Eeeeeee. Eeeeeee."

"You want me to have a word with him."

"Eeeeeee. Eeeeeee."

"Okay, in a minute."

But dad couldn't wait that long.

"Eeeeeee. Eeeeeee."

"Alright dad, I'll go over there now."

The nurse couldn't have been more sympathetic to dad's condition but the fact remained he had bruised the orderly's wrist when losing his temper. Why? She'd suggested he took advantage of the sunny weather and sat outside. It would do him good, she preached in a patronising manner. She continually repeated this assertion until dad lost his cool and slammed the wardrobe door against her wrist.

Because of the incident she'd gone off duty – although hopefully a bruising would be the limit of her misfortune. Nick apologised profusely and the nurse assured him that dad had shown great remorse once he realized the injury he'd caused. But notwithstanding that the incident would have to be reported in the day book. Nick nodded. Dear oh dear, poor old dad – and the orderly of course.

"Eeeeeee. Eeeeeee."

"Yes, he told me," said Nick.

Dad shrugged his shoulders and looked guilty. Like a child after they'd been found out.

"She'll be alright dad. But you don't know your own strength. You must be careful."

Dad nodded then looked around at everybody enjoying themselves and angrily stuck two fingers up. Then he pointed indoors.

"You didn't want to come outside but she said you had to?"

"Eeeeeee. Eeeeeee."

"I suppose they thought it'd be good for you sitting in the sun."

"Eeeeeee. Eeeeeee."

"You would have preferred watching the television. Do you want to go in now?"

"Eeeeeee. Eeeeeee."

Dad nodded and the pair of them made their way inside the imposing building.

Once inside his room dad relaxed. He took off his shoes sat on the bed and gestured to Nick to feel his face and comment on the shave he'd had.

"Yes, that's not bad at all. I couldn't have done better myself."

"Eeeeeee. Eeeeeee."

"Shall I give the razor a clean?"

Dad nodded and Nick took the head apart and emptied its contents into the waste bin.

"I don't think this has been done for some time. Look at all that gunge."

Dad smiled. No, it probably hadn't. In fact he couldn't remember the last time.

"I'm just the same with my razor. It's so fiddly cleaning it."

"Eeeeeee. Eeeeeee."

"That should keep it going for another year. You never miss a shave, do you?"

Dad looked puzzled. Of course he didn't. Shaving was something you did no matter how depressed you might feel. You had to keep up your appearance.

"Sometimes at the weekend I might miss a day," said Nick. "I can't be bothered."

"Eeeeeee. Eeeeeee."

Dad took umbrage with that lazy attitude and Nick thought it best to retract a degree or two.

"It's not very often I do that though. I try and make the effort."

243

"Eeeeeee. Eeeeeee."

"What do you mean?"

Dad moved his finger across his top lip.

"You used to have a moustache?"

"Eeeeeee. Eeeeeee."

"When you were in the army?"

"Eeeeeee. Eeeeeee."

"Did you have it when you got married?"

"Eeeeeee. Eeeeeee."

"That's right. I've seen a photograph of you and mum coming out of the church. A pencil moustache, wasn't it?"

"Eeeeeee. Eeeeeee."

"Not like my one."

"Eeeeeee. Eeeeeee."

"I've had mine for ten years now. About time I got rid of it. Did you ever have a beard?"

"Eeeeeee. Eeeeeee."

"No, neither have I. You don't see many beards nowadays."

The door opened and in walked a nurse with the tea trolley. She looked wary of dad, made a quick inspection of the wardrobe door, and tutted.

"Would you like a cup of tea?" she asked.

"Yes, please. What about you dad?"

Dad nodded sheepishly and they watched as she poured two cups.

"It's a nice day for a fete," said Nick.

"If you like fetes I suppose it is," said the nurse.

"You don't like them?"

"I'd much rather be at home on the sun bed. Do you want a piece of fruit cake?"

"Yes, please. What about you dad?"

Dad nodded and she handed out one plate with two portions of fruit cake.

"What time do you finish?" enquired Nick.

"Too late for the sun bed."

"Oh well, there's always tomorrow."

"Have you seen the forecast?"

And with that she departed.

"What a bundle of laughs," said Nick.

Dad nodded but had a feeling her brusque attitude had something to do with his aggressiveness towards her work colleague. He'd have to accept from now on his stay wouldn't be as comfortable as prior to the incident.

"Look at the colour of that tea," said Nick. "Talk about weak. I can't drink that. It should be straightforward making a cup of tea."

Dad nodded and smiled.

"Do you remember Kit and Mary's tea?"

"Eeeeeee. Eeeeeee."

"Now that was the strongest in the world. You could stand a digestive up in it."

"Eeeeeee. Eeeeeec."

"Have I seen them lately? No, I'm hoping to bring them up to see you sometime."

"Eeeeeee. Eeeeeee."

"No, just for the day dad. Now don't start worrying about where they're going to sleep."

Dad smiled again but then looked agitated.

"Eeeeeee. Eeeeeee."

"When do you go home? Wednesday, that's another four days."

"Eeeeeee. Eeeeeee."

"You can't wait. No, there's no place like home."

"Eeeeeee. Eeeeeee."

"Why are you in here?

"Eeeeeee. Eeeeeee."

"Because mum's visiting Iris."

"Eeeeeee. Eeeeeee."

"She goes up every year."

"Eeeeeee. Eeeeeee."

"Oh dad it's only for one week in the year."

"Eeeeeee. Eeeeeee."

"Do you remember visiting Iris and the family when we were on holiday in Saltburn?

245

Dad shook his head.

"I think we stayed at a B & B on the front called Stanley House. You don't remember?"

"Eeeeeee. Eeeeeee."

"Well what about that place in Weymouth? The last holiday we had together in nineteen sixty two."

Dad shook his head again.

"That awful Mrs Cuthbert who owned the bed and breakfast."

"Eeeeeee. Eeeeeee."

"You don't remember her stupid dog. It used to nick our sausages at breakfast."

"Eeeeeee. Eeeeeee."

"You hit her."

"Eeeeeee. Eeeeeee."

"No, not Mrs Cuthbert the dog."

"Eeeeeee. Eeeeeee."

"You swatted it with the paper."

"Eeeeeee. Eeeeeee."

"No, no harm done."

"Eeeeeee. Eeeeeee."

"You still don't remember. Well do you remember seeing Morcambe & Wise and Matt Monroe?"

"Eeeeeee. Eeeeeee."

"Then you went to the cinema to see El Cid and saw a bloke in a flat hat in one of the crowd scenes."

Dad stared in disbelief.

"You did dad. Well that's what you said. You wanted us to go along the next day to see for ourselves."

"Eeeeeee. Eeeeeee."

"You don't remember the film?"

"Eeeeeee. Eeeeeee."

They were interrupted by the nurse again.

"I take it you've finished," she said.

Neither of them had made much of an attempt with the tea and were still munching their way through the fruit cake.

"Not quite," said Nick.

The nurse looked most indignant. "In that case I'll be back in five minutes."

"That'll be fine," said Nick.

They finished off the cake in double quick time just in case she returned early.

"Well at least it was better than the tea," said Nick.

"Eeeeeee. Eeeeeee."

"What's the food like in here?"

Dad shrugged his shoulders. He wasn't a fussy eater and ate most things presented.

"I bet you don't get ravioli for lunch?"

"Eeeeeee. Eeeeeee."

"No, I thought not. That'd be too good to be true."

"Eeeeeee. Eeeeeee."

"What do you mean dad?"

"Eeeeeee. Eeeeeee."

"You get fed up having that everyday at home. Well does mum know?"

"Eeeeeee. Eeeeeee."

"I know what you mean. It probably wouldn't make any difference."

"Eeeeeee. Eeeeeee."

"Something you had for dinner?"

"Eeeeeee. Eeeeeee."

"One of your favourites. Liver and Bacon?"

"Eeeeeee. Eeeeeee."

"Did it compare with mum's?"

Dad nodded and gave the thumbs up just as the nurse returned.

"Have you finished?" she asked.

"Yes, we've had enough thank you. The fruit cake was really nice."

"I'm pleased about that."

And with that she collected the cups and disappeared.

"I bet she'll be back. She'll find some excuse. It could be raffle tickets. I'm surprised nobody's tried to flog us any yet."

Dad smiled but looked tired. He motioned to Nick he'd like to take a nap. He passed him the National Geographic.

"Okay Dad, I'll have a read."

It didn't take long for dad to start snoring. Nick put down the magazine and looked at his father. He smiled. He felt proud of him. No, of course he shouldn't have lost his temper. But then his brain wasn't functioning properly. You had to make allowances. All those years he'd suffered. God, what must it be like? And how many more years would there be?

The door opened and in walked the nurse again. That woke dad up.

"Would you like any raffle tickets?" she enquired, this time in a more benevolent tone."

"No, thank you," said Nick.

But dad wasn't so dismissive. "Eeeeeee. Eeeeeee."

"You want me to buy some?"

Dad nodded. That was the least he could do to attempt to repair the damage done by his assault on the staff.

"How much are they?"

"Twenty pence each or five, sorry, six for a pound."

"I'll have a pound's worth then."

"Thank you."

"What's the first prize?"

"A 14 inch black and white television."

"That's the first prize?"

"Yes."

Dad and Nick looked at each other but said nothing. This was one of those occasions when Nick knew exactly what dad was thinking. *A 14 inch black and white television! You must be joking?*

"I can't remember what the other prizes are," she said.

"I'm sure they're all worthwhile," said Nick.

"Well, whether they're worthwhile or not they're all for a good cause. The refurbishment of the hospital."

Nick gave her a pound and she departed.

"Now don't lose the tickets," said Nick.

Dad looked at Nick and shrugged his shoulders. What would it matter if he lost the tickets?

"Yes, you're right dad. It wouldn't matter at all."

# TWENTY EIGHT

Encouraged by her sisters mum had produced a box of family photographs. Some dated back to the turn of the century. Great grandparents posing, as they did in Victorian times, seated and wearing their Sunday best apparel with an assortment of stern faces, moustaches and bonnets. What marvellous family memories they provided. Mum and dad strolling along the sea front at Ryde in the Isle of Wight in nineteen thirty eight looking the quintessential courting couple. What style and elegance.

"You always looked great in a hat Joan," said Joyce.

"Yes, not many people could carry it off like you," said Iris.

"Well I did enjoy wearing one – especially on big occasions."

"Do you remember what colour it was?"

"Now you're asking. Isle of Wight nineteen thirty eight? I would say navy blue."

"Doesn't Stan look smart in his three piece," said Joyce.

"Yes, its funny how times change. Could you imagine anybody today strolling along the sea front in a three piece suit, pocket handkerchief, tie and trilby."

"Not unless they were going to the Ritz," said Iris.

"We certainly weren't going anywhere posh like that. Just having a midday promenade stroll. You notice Stan's carrying the box camera."

"I have. That was quite a luxury in the thirties."

"I think we'd just bought it. Well actually it was Stan's surprise. He never did let on how much it cost."

"I should think not. That's not the idea of a surprise."

"No, but I couldn't help being curious. They were probably more expensive than they are today. You know, compared to the cost of living."

"It probably cost him a week's wages," said Joyce.

"I was worth it," said mum smiling.

"And you're wearing sunglasses. Another luxury in those days?"

"Yes, they look quite smart, don't they? Stan bought those as well."

"Another week's wages," said Iris. "You were a lucky girl."

"I know. We had a lovely time. We were so lucky with the weather. That's when we started making wedding plans."

Mum smiled. She thought of all the good times they'd had together. She should be thankful for those years and not dwell on the post stroke era.

"Am I right in thinking there are no photos of Stan taken after his stroke?" said Joyce.

"Yes, I've never been able to look at a photo of him after sixty three. I just found it so upsetting."

"But you wouldn't know by looking at the photo that Stan had had a stroke."

"No, but I'd know."

"Did Stan mind having his photo taken?"

"No, it never bothered him. Nick's got one taken in the garden at Nottingham road. He looks well but I hate it. It doesn't help that he's wearing a baggy orange cardigan that's seen better days. Nick hides the photo if I'm visiting."

"I remember that cardigan," said Iris.

"Didn't he have a dark green one as well?" asked Joyce.

"Yes, that's still in his wardrobe. He wore it most days towards the end. I'll have to think of what to do with his clothes."

"Oh you've got plenty of time for that."

"I suppose so but I'd rather get it done now. I know Nick wants his Crombie overcoat."

"That'll be too big for him," said Iris.

"That's what I said but he's promised to put on a stone,"

"A stone! He'll need to put on more than that."

# 1986

Mum sat down in her chair smiling. She felt tired but relaxed. Dad had enjoyed a good day. He'd even been out for a walk – his first for ages. She had worried he wouldn't remember the location of the pillar box but he'd returned without the letter. Hopefully he hadn't discarded it elsewhere. Although because she'd taken the precaution of giving him the Readers Digest Competition reply (The No envelope) to post it wouldn't matter if it went astray. They'd cope without the £200,000.

Nick had been up for the weekend with Abiodun, the Nigerian girl him and Nicole used to look after. She got on well with the grandchildren. They'd all been round and made a fuss of her. Mum smiled when she recalled the episode of Abiodun asking dad whether he preferred coffee or tea. "So what does Uncle Stan want?" she asked when Abiodun came running into the kitchen. "Eeeeeee, Eeeeeee," she replied. Everybody laughed. Although Abiodun, being only four, looked perplexed at the joviality she'd caused.

Dad had just gone to bed – and amazingly still on good form. Hopefully he'd have a peaceful night. Lately he hadn't disturbed mum quite so often. Indeed there'd been one particular night when he hadn't interrupted her sleep at all. Mum had marked the date on the calendar in red biro. But she had a feeling it wouldn't last. She picked up the paper to finish the crossword she'd been unable to finish with her morning coffee. Then the phone rang.

"Hello," said mum. "Who is it? Mrs Walker? What Mrs Walker from Henry Taylor's? How are you? It's been such a long time."

She ended up speaking to her old work colleague for half an hour. She learnt more about her and her family than she ever did when they worked together. She caught up on all the latest men's outfitters gossip. How the school uniforms were selling or otherwise. How she'd been sorely missed. How useless her replacement was – and if it was down to her she'd be sacked immediately.

Mum smiled as she put down the phone. She'd enjoyed the chat and at Mrs Walkers insistence promised to call in when she next visited London. Unfortunately as she sat down to complete the crossword dad walked in.

"What is it Stan?"

Her aggressive tone of voice betraying the fact the interruption annoyed her. Dad quickly picked up on it.

"Eeeeeee. Eeeeeee."

"Sorry, I didn't mean to shout."

"Eeeeeee. Eeeeeee."

"On the phone? Mrs Walker. I worked with her at Henry Taylor's."

Dad nodded and crooked two fingers as though to shoot somebody.

"What, Mrs Walker?"

"Eeeeeee. Eeeeeee."

"What do you mean?"

"Eeeeeee. Eeeeeee."

"I don't understand Stan."

"Eeeeeee. Eeeeeee."

"I said I'd like to see her shot? Stan, I've never said anything of the sort."

"Eeeeeee. Eeeeeee."

"Why would I say that?"

"Eeeeeee. Eeeeeee."

"Yes, I used to talk about her but we got on okay. There wasn't a problem."

"Eeeeeee. Eeeeeee."

"So you say but I don't remember saying that."

"Eeeeeee. Eeeeeee."

"Okay Stan, I'll take your word for it."

"Eeeeeee. Eeeeeee."

"Yes, I'll see you in the morning."

But dad had other plans. "Coffee," he requested in his inimitable style.

Mum looked speechless. Dad asking for a second coffee hadn't been on the cards. He never asked for a coffee after retiring for the night.

"You had your coffee an hour ago."

"Eeeeeee. Eeeeeee."

"You want another one?"

Dad nodded and mum sighed. She had no wish to start a second coffee precedent. But then she relented. She took into consideration dad's demeanour during the day. Yes, on this occasion he deserved a second coffee.

"Well okay Stan, just this once. But I don't want you getting in the habit of expecting a coffee this late. It'll keep you awake at night."

As mum got up to make the coffee she realized the absurdity of the comment. Dad didn't need a coffee to continuously interrupt mum's sleep pattern.

When she returned with dad's coffee, and a couple of ginger nuts, she found him reading her paper. That irked her. She needed to finish the crossword.

"Here you are Stan. Could I have the paper please?"

Dad looked at mum in surprise. Wasn't he allowed to read the paper?

"Eeeeeee. Eeeeeee."

"I want to finish the crossword."

"Eeeeeee. Eeeeeee."

"Well can I have the page with the crossword in then?"

Dad begrudgingly handed mum the paper and waited for her to sort out the crossword page and hand the remainder back. It seemed to take her an age.

"Eeeeeee. Eeeeeee."

"I'm being as quick as I can."

"Eeeeeee. Eeeeeee."

"Don't snatch."

"Eeeeeee. Eeeeeee."

"Yes, you did."

Ten minutes later mum still hadn't completed the crossword and dad hadn't made a start on the coffee – although the ginger nuts had been disposed of. He seemed quite content to wile away the time reading the paper. That was unusual because these days dad didn't bother about the news.

"You haven't started your coffee Stan."

"Eeeeeee. Eeeeeee."

"It's too hot! Oh come off it."

Dad took exception at mum's disbelieving attitude and handed her the cup to check for herself. Mum took a sip, shook her head and handed the cup back.

"That's not hot Stan."

"Eeeeeee. Eeeeeee."

But Dad wasn't about to be pressurised into drinking the coffee. He put down the cup and nonchalantly picked up the paper again.

Ten minutes later, as mum completed the crossword, dad resumed his coffee.

"Those clues were difficult today. Is that okay now Stan?" she enquired.

"Eeeeeee. Eeeeeee."

"That's good. Do you see how late it is? Eleven fifteen. You're usually asleep by now. Don't you feel tired?"

Dad shook his head. He knew what she was intimating but he'd take his time. He felt quite relaxed reading the paper. It made a pleasant change from the National Geographic. Some days he found that heavy going. You could have too much wildlife served up on a plate. A boxing story caught his eye. The forthcoming title fight between the Champion Trevor Berbick and the cocky upstart Mike Tyson. It reminded him of Cassius Clay's title fight against the champion Sonny Liston all those years ago. Nobody had given Cassius a chance but against all the odds he'd knocked the supposedly invincible Liston out. Perhaps history would repeat itself. If it did Mike Tyson would become the youngest ever heavyweight champion at the tender age of twenty. Dad smiled, his money would be on the challenger.

"Have you finished your coffee?" asked mum.

Dad nodded but continued reading.

"Do you think its time for bed now Stan?"

"Eeeeeee. Eeeeeee."

"It's eleven thirty"

"Eeeeeee. Eeeeeee."

"You don't feel tired. No, but you will in the morning."

"Eeeeeee. Eeeeeee."

"What me? No, I'm not ready for bed yet."

Actually mum did feel tired but no way would she be retiring before dad. That hadn't happened since the stroke and tonight wouldn't be an exception.

By eleven forty five mum was finding it increasingly difficult to keep her eyes open. And what's more dad had noticed.

"Eeeeeee. Eeeeeee."

"No, I wasn't asleep Stan."

"Eeeeeee. Eeeeeee."

"Well you're mistaken. I don't feel particularly tired. I never go to bed before midnight."

She exaggerated a little in the hope that dad would call it a day. But unfortunately dad continued reading the paper.

Shortly afterwards mum could no longer delay the inevitable and dozed off. Soon she snored loudly. Dad found it amusing and started laughing aloud. This woke mum up.

"What are you laughing up?"

"Eeeeeee. Eeeeeee."

"I don't know what you mean."

Dad mimicked mum's snoring.

"I wasn't snoring Stan. I don't snore. You're the one who snores. You should hear yourself sometimes."

"Eeeeeee. Eeeeeee."

"You're going to be so tired in the morning. It's almost midnight."

But dad just shrugged his shoulders and returned to the paper. And mum not wanting to be caught snoring again picked up the National Geographic. That also made dad laugh.

"Eeeeeee. Eeeeeee."

"What are you laughing at now?"

"Eeeeeee. Eeeeeee."

"The National Geographic?"

"Eeeeeee. Eeeeeee."

"I read it sometimes."

"Eeeeeee. Eeeeeee."

"Yes, I do. Just because you haven't noticed doesn't mean I don't."

"Eeeeeee. Eeeeeee."

"I don't care what you think."

But if truth be told this was only the second time mum had picked up the magazine since Nick introduced it into the household five or six years ago. It just wasn't her cup of tea. She much preferred the Daily Mail, or rather, the Mail's quick crossword. That suited her perfectly over a morning cup of coffee and a biscuit. Although if, like today, she couldn't complete the crossword before midday it irked her.

"Eeeeeee. Eeeeeee."

At twelve fifteen Dad took pity on mum and handed her the paper in exchange for the magazine. He'd decided to retire for the night.

"Are you off to bed now?"

"Eeeeeee. Eeeeeee."

"Well I hope you have a good night Stan."

"Eeeeeee. Eeeeeee."

Dad got up and gave mum a kiss on the cheek.

"You've had a good day today."

"Eeeeeee. Eeeeeee."

"I can't remember the last time you went for a walk."

Dad nodded then put his hand to his mouth. Something had occurred to him.

"Eeeeeee. Eeeeeee."

"What is it Stan?"

Dad signalled to mum to stay put while he disappeared for a few minutes.

He returned holding the Readers Digest letter mum had given him to post that morning. He held up his hand in apology then handed it to mum. He waited for her negative reaction. But surprisingly mum just smiled.

"Oh that's okay Stan. It wasn't that important. Only the Readers Digest competition. Tomorrow will do. At least you got some exercise today."

"Eeeeeee. Eeeeeee."

"No, you don't have to go out tomorrow. I can post it when I go into the city."

"Eeeeeee. Eeeeeee."

"Stan, if you feel like going for a walk that's okay."

"Eeeeeee. Eeeeeee."

Now it irked Stan that mum hadn't given him an important letter to post. Could that be intentional because she didn't trust him? But then again she'd been proved right because he'd forgotten to post the unimportant letter. He'd actually stuffed it into his pocket on the way out and there it'd remained until a few minutes ago.

"What do you mean Stan?"

"Eeeeeee. Eeeeeee."

"Posting the letter?"

"Eeeeeee. Eeeeeee."

"That's the only one I had."

"Eeeeeee. Eeeeeee."

"That's not true. If there's a letter to post you can take it."

"Eeeeeee. Eeeeeee."

"I mean that Stan. Now you've had a good day today. We don't want to end it with an argument."

Dad nodded and held his hand up in apology.

"Eeeeeee. Eeeeeee."

"That's okay Stan. I'll see you in the morning."

This time dad went out without kissing mum. But then remembered he hadn't kissed her and returned and planted a noisy whopper on her cheek.

"Thank you," shrieked mum "That was a wet one."

Dad smiled and gave the thumbs up before crooking his fingers as though to shoot somebody.

"I didn't say that about Mrs Walker."

"Eeeeeee. Eeeeeee."

"Yes, goodnight Stan."

# TWENTY NINE

Over yet another cuppa Nick and Joanna were having a sombre discussion on whether dad had ever hit mum. They agreed he'd pushed her on more than one occasion but had he actually hit her. They tended to think not – but obviously mum would be the one to ask.

"Mum," said Joanna. "Did dad ever hit you?"

"Yes, just the once. He slapped me round the face. I'll tell you when."

"No, it doesn't matter now mum."

But mum had already gone to check in her dairy diary.

"That's a surprise," said Nick. "Perhaps she didn't mention it."

"No. I remember her having stitches in her hand after he caught it in the door. We spent a couple of hours up the hospital on a Saturday afternoon."

"Yes, then there's the time mum visited Iris and dad went into respite. He lost his temper because the orderly wanted him to sit outside. He slammed the wardrobe door against her wrist and she had to take some time off. Thankfully we never heard any more about it."

"Can you imagine if they'd taken it further?"

"But what could they have done? I mean dad couldn't have appeared in court. Or could he?"

"I don't know. It doesn't bear thinking about."

As they pondered the scenario of their dad appearing in court on an assault charge mum returned with her diary.

"I've found it," she said. "The third of December last year. I knew it wasn't that long ago."

"I don't remember that," said Joanna.

"Well I must have mentioned it. I'd had a bad night because of his interruptions and said something petty to get my own back. It didn't help the situation but it made me feel better. The slap came as a shock because he hadn't done that before. You could tell he regretted it straightaway. Poor old Stan, I didn't help matters sometimes."

"Mum you couldn't expect to say the right things all the time."

Mum smiled. She appreciated the children's support but there were still issues to be resolved.

"I know, but dad did deteriorate after going into the home. You can't get away from that."

"Yes, but he should have gone in earlier," said Joanna. "You couldn't cope with his behaviour."

"Well he was getting more and more unpredictable."

"So there wasn't another solution," said Nick.

Mum nodded. She felt tired. She looked forward to a good nights sleep. Give it another hour and hopefully everybody would have either departed or gone to bed.

"What about when you had to call the police?" said Joanna.

Mum shook her head reliving that occasion.

"Oh, that was awful. He looked really scary that day. I can still see his smirking face."

"So can I," said Joanna. "I thought the police handled it really well."

"They did," said mum. "I don't know what we'd have done without them. The doctor wasn't much help."

"No. Now who did he remind you of?"

"The steak and kidney on a Wednesday man," said Nick.

"Exactly."

# 1987

While dad got up full of the joys of spring mum felt terrible. She'd had one of those nights when he'd continuously interrupted her sleep pattern. Seeing him so chirpy just exasperated her. If she was suffering then why wasn't he? It certainly wouldn't take much for her to antagonize him. She took in his coffee and ginger nut prepared for battle.

"Did you sleep okay?" she asked sarcastically.

He smiled and gave the thumbs up. That exasperated her even more. How on earth could he say that with the constant waking up and barging into her bedroom? It didn't make sense.

"Don't you remember waking me up?"

"Eeeeeee. Eeeeeee."

"I can't believe that Stan. You must have come in my bedroom at least a dozen times."

Dad just shrugged his shoulders and held his hands up in apology. On another day mum might have accepted that and moved on – but not today.

"I feel awful," she said. "I hardly slept at all. I keep telling you the beds not wet but you don't believe me."

"Eeeeeee. Eeeeeee."

"Why don't you believe me Stan?"

"Eeeeeee. Eeeeeee."

"The bed's not wet."

Dad looked apologetic but unfortunately couldn't recall the previous night's escapade.

"The beds not wet," she reiterated.

"Eeeeeee. Eeeeeee."

"It never has been."

"Eeeeeee. Eeeeeee."

"It's just a feeling."

"Eeeeeee. Eeeeeee."

"Do you understand what I'm saying Stan?"

"Eeeeeee. Eeeeeee."

By now dad had had enough of mum's ranting.

"You don't have to shout Stan."

"Eeeeeee. Eeeeeee."

But dad felt quite entitled to shout in view of mum's aggressive attitude. Enough was enough.

"I said don't shout."

"Eeeeeee. Eeeeeee."

This time dad pointed aggressively at mum as well as shouting. Mum decided to back off. She'd succeeded in riling him but shouldn't push her luck further. She left him shouting and gesturing and went into the garden.

An hour later she'd relaxed sufficiently to return indoors. Spending time outside had been excellent therapy. Her well kept garden gave her many hours of pleasure. Particularly the beautiful silver coloured magnolia bush. Now she felt compassion for dad. She knew the wet feeling was simply a symptom of his stroke condition. Something he had no control over. She promised herself to be on her best behaviour for the rest of the day.

But when she tried the back door she found it locked. The same went for the front door. That didn't make sense – unless Stan had deliberately locked them. But why would he? She went round the bungalow peering in the windows but couldn't see him. She stooped to peer through the letterbox. She froze because there he stood, standing in the hallway, staring and pointing at her. To say he was sneering would have been an understatement. She'd never seen him looking quite so frightening. As though he'd finally taken leave of his senses and opted for the role of Jack Nicholson in the Shining. She felt quite intimidated by his appearance.

"Stan," she shouted. "Could you open the door please?"

"Eeeeeee. Eeeeeee."

"Come on Stan."

"Eeeeeee. Eeeeeee."

"I'm sorry if I made a fuss about your wet feeling. I know you can't help it."

"Eeeeeee. Eeeeeee."

"Could you open the door please?"

"Eeeeeee. Eeeeeee."

But dad didn't seem in a conciliatory mood. Indeed he stuck two fingers up. She stood up to consider her next move. She wouldn't do anything hasty. She'd return to the garden, find something else to prune and give dad time to cool down.

But when she tried the doors half an hour later they remained locked. She peered through the letterbox again. Dad stood in exactly the same position. Perhaps he'd been there all along. He sneered and pointed when he saw her.

"Could you open the door now Stan?"

"Eeeeeee Eeeeeee."

"Please Stan. You'll have to open it sometime."

"Eeeeeee. Eeeeeee."

"I said I'm sorry Stan."

"Eeeeeee. Eeeeeee."

"Come on Stan."

"Eeeeeee. Eeeeeee."

But dad seemed as determined as ever to teach her a lesson. Mum pondered her next move. She decided to phone Joanna. She had the spare key. Unfortunately that meant knocking on Mrs Bunn's door and asking to use her phone. An obvious giveaway that something must be amiss. But that couldn't be helped.

Fortunately Joanna had just returned from the city and promised to be round as quickly as possible. Mum thought she'd relay that information to dad in the hope it could be used as a bargaining tool. But dad didn't seem impressed by the revelation. Indeed he laughed sarcastically. As though to say, "Is that the best you can do? Seek the help of Joanna. It'll need more than that to get back inside the house."

So mum returned to the garden. But this time to sit on a deckchair and relax. Well as much as she could with dad locked up and the outcome unsure.

By the time Joanna arrived dad had been inside for almost two hours.

"Are you alright mum?" she asked.

"Well I'll be better when dad's unlocked the door."

"Has he ever done that before?"

"No, I'm afraid I annoyed him by going on about his wet feeling."

"You had another bad night?"

"Yes, I felt awful this morning and took it out on dad."

"Oh mum. Well let's see if he'll listen to me. I think that's better than using the spare key straightaway. You never know how that might affect him."

She peered through the letterbox but couldn't see dad.

"Dad," she shouted. "Could you open the door please?"

It was eerily quiet inside.

"Dad, can you hear me? Please open the door."

Suddenly he appeared in the hallway and pointed at her in a menacing manner.

"Eeeeeee. Eeeeeee."

"What's the matter dad?"

"Eeeeeee. Eeeeeee."

"Please open the door."

"Eeeeeee. Eeeeeee."

"I don't know what you mean dad. Open the door and we can talk about it."

"Eeeeeee. Eeeeeee."

"Mum didn't mean to shout at you."

"Eeeeeee. Eeeeeee."

But dad's resolve didn't appear to be weakening. Joanna decided to play her ace hand.

"I've got a spare key with me."

Dad laughed and mum and Joanna looked at each other.

"Are you thinking what I'm thinking?" said Joanna.

"Yes, he's put the safety chain on. He's actually thought of doing that. Well I never."

"That never occurred to me."

"Nor me."

They were proved right because when Joanna tried the key the door opened barely six inches.

"Eeeeeee. Eeeeeee."

"Very clever dad," said Joanna. "We'll have to call the police now."

"Eeeeeee. Eeeeeee."

But the threat didn't seem to deter dad and again he stuck two fingers up.

"Oh Joanna," said mum. "Should you have mentioned the police?"

"Well what else can we do?"

"What about the doctor?"

"I don't think they'll want to get involved."

"I'd rather try them first. Phoning the police seems a bit drastic."

"Well okay but I don't see what they can do if dad refuses to budge."

"Perhaps dad will listen to the doctor. Let's have one more go and then I'll knock at Mrs Bunn's again."

But now dad had moved out of view. That unnerved her. He wondered what he might be up to.

"Stan," she shouted. "Can you hear me? Please open the door."

There was an eerie silence and mum stood upright again.

"I'll see if I can see him through the window," she said.

"Well you go round the front and I'll go round the back," said Joanna.

But a few minutes later they met back at the front door without catching sight of dad.

"He must be in the bathroom," said mum.

"Yes, well I think it's time to call the doctor."

"I suppose you're right."

The receptionist at the surgery was sympathetic without offering much hope. They would despatch a doctor – although it wouldn't be dad's because of holiday commitments. But if he refused to co-operate there wasn't much else they could do. The only option then would be to contact the police.

"I hate the idea of the police being called," said mum.

"Well let's hope Stan listens to the doctor," said Joanna

"Yes, he might do, although there'd have been more chance with his own. I wonder who they'll send."

The young male doctor who turned up thirty minutes later wasn't familiar to either of them. Joanna explained the situation and the doctor immediately took umbrage. He testily retorted that the police should have been called. It wasn't a doctor's problem. That was it – end of discussion. No attempt whatsoever to make contact with dad. Just a brusque retort that the receptionist shouldn't have requested his attendance. She should have known better and he'd relay that fact to her in no uncertain terms. But the good news – he would pass on the details to the police. Then off he went.

"Now who did he remind you of?" said Joanna.

"Yes, exactly," said mum. "But at least he's going to contact the police."

"Do you really think so? No, I'll go next door and phone myself. Then we'll know for certain."

Joanna tried to explain to the police as unemotionally as possible their predicament. But the fact was she did feel emotional. The police were being contacted because of the unpredictable behaviour of her father.

"Were they interested?" said mum when Joanna returned.

"Yes, of course they were mum. They promised somebody would be here within half an hour."

"That's a relief. I think I'll sit in the garden. It's not worth talking to Stan again."

"No, let's leave it up to the police now."

"I just hope they can persuade him without breaking down the door."

The police turned up after forty minutes. Two young constables who were probably dreading the thought of interfering in this family domestic. After Joanna explained the situation they circled the bungalow a couple of times hoping to catch sight of dad. But he remained out of sight. So they opted for the tried and trusty method of shouting through the letterbox. They sounded both firm and sympathetic. They sounded professional. They said it would be in dad's best interest to open the door.

Well, amazingly, almost immediately dad removed the chain, unlocked the front door, and came out with hands raised in a resigned manner. As though he realized he'd been a naughty boy and expected to be reprimanded. Immediately mum ran and hugged him.

"Are you alright Stan?" she said.

"Eeeeeee. Eeeeeee."

"That's okay Stan. It's both our faults."

"Eeeeeee. Eeeeeee."

"The police? I don't know what they're going to do."

"Eeeeeee. Eeeeeee."

"I know you don't."

The police seemed unsure of their next move. Should they take the matter further or count their blessings that the situation had been resolved quickly and quietly.

"You must be hungry Stan?"

"Eeeeeee. Eeeeeee."

"Yes, I'll do your ravioli in a minute."

Thankfully the police decided to take no further action. They deduced it wouldn't help matters despatching dad off to the station or hospital. But they conveyed to him the importance of not going down that avenue again. That the next time the outcome would be different. Dad nodded. It appeared he realized he'd had a lucky escape.

"I thought the police were great," said mum over a cup of tea, after ensuring dad was comfortable in front of the tele with his rather late lunchtime ravioli.

"Yes, you're right," said Joanna. "They knew exactly what to do. More helpful than the doctor."

"Well they couldn't have been less."

"I wonder whether they were related."

"Related? What do you mean? Oh of course. Yes, it wouldn't surprise me."

"I reckon it was his grandchild. He looked like a chip off the old block. Probably spends his day tearing up prescription pads and has steak and kidney on a Wednesday."

"We will never know."

"But seriously mum, you'll have to think of admitting dad to a home. His behaviour's getting too unpredictable. You don't know what might happen next time."

"I know Joanna. I know."

# THIRTY

"I've just had a call from Ralph that they arrived home safely," said mum.

There was astonishment on the faces of those that knew how long the journey took between Norwich and Leytonstone.

"He must have been pushing it," said Nick. "My best time is one hour fifty two minutes. And that was early on a Sunday."

"I don't think I've done it in under two hours," said David.

"I've never thought of Ralph as a quick driver," said Joanna.

"No, he can drive fast when he wants to," said mum. "I remember him giving me a lift to Henry Taylor's. He didn't hang about up Hoe Street. I had to tell him to slow down."

"I wish they could come up for Christmas again," said Robert. "Uncle Ralph was so funny the last time. Do you remember his charades?"

"How could we forget?" said mum. "You never know we might see them up here again."

But she knew that wasn't likely to happen. She hadn't hosted a Christmas for years. Dad's unpredictability had seen to that. Naturally this Christmas, her first without Stan, she'd be round Joanna's. And with the four boys and David's parents present theycouldn't cope with Ralph and Joan.

"Will Uncle John ring when he gets home?" said Robert.

"I wouldn't have thought so," said mum. "He'll be too busy telling Eileen off about her driving."

"Is she a bad driver then?"

"No, she isn't. It's just my brother's funny way. I wish I'd learnt all those years ago. I really envy Eileen's independence."

"I can't imagine you driving," said Robert.

That bought a smile to everybody's face.

"And why not?" said mum.

"Well you're my nana."

"Does that make a difference?"

"I think so."

"Did you know your grandpa used to drive?"

"Grandpa! Really?"

"Yes, during the war."

"In Germany?"

"No, Robert. In this country. Actually it'd be easier taking you to the seaside if I had a car. But I realize I'm too old to start driving now."

"Oh mum," said Joanna. "Isn't the train journey all part of the fun? That's what the boys look forward to."

"Well, what do you think Robert? Would you prefer going to Yarmouth by car?"

"What, with you driving nana?"

"Yes, with me driving."

"I don't know."

"Of course I'd have to pass the test first. Although grandpa never did."

"Didn't he?"

"I've never believed that," said Nick. "That dad could have driven without taking a test because he drove during the war."

"That's what he always said."

"I know he said that. So there could be thousands of elderly ex army drivers out there who've never taken a test in their life."

"That doesn't sound right," said David.

"No, it doesn't. We should have asked Ted when he was here."

"I have," said mum. "He backed up Stan. So what would you prefer Robert, the train or car?"

"I think the train is more fun. We can all play Newmarket then. You couldn't do that in the car. Well you wouldn't be able to join in nana."

"That's a good point Robert."

"Mum," said Joanna. "Are you telling me you play cards on the train with my boys?"

"Only if they behave themselves," said mum.

# 1988

Mum sat down with her morning coffee and reflected on an enjoyable weekend. She'd driven down with Joanna to her nephew Alan's wedding in Essex. She'd been able to relax and reminisce without worrying about dad. David had kept a watchful eye on him. He'd reported back on a quiet uneventful weekend. In other words, dad played ball at all times.

She smiled. It'd been really nice seeing so many of the family. She counted the number of nephews and nieces present. She made it seven. Iris's two girls, Sue and Lyn, had giggled throughout the service. They'd attracted some adverse attention but for the majority of the time just about kept their laughter at a manageable level. In other words it wasn't as intrusive as Stan and his brothers at Fred's funeral. Mum dearly wanted to know what tickled them. Iris didn't, she thought her daughters should have known better.

But when mum finished her coffee and contemplated what lay ahead her mood changed. She'd finally decided to put dad into a nursing home. After months of toying with the idea but unable to go through with it because of guilt she'd reached the decision. With dad's continuing deterioration she knew it to be the right move – but that didn't make it any easier. How could it, her Stan going into a home for the remainder of his life.

So that afternoon she was accompanying the social worker for viewings at three nursing homes. All had vacancies so if mum gave the green light the move could be instigated quickly. The social worker had been really supportive. In the first instance she'd come round and chatted about the procedure. How mum felt about the decision. That it'd be natural to feel guilty. But in the long run she'd realize it was for the best. That dad needed to be in a place where he could receive the appropriate nursing care. That did make sense to mum.

But what did dad think about the move? Well strangely it didn't seem to bother him. Mum had sat down and raised the subject but he'd just shrugged his shoulders. Perhaps he didn't really understand the significance. Or he didn't want to understand. But that would be the worse time, the day dad actually moved out. Mum shook her head thinking about it. How would he cope? Would he go quietly? Perhaps he'd lock himself inside the house again and she'd have to call the police. No, she shouldn't start worrying that far ahead. Let's get today out the way first.

Dad came out of the bathroom and sat in his armchair. He picked up the paper and started to read. Mum tried to gauge his mood. She had already mentioned their nephews wedding. He'd been quite receptive. He'd even asked a few questions about the bride and groom. So would now be a good time to remind him where she was going that afternoon?

"Stan, have you remembered where I'm going this afternoon?"

Dad shook his head.

"I'm going with the social worker to look at some nursing homes."

"Eeeeeee. Eeeeeee."

Dad looked puzzled.

"I have mentioned it before Stan. We think its best if you go into a home."

"Eeeeeee. Eeeeeee."

It didn't seem to register with dad what mum had said. What a momentous decision had been taken. That suited mum because the last thing she needed now was a big scene. So she didn't pursue the subject.

"Eeeeeee. Eeeeeee."

"Yes, I'll be back in time for dinner."

"Eeeeeee. Eeeeeee."

"What have we got? Shepherds Pie. Your favourite Stan."

Dad smiled. That's what mum invariably said when he asked her what was on the menu. But unfortunately he'd had Shepherds Pie yesterday. He would have preferred something different.

"Eeeeeee. Eeeeeee."

"What do you mean Stan?"

"Eeeeeee. Eeeeeee."

"You had that yesterday? I thought Joanna said you were having liver and bacon."

"Eeeeeee. Eeeeeee."

"Are you sure? Well I'm sorry about that Stan."

"Eeeeeee. Eeeeeee."

"No, I've already made it."

Dad looked a little peeved but not enough to make a big issue about it. She left him reading the paper and went to vacuum the bedroom.

The morning dragged for mum – a real anti-climax to the afternoon's event. She couldn't wait to set off. While in the house there was always a chance dad might bring up the subject of her impending visit. That the penny would drop and he'd want an explanation. So she kept out of his way as much as possible. When she served up ravioli at lunchtime she didn't hang about.

"Eeeeeee. Eeeeeee."

But she wasn't that quick. Her face dropped. "What is it Stan?"

"Eeeeeee. Eeeeeee."

"I don't know what you mean."

"Eeeeeee. Eeeeeee."

"I'm sorry Stan."

"Eeeeeee. Eeeeeee."

She could have continued along this line but thought it unfair. Dad deserved an explanation if nursing homes were on his mind. She'd have to bite the bullet and bring up the subject.

"Do you mean where I'm going this afternoon?"

Dad shook his head and mum sighed with relief.

"Eeeeeee. Eeeeeee."

This time he mimed as though he was eating.

"Oh, you mean dinner?"

"Eeeeeee. Eeeeeee."

"It's Shepherds Pie."

"Eeeeeee. Eeeeeee."

"Yesterday. Yes, you said you had Shepherds Pie."

"Eeeeeee. Eeeeeee."

"Oh you didn't. You made a mistake. So was it liver and bacon?"

Dad gave the thumbs up.

"I'm glad about that. You'll enjoy it better tonight now."

"Eeeeeee. Eeeeeee."

"Right, well I'm off now."

"Eeeeeee. Eeeeeee."

"No, I won't be late back. Dinner will be on time."

"Eeeeeee. Eeeeeee."

"Yes, I'm sure. Now don't start worrying."

Mum wondered even at this late stage whether he'd suddenly bring up the subject of her afternoon visit. But no, he waited for her to kiss him on the cheek then returned to the latest issue of the National Geographic.

A couple of hours later Mum returned from her afternoon excursion with mind made up. All three nursing homes had been satisfactory. All were relatively clean with staff that appeared to be used to dealing with residents of a similar disposition to dad. And none had that whiff of urine that could sometimes greet you when you entered a home.

Of the three, the home at Welbourne had the edge because of its location. Importantly mum would be able to visit without relying on a lift from Joanna. A bus from outside the bungalow would drop her off about a mile from the home. Granted she then had to walk down a country lane – but that would be manageable. She sighed with relief that the decision had been made. Now she had to wait for the social worker to give her a date. But all being well it should be within the month. She decided it wasn't worth mentioning anything to dad at this stage.

"Hello Stan," she said. "I'm back."

Dad had been snoozing and woke with a jump.

"Sorry Stan, did I wake you up?"

Dad acknowledged mum and shut his eyes again – but not for long.

"Would you like a cup of tea?"

Dad opened his eyes again. Peeved at being woken again but happy to be offered a cup of tea.

"Eeeeeee. Eeeeeee."

"What about a piece of fruit cake?"

Dad looked perplexed. A piece of fruit cake! Now that was something he didn't expect with an afternoon cuppa.

"Eeeeeee. Eeeeeee."

"What do you mean Stan?"

"Eeeeeee. Eeeeeee."

"You don't have cake very often? I wouldn't say that."

"Eeeeeee. Eeeeeee."

But dad knew there must be an ulterior motive. He just couldn't think what it might be. Meanwhile he might as well enjoy the treat.

"Did you enjoy that Stan?" asked mum as he finished his second piece of cake.

Dad nodded. Yes, it'd made a pleasant change. But enough was enough. A third piece might spoil his dinner. He picked up the National Geographic and returned to the article about the Grand Canyon.

"Is it interesting?" said mum.

Dad sighed with annoyance. He didn't want to start talking about the magazine, he just wanted to read it. Mum picked up on his negative vibes and left him alone while she went to check on the location of Welbourne in the A-Z. Then she'd ring Joanna and inform her of the afternoon's events.

Unfortunately the "Your eyes are bigger than your belly" syndrome reared its ugly head at dinner. As hard as he tried dad couldn't do the shepherds pie justice and gave up after eating a fraction of it. He looked at mum sheepishly. He knew how much she hated him leaving his dinner. But what could mum do? She'd egged him on in the first place to have a second piece of fruit cake.

"That's alright Stan,"

"Eeeeeee. Eeeeeeee."

"Perhaps I'll warm it up for tomorrow."

"Eeeeeee. Eeeeeee."

"I don't suppose you want any rice for desert?"

Dad smiled and shook his head. He excused himself and returned to his favourite magazine of the moment.

Well would you believe it, but shortly before dad retired for the night he raised the subject of her afternoon excursion. She sighed, the last thing she wanted to discuss this late were nursing homes. From her experience if they had words prior to him sleeping he didn't and she'd suffer. But what else could she do?

"Oh, do you mean where I went this afternoon?"

"Eeeeeee. Eeeeeee."

"I visited three nursing homes."

"Eeeeeee. Eeeeeee."

"Why. Because that's where you're going to live Stan."

Dad looked quizzical but didn't say anything.

"Did you understand what I said?"

"Eeeeeee. Eeeeeee."

"No, not when I'm on holiday Stan. I mean all the time."

Dad still didn't seem to take it in.

"Eeeeeee. Eeeeeee."

"Where is it? At Welbourne. That's not far from Norwich."

"Eeeeeee. Eeeeeee."

"In about a month."

"Eeeeeee. Eeeeeee."

"It looked very nice Stan. I think you'll be happy there."

Mum cringed as she said that. How did she know how he'd feel there?

"I'll be able to visit you regularly," she added.

Dad looked at mum but said nothing. She wondered what he might be thinking. As she regularly had over the years. How much of his damaged brain was functioning? She hadn't a clue in this instance.

"Did you understand what I said Stan?"

"Eeeeeee. Eeeeeee."

"What do you mean?"

"Eeeeeee. Eeeeeee."

"No, I'm sorry Stan."

"Eeeeeee. Eeeeeee."

"Did you understand?"

Dad shook his head, stood up and sloped off to bed without the customary kiss. So the likelihood was he'd digested the bad news. She waited for a door to slam. It didn't. She wondered how many times he'd interrupt her sleep that night. But who could blame him after being informed of his imminent admittance to a nursing home. Then she heard him crying.

# THIRTY ONE

"I think we'll be going now," said Joanna.

"Okay," said mum. "Thanks for all you help. It was really good seeing all the boys at the funeral. Stan would have appreciated it."

"They wanted to attend mum. I know you were concerned about Robert."

"Well I did think he was a bit young."

"He's been fine. He told me he's glad he came."

"Oh that's good."

"Are you ready boys?" Joanna shouted.

Tim, Duncan, William and Robert queued up to say their goodbyes to mum. They were followed by Nicole. She was staying overnight with Joanna and realized this would probably be the last time they had contact with each other.

"Thanks for coming Nicole," said mum.

"I'm glad I did. And I'm sorry about – well you know what I mean. Nick's a good man."

"Yes, he's a good son. I wish you well for the future. I really do."

"Thank you. I expect Nick will be moving up to Norwich in the future."

"That would be nice."

After they'd gone mum, Nick, Joyce and Iris decided there was just enough time for one last round of beverages before calling it a day.

"I'm sure I'm going to sleep well tonight," said mum. "I feel drained. What time are you off in the morning?"

"Well the train leaves at ten thirty," said Iris.

"I'll give you a lift to the station," said Nick. "Ten o'clock will be plenty of time."

"Oh thanks Nick," said Joyce. "When are you going home?"

"Sunday evening. I'm back at work on Monday."

"I'd like to go to Homebase sometime over the weekend," said mum.

"That shouldn't be a problem," said Nick. "What are you after?"

"Creosote for the back fence."

"Creosote, you don't hear that word very often. I remember using that in Nottingham Road."

"Yes, Ted's used that a few times over the years," said Iris.

"And Sid," said Joyce.

"Stan always had to do two coats," said mum. "I'm sure it didn't need it."

"That's right," said Nick. "I remember him telling me off because I tried to get away with one coat on the shed."

"It's got such a distinctive smell," said Joyce.

"The smell of springtime," said mum.

"I don't know about that," said Iris. "I can think of pleasanter springtime smells."

"Do you need a brush as well?"

"No, I've got plenty of old brushes. Some of them date back to Nottingham road but they're all clean."

"What was Stan like with the D.I.Y?" said Joyce.

"Well he wasn't a natural but he had a go. Actually his painting was pretty good. A bit on the slow side but the results were okay."

"That's who I take after then," said Nick. "I paint a great door but it takes me ages. It'd be a waste of time doing it for a living. I wouldn't earn anything."

"Stan always said the preparation was the most important thing," said mum. "And you must use an undercoat."

"That's something Ted's always championed," said Iris.

"When Sid was decorating back in the sixties there wasn't an alternative to undercoat," said Joyce.

"Now you can do it all with one coat," said Nick.

"I wonder if you can still buy undercoat?" said Iris.

"That's a good question. When we're in Homebase I'll have a look."

"We've got some in the shed," said mum. "I don't know how long it's been there though. Poor old Stan."

# 1989

Dad's admittance to Welbourne Nursing Home actually occurred nine months after mum's visit. As had happened on previous occasions she'd deferred the decision because of guilt. But it's funny how these things turn out because the move itself didn't cause a problem. There were no doorstep protestations. No tears and regrets. Why? Well three days before the move dad had been admitted to hospital following a funny turn. So in fact he went straight from the hospital to the home. A blessing in disguise, thought mum. God really did move in a mysterious way. A potentially stressful situation had been averted.

Three months on and dad had settled in as well as could be expected. Mentally his deterioration had stabilized. Indeed he seemed calmer and more relaxed. Or perhaps that should be resigned. Resigned to the fact that without mum's twenty four hour care he wouldn't be around much longer. But, importantly, nowadays he rarely lost his temper. And when he had – hadn't hit anybody. He ate pretty well, watched the tele, read the National Geographic and continued to shave daily.

For most of the time he remained in his room. He felt more comfortable there than the day room. Occasionally he exercised around the grounds but without a letter to post that activity didn't have the same appeal. He looked forward to mum's visits but became extremely agitated if she was late. Her perfectly reasonable excuse of the bus being late, treated with a derisory smirk and a shake of the head. And nobody smirked like dad.

Physically though he'd deteriorated. He'd lost weight and aged. Up until his admission mum always reckoned he looked good for his age. But now he looked his seventy six years. And he resembled somebody who'd suffered a severe stroke. I.e. not quite the ticket. As for the care he received, that depended on the staff on duty. Some were excellent and some not so. Some didn't give a damn when his razor went missing while others pulled out all the stops to discover the culprit.

Mum usually visited twice a week. The walk up the country lane had lost its initial, "Isn't the countryside wonderful" appeal – and with winter approaching looked more and more foreboding. But at least she was independent. And with dad off her hands, so to speak, she once again felt that deep love for him. She could sympathize for his lot as a stroke victim. How at the age of forty nine his world had come tumbling down.

But as yet she wasn't sleeping better. The years of continual interruptions had taken their toll. There continued to be nights when she managed hardly any sleep whatsoever. She tried to be positive. She'd been warned by the doctor that it would take time to adjust to a different pattern. As for dad's nights, well he said they were okay and the staff backed that up. When she mentioned this wet feeling he'd experienced over a number of years they shook their heads. No, they couldn't relate to that. Mr Wisbey slept like a log. Mum thought that really odd. What could be the explanation?

Today would be her first visit for a week. She'd spent a couple of days in hospital having the top joint of her finger amputated. Normally with Dupuytren's Contracture the finger can be straightened with a simple operation. But unfortunately mum had ignored the symptoms because of her preoccupation with dad's well being. When she finally visited the doctor he advised the operation might not be as successful as hoped. Okay, but amputation hadn't been mentioned and that's what the surgeon recommended as mum waited to go down to theatre. Mum had been too drowsy to argue the point but subsequently wanted to know why the amputation option hadn't been mentioned earlier?

"What do you think of my finger?" said mum.

Dad studied mum's left index finger with the top half missing.

"Eeeeeee. Eeeeeee."

"I had an operation in hospital. It's called Dupuytren's Contracture."

Dad looked none the wiser.

"It's where the fingers bend towards the palm. It means I've got Viking blood."

Dad looked even more puzzled.

"You remember when the Vikings invaded all those years ago?"

He wondered what she was talking about.

"I'll have to keep a check on the other fingers. Margaret Thatcher had the same problem."

"Eeeeeee. Eeeeeee."

"No, she didn't have the finger off. They managed to straighten hers."

"Eeeeeee. Eeeeeee."

"What, because she was the Prime Minister? Oh, I don't think that made a difference Stan. She probably went to the doctors earlier."

"Eeeeeee. Eeeeeee."

"I never got round to it."

"Eeeeeee. Eeeeeee."

"I never found the time."

"Eeeeeee. Eeeeeee."

"Oh don't go on about it Stan."

"Eeeeeee. Eeeeeee."

Mum could have mentioned the reason why she hadn't got round to it. A question of priorities and his care and attention being the number one. But that would have been unfair – making him feel guilty. Although a year earlier when they were living under the same roof, with all the tension that created, she could easily have used that jibe to get back at him.

"How have you been Stan?"

Dad shrugged his shoulders and opened his hands in front of him.

"Are you still sleeping okay?"

"Eeeeeee. Eeeeeee."

"That's good. You don't get that wet feeling anymore?"

Dad looked puzzled. A wet feeling! What was she on about?

"You used to think the bed was wet."

Dad shook his head.

"And you're eating okay?"

"Eeeeeee. Eeeeeee."

"That's good. What did you have for dinner yesterday?"

Dad shrugged his shoulders. As if he could remember that far back.

"Eeeeeee. Eeeeeee."

He motioned her to feel his face. To give approval of his shave that morning.

"Yes, that feels fine Stan."

She wasn't quite telling the truth. His standard of shave continued to deteriorate but the fact he shaved at all was the important thing. Even when his razor went missing he'd managed courtesy of the staff and their safety razor. Not that they'd been bothered whether he shaved but he made such a fuss about missing a day that they felt compelled to assist.

"It was a good idea putting your name on the razor. It should deter somebody taking it again."

"Eeeeeee. Eeeeeee."

"You know who took it the last time? I didn't think they caught anyone."

"Eeeeeee. Eeeeeee."

"That man you don't like?"

"Eeeeeee. Eeeeeee."

"Oh, you don't mean him."

"Eeeeeee. Eeeeeee."

"Who do you mean?"

"Eeeeeee. Eeeeeee."

"A woman! Are you sure?"

"Eeeeeee. Eeeeeee."

"That very elderly woman?"

"Eeeeeee. Eeeeeee."

"Oh I can't imagine her taking it."

"Eeeeeee. Eeeeeee."

"Yes, if you say so Stan. I believe you."

But she didn't. The woman in question being at least ninety, painfully slow on her feet even with the aid of a frame, and the most important detail, a real sweetie. No way could she be guilty. Whereas the man dad hadn't taken to looked for all the world like your ideal suspect. He'd even popped into dad's room while she'd been visiting on the pretext of being lost. Yes, a likely story.

"Did Nick come and see you at the weekend?"

"Eeeeeee. Eeeeeee."

"How was he?"

"Eeeeeee. Eeeeeee."

"Any news?"

"Eeeeeee. Eeeeeee."

"No."

She asked because Nick had recently informed her that Nicole and he were separating and he couldn't decide weather to inform dad or not. Obviously he hadn't so she didn't think it right to mention it.

"Eeeeeee. Eeeeeee."

"What do you mean Stan?"

"Eeeeeee. Eeeeeee."

"Nick?"

"Eeeeeee. Eeeeeee."

"What about Nick?"

Now she had the feeling he might have mentioned something.

"Eeeeeee. Eeeeeee."

"Do you mean him and Nicole separating?"

Dad nodded and shrugged his shoulders.

"I'm glad he told you."

"Eeeeeee. Eeeeeee."

"No, I don't know any more than you Stan."

"Eeeeeee. Eeeeeee."

"You liked Nicole?"

"Eeeeeee. Eeeeeee."

"Yes, she always took the time to talk to you."

"Eeeeeee. Eeeeeee."

"I suppose she'll go back to Canada."

"Eeeeeee. Eeeeeee."

"Nick? Well he did mention about moving up to Norwich before."

"Eeeeeee. Eeeeeee."

"Yes, that would be nice."

Just then the door opened and in shuffled the elderly woman dad had accused of taking his razor. Well, well, well, thought mum. Perhaps he had a point after all.

"Can I help you?" said mum.

The woman, who appeared very unsteady even with the frame, looked put out by mum's presence. She remained rooted to the spot and glared at mum.

"Can I help you?" repeated mum.

The woman continued to stare at mum. Now she didn't resemble the sweetie that mum had recognized previously.

"Are you lost?" asked mum losing patience.

The woman suddenly about-turned and shuffled out again without so much as a hello or goodbye. Just plain guilt written all over her face.

"Eeeeeee. Eeeeeee."

"Yes, perhaps you were right. Well I never. It might be a good idea to hide the razor."

"Eeeeeee. Eeeeeee."

"You have. Well where is it?"

Dad looked puzzled. He was having trouble remembering. Then he got up and went across to the television. He reached behind it and produced the razor.

"That's a good place Stan. Nobody would think of looking there."

"Eeeeeee. Eeeeeee."

"Yes, so long as you don't forget. Perhaps it'll be better to tell the staff just in case?"

"Eeeeeee. Eeeeeee."

"Why not?"

"Eeeeeee. Eeeeeee."

"You don't trust them. Oh Stan I'm sure you can. What would they want with your old razor?"

"Eeeeeee. Eeeeeee."

"Alright, don't tell them."

"Eeeeeee. Eeeeeee."

"No, I won't. Not if you don't want me to. Can you remember where you left it when it disappeared before?"

Dad shook his head.

"Hopefully it wasn't behind the television."

"Eeeeeee. Eeeeeee."

"Alright Stan you don't have to shout."

The door opened again and in walked a member of staff. He looked embarrassed. One of the residents, a very elderly lady, had just reported seeing a suspicious person in dad's room. He felt obliged to investigate. He apologized for the interruption and quickly departed.

"What a cheek," said mum.

But dad found the incident amusing and started laughing.

"I'm glad you find it amusing. Telling stories like that could land somebody in trouble."

"Eeeeeee. Eeeeeee."

"Has Joanna been up lately?"

"Eeeeeee. Eeeeeee."

Dad shook his head. But mum knew that wasn't the case. She'd spoken to Joanna earlier. She'd visited twice in the last week. Mum didn't think it worthwhile making an issue over it. He might have genuinely forgotten.

"It's half term next week so you might see the boys," said mum.

Dad didn't appear particularly enthralled with that bit of news.

"Oh don't look so interested," said mum.

"Eeeeeee. Eeeeeee."

"They think a lot of you Stan."

"Eeeeeee. Eeeeeee."

Silence ensued as dad returned to the National Geographic and mum finished the Mail crossword. After a while she looked at the clock. Time dragged. Governed by the bus timetable she invariably stayed for ninety minutes. This afternoon that felt an age. Then dad looked at his watch. Perhaps he was thinking along the same lines.

"Eeeeeee. Eeeeeee."

"What do you mean Stan?"

"Eeeeeee. Eeeeeee."

"You want me to go?"

Dad nodded.

"I would Stan but the bus isn't due for forty five minutes."

"Eeeeeee. Eeeeeee."

"What, go to sleep? Yes, if you want to. I can watch the tele."

So dad removed his dressing gown and got into bed while mum made herself comfortable in front of the television. Once in bed he pursed his lips pretending to kiss mum. She got up and kissed him on the cheek.

"Goodnight Stan. I'll try not to wake you up on the way out. I love you."

Dad gave the thumbs up.

# THIRTY TWO

Iris and Joyce had retired for the night and mum and Nick were about to.
After one last cup of coffee that is. They relived the day's events. They
thought the service had been as satisfying as a cremation can be when
the time is governed by the next funeral party waiting in the wings. That
the vicar had spoken sincerely even though he hadn't known dad. That
everybody dad would have wanted to attend had. There'd been lots of
reminiscing about the good old times – those years prior to the eighteenth
of February nineteen sixty three. You had a picture of dad as an honest
and caring human being greatly respected in the army and at the office.
But, more importantly, he'd be remembered as a dedicated family man.
Mum and Nick smiled. Of course they were biased.

And now they could smile at the reality of how close Ralph came
to reversing over Mr Talisman.

"Can you imagine if he had?" said Nick.

"I don't want to," said mum.

"I shouldn't think it happens very often."

They laughed at the tragic absurdity of a mourner running over
the undertaker.

"So did he have a wooden leg?" said Nick.

"I've no idea."

"We will never know."

"No."

"Unless you bump into him in Sainsbury's with the trolley."

"That's a good idea. Now can you make sure you get Iris and
Joyce to the station in good time?"

"I will, don't worry."

"I mean with no rushing."

"There won't be any rushing."

"That's good."

"This may sound like a silly question," said Nick. "But what did dad actually die of? I mean what was on the death certificate?"

"Pneumonia."

"Pneumonia! Nothing to do with the stroke then?"

"Well yes, but according to Joanna they often put pneumonia as a cause of death for the elderly. Or at least a contributory factor."

"Is that right?" said Nick. "But he had deteriorated physically since going in the home. He'd lost weight and aged. He seemed to give up. And he had those chest infections. It still came as a shock though."

"It was," said mum. "When I visited on the Tuesday he seemed okay. I thought he'd got over the latest chest infection. The staff didn't make a big thing about it."

"Probably a combination of things then."

"It's a shame they couldn't have used any of dad's organs. Especially when he had three kidneys. "

"No, they said they weren't suitable – whatever that meant. Do you carry a donor card?"

"No, I haven't got round to it."

"You should mum. I've got to change mine. I've still got Nicole as my next of kin. I'm sure she doesn't want that responsibility."

"I'll think about it. Sometimes I think a dog would be good company."

"Yes, I can imagine you with a little terrier."

"We'll see. It's a bit early to make a big decision like that."

"But you'll have to make the fence more secure if you do. Can you imagine Mrs Bunn's reaction if she finds a dog in her garden?"

"I know that. Now I don't want you to keep on about a dog just because I've mentioned it once."

"I won't say another word."

"Good. I think I'll go to bed now. I feel shattered. I just hope I sleep okay."

"Okay mum. I'll see you in the morning. Do you think dad's talking up there?"

Mum smiled. "I expect so. He's got a lot of catching up to do."

# 1990

Mum, Nick and David had booked on the Carlisle to Settle railway excursion. The most scenic railway line in the country, if not the world. And for one day only, tomorrow, with a connection from Norwich. A treat too good to miss the family decided. Nick had taken the Friday off work and arrived at mum's shortly after lunch. She looked in shock as she opened the door.

"What's up mum?"

"Dad's died," she replied. "The home rang half an hour ago. Joanna's on her way over."

Nick couldn't take in what mum had said. "Died? But he wasn't seriously ill. Did he have another stroke?"

"No, they just said he quickly deteriorated. He had a chest infection at the beginning of the week. They rang yesterday to say he'd worsened but didn't make a big thing about it. I saw him on Tuesday. He didn't look too bad. Actually he seemed quite with it."

"Oh mum, poor dad."

"I'm going to the home when Joanna gets here. Will you come?"

A little while later mum, Joanna, Nick, Duncan and William arrived at Welbourne to pay their respects. Dad looked peaceful lying in bed. He looked asleep. He looked younger. The family took it in turns to hold his hand and say their goodbyes. The grandchildren were emotional. This was their first experience of a dead person.

The staff confirmed it wasn't unusual for somebody of that age and medical history to deteriorate quickly. They added they thought his resistance was low. That perhaps he'd given up the will to live. Mum could certainly relate to that. They asked mum if she'd consider donating his organs, if suitable that is. Mum agreed. They'd have a pleasant surprise when they discovered his third kidney. Then the family departed debating the pros and cons of a cremation against a burial.

"You and David can still do the rail journey," said mum over a cup of tea and a ginger nut. "I'll be alright."

"But I don't feel like doing it," said Nick.

"There's not a lot to do until Monday."

"I wouldn't enjoy it. Anyway we might be able to sort out the funeral tomorrow. Have you decided on a burial or cremation?"

"I'd prefer a cremation," said mum.

"That's okay with me," said Joanna.

"I know you'd prefer a burial."

"Yes, but it's what you want mum."

"I just think a cremation is less harrowing. I don't like the idea of standing round the graveside watching the coffin lowered. Especially at this time of year when it's so muddy. I'm sure Stan would be happy with a cremation."

"Right, well let's try and get an appointment for tomorrow then" said Nick.

Ironically mum slept well that night and woke feeling focused on the task ahead. With Joanna's help she'd already contacted the immediate family and when they returned from their appointment with the undertaker she'd complete the job.

"Are you sure you don't want to do the rail trip?" said mum when Nick appeared for breakfast.

"Mum, I've told you. I wouldn't enjoy it. We're off to the undertakers. Remember?"

"What about the money you've paid?"

"Well I'll give them a ring later. See if we're due a refund."

"Thanks for that Nick. Well as soon as Joanna arrives we'll leave."

It was all very straightforward. The funeral director, the very elderly, statesmanlike and walking stick assisted Mr Talisman, couldn't have been more supportive and reassuring. The funeral would take place at one thirty the following Friday at the City crematorium. One car would be provided and both flowers and donations to the Stroke Association would be appreciated.

"Did you think he had a wooden leg?" said Joanna as they returned to the car.

"A wooden leg?" said a surprised mum. "It hadn't occurred to me. Why do you say that?"

"I don't know. I just thought when he bashed his leg against the filing cabinet it sounded strange. As though it could be wooden."

"He certainly hobbled," said Nick. "But would you have a walking stick with a wooden leg?"

The three of them weren't sure what to make of that conundrum.

"I couldn't believe all those urns lined up on the shelves," said mum. "Did he say some of the ashes had been there over twenty years?"

"That's right," said Joanna. "They have to keep them in case the family suddenly turn up."

"Yes, but twenty years," said Nick. "You'd think they'd inform the families that if they haven't collected them within twelve months they'd be disposed of. All that space they take up."

"Well one thing's for sure," said Joanna. "Funeral directors don't retire at sixty five. He looked tens years older than dad."

"I think you're exaggerating," said mum.

"Maybe, but he was pretty old."

"It is a family firm. I suppose there's no rule about retiring. Did he say his grandson would be assisting?"

"That's right."

"Well it won't take long from home to the crematorium."

"Ten minutes at the most," said Nick. "They've usually got it down to a fine art."

"I'm glad that's all done," said mum. "It's a relief to have everything arranged."


When they arrived back in Norwich Nick rang the travel company to enquire about a refund. To his surprise the company couldn't have been more sympathetic. They offered their condolences and promised a refund by return of post.

"That's really decent of them," said mum.

"Yes," said Joanna. "At times like these you appreciate goodwill like that. It's the little things that count."

"It'll probably make us more inclined to do the trip later."
The remainder of the day mum spent on the telephone. By the evening everybody she could think of informing had been. That included Henry Taylor's where she'd enjoyed a twenty minute one-way conversation with Mrs Walker. At the end of which mum couldn't be sure whether she'd actually mentioned Stan passing away – such had been Mrs Walker's enthusiasm for divulging the latest in store gossip.

On Monday she'd ring Stan's old workplace, Vavasseurs. Granted it'd been twenty eight years since he'd been employed there but she knew Stan would have wished it. And you never know, there might be somebody there who remembered him.

She felt in control of her emotions. Well she hadn't had time to dwell on Stan's passing. She knew it to be for the best. She'd been praying for this outcome for years – just like Stan. When she looked back on the time since sixty three she sincerely believed he should have died after the second stroke. That should have been the final chapter. His quality of life since simply hadn't been worth the pain. Everybody could see that. But then life didn't always pan out the way you expected it to.


"Not Casualty," groaned Nick when mum turned the tele on.

"There's nothing else on a Saturday night," said mum. "The television's diabolical. It has been for years."

"You would think it'd be the best night of the week."

"At least on Sunday you've got Last of the Summer Wine."

"Mum, that's just as bad."

"Nana used to love that."

"I know she did. Meringue with strawberries and cream watching Last of the Summer Wine. What else would you want on Sunday after church?"

"Look, if you want to go round Joanna's that's not a problem."

Nick was sorely tempted but decided in the circumstances he should spend the evening with mum. Give her his support.

"No, that's okay."

"Well if you are staying I don't want any of your comments. Just watch it in silence."

"What do you mean?"

"You know full well what I mean."

And he did.

Mum didn't sleep as well as the previous night. She took an age to drop off. All sorts of things were going around her head. Not least how dad had felt on his last day. Had he been in any pain? Had he realized his time was up? Did he think of her? She wished she could have said goodbye. Perhaps she hadn't picked up the correct signals when the home rang earlier. Were they warning her that his time might be up?

She decided to go to church. Since moving to Norwich she'd visited three or four without feeling at home. But today she needed the comfort of a service. She needed to pray for Stan and herself.

"I'd like to come," said Nick. "Do you think Joanna would fancy it?"

"I don't know. She doesn't go very often. You could ask her."

As it transpired everybody went along to St Michael's near Earlham Park. The party of eight making up a fair percentage of the congregation.

"I bet they don't know what's hit them," said Nick as they took their pew and waited for the service to begin.

"No, it'll make a difference with the collection," said David.

"Yes, boys," whispered Joanna. "Don't forget to put in the collection."

As she'd ensured beforehand they were all carrying loose change that shouldn't pose a problem.

"Where's the choir?" enquired Duncan.

"Sssh," said Joanna. "Not all churches have choirs."

"Why not?"

"Perhaps they can't get the volunteers."

"They don't pay them enough," said William.

All the boys started laughing.

"Less of that please," said Joanna.

The vicar referred to his larger than normal congregation in his sermon. That he hoped to see some of the new faces again. The family nodded but in truth mum would be the only one who might visit again. On the plus side the sermon lasted fifteen minutes, which mum could cope with on a regular basis, and it'd been fairly interesting. Indeed on a par with St Paul's Leyton at any time in the last forty years.

Afterwards there'd been the bonus of a coffee, a biscuit and a natter. Although having said that the youngsters would have preferred a coke.

"Robert, you do not ask for a coke," said Joanna.

"There should be something suitable for us," said William.

"They used to provide orange squash at St Paul's," said Nick.

"Big deal," said Timothy.

"I think it's time to go," said Joanna.

The Sunday roast round Joanna and David's was just what the doctor ordered. The family together and supportive. Lots of laughter and tears. Memories from mum, Nick and Joanna from a bygone era when Dad could speak. His boxing and swimming exploits, the family holidays, the Christmas get-togethers. The fun days out to the Lords and Oval test matches. The everyday normal family affairs.

"I wonder whatever happened to Dr Jarvis?" said Nick.

"Well he would have retired by now," said mum.

"Yes, he looked old in the sixties," said Joanna. "Do you feel bitter mum?"

"Not really. I have done in the past. There's been times when I've thought how different our lives might have been. We were just unfortunate our doctor wasn't up to much."

"I wonder if he ever blamed himself for dad's stroke?" said Nick.

"I don't know," said mum. "Sometimes when I visited the surgery I got the impression he had something on his mind."

"The trouble is," said Joanna. "When you make a mistake in that profession the consequences can be catastrophic."

David dropped mum back home in time for Last of the Summer Wine. Nick had already returned to London for work. He'd talked about staying overnight and leaving at five in the morning but had than spotted the late night film on the tele. El Cid. How amazing, he thought. How appropriate. So he'd decided to watch it at home in the hope of catching sight of the bloke in the flat cap.

Mum made herself a cup of tea and stood in front of dad's framed Institute of Export certificate hanging inside the front door. She smiled. That certificate said it all. He'd worked so hard to achieve that qualification. He'd set his heart on it and persevered. She noticed some dust on top of the frame. She'd polish that straightaway. She had ten minutes to spare before Last of the Summer Wine.

"So long Stan, I hope you're in peace. And if I stay up to watch EL Cid and see the man in the flat cap I'll let you know. I loved you Stan. You made me so proud."